Comparative Studies in

COMMUNITY PROPERTY LAW

Comparative Studies in Community Property Law

Edited by
JAN P. CHARMATZ
and
HARRIET S. DAGGETT

GREENWOOD PRESS, PUBLISHERS
WESTPORT, CONNECTICUT

Library of Congress Cataloging in Publication Data

Charmatz, Jan P ed.
Comparative studies in community property law.

Reprint of the 1955 ed. published by Louisiana State University Press, Baton Rouge.
Articles originally appeared in vols. 14 and 15 of the Louisiana law review.
Includes bibliographical references and index.
1. Community property--United States--States.
I. Daggett, Harriet Spiller, 1891- joint ed.
II. Title.
[KF526.Z95C43 1977] 346'.73'042 77-1740
ISBN 0-8371-9523-3

Originally published in 1955 by Louisiana State University Press, Baton Route

Reprinted with the permission of Louisiana State University Press

Reprinted in 1977 by Greenwood Press, Inc.

Library of Congress catalog card number 77-1740

ISBN 0-8371-9523-3

Printed in the United States of America

Foreword

*Jan P. Charmatz**

The community property system, which has become an integral part of the law of seven common law jurisdictions in the United States in addition to Louisiana, should be of considerable interest to every student of comparative law and to every practicing attorney. The ever increasing importance of some of the eight community property states, like California, Louisiana, and Texas, in the life of the nation and the problems arising from the ever increasing mobility of the population have produced in the last few years a marked interest in this legal institution. There is hardly a practicing attorney in a non-community property state who is not faced at one time or another with the peculiar problems arising from the operation of the community property system.

For some states, like Arizona, Nevada, and Washington, the contributions in this volume represent the first attempt to offer a comprehensive treatment of their community property law. For those states where monographs on community property law are available, as in the case in California, Idaho, Louisiana, and Texas, the contributions are concerned with basic policy questions and specific problems.

The fact that the system is with us to stay does not, however, mean that it is not subject to change or that its basic premises should not be made the object of a critical appraisal. Some of the present contributions show the necessity for a thorough re-evaluation of its bases and the efforts which are being made to keep the system in line with the requirements of our modern society.

A contribution by the Secretary General and the Secretary of the French Commission for Revision of the *Code Civil* has been included in order to show the present efforts in France to adapt its traditional community property *règime* to social change.

It is hoped that the publication of these articles reprinted from Volumes XIV and XV of the *Louisiana Law Review* will contribute to a better understanding of the community property system in this country and abroad.

---

* Faculty Editor, *Louisiana Law Review*.

Preface

*Harriet S. Daggett**

The wealth of material recently appearing in both professional and popular journals regarding marital property, problems arising in connection therewith and their repercussions upon family life of the present, attests the widespread and growing interest in the subject. Further manifestations of concern are evidenced by programs for lectures and for study arranged for a great variety of groups at almost every level of community organization. Obviously, this reaction would be expected at a time of transition of thought attempting its adjustment to the changes wrought by the upheavals of the era as they reach down to the smallest unit. According to Norman Cousins we are "in the middle of a century which has already seen more change than has been accumulated in the previous thousand years."

Community property, one of the oldest and the most generally accepted answers of the civilized world to the question of regulation of property in the family's best interest, furnishes a pattern not too well known in the United States. Thus, at this time of quest, the Louisiana Law Review by a series of articles and now the Louisiana State University Press by incorporating these articles into a volume may be offering a real public service. The materials comprise a general resumé together with expression of varied points of view by writers from the eight states of the Union using the system, and from one foreign parent state.

Exchange of ideas among the states operating under the system with its many variations of detail even in the Union should be most valuable to technicians. Wealth of information in regard to the general platform of the system should be of great interest to the uninitiated within and without states providing for this method of regulation. Perhaps suggestions for more satisfactory adjustments may take root in favorable season.

All is not well by any means in community property states. Even believers see a need for repair varying from slight to major

---

* Professor of Law, Louisiana State University.

reform. Abandonment because of complexity together with other reasons may be an issue. France, one of the two immediate parents of the system in the United States, evidences discontent and the present committee for possible official revision suggests compromise measures. Moreover, a new type of prenuptial contract is said to be gaining popularity in France, the essence of which seems to be separate *régime* during marriage with provision for community division at dissolution of the association.

It is of considerable interest that the Oklahoma plan for a community *régime*, later abandoned when it ceased to be advantageous for tax purposes, expressed in general the same idea evolved in France for a form of marriage contract. Thus, the new and the old, widely separated in time and space, met in thought directed toward adjustment for changed economic and social conditions. Whether this likeness came about through communication or whether it arose spontaneously as a just method of meeting present contingencies, as the community property idea is said to have originated in early days in different countries, is problematical.

Certainly this solution answers some of the problems of the day. When both spouses are gainfully employed outside the home, which increasingly is the case, particularly in urban and industrialized communities, a need is felt for individual protection and creditors' security and convenience in connection with each business. Yet, a sharing of accumulations at the dissolution of the marriage seems fair to the parties.

Everywhere, increasing urban communities seem to produce more divorces, many of which must involve discontents arising out of property questions. Early marriages are on the increase in the United States and need little sanction by parents. Property questions are not considered and prenuptial contracts are rare. As the spouses mature, it might be that allowance of contracts between the spouses during marriage might cause lessening of strain. The old idea that marital discord and unfair practice would necessarily result may have been sound in a day of lack of education and experience and few opportunities for employment for wives and in dominant areas of rural population. It would appear that presently, these factors being no longer present, the rule must also shift if undesirable results are to be avoided, the reason for the rule having ceased to exist.

PREFACE

It has been said that it is harder to regulate a household than to govern a people. Spouses are human. One is usually stronger than the other. To permit them to regulate their affairs within the law might be the wiser course today, with a reserve of protection for the weaker or less fortunate, always with the best interests of the family unit in mind. Emotional insecurity and uncertainty in general mark the pattern of today. Whatever may be done to consolidate internal forces, particularly within the basic integer, the family, property problems should be given a high place in the thinking and planning of our leaders.

If primitive tribes were able to work out a just distribution of the spoils of war for the spouses that labored together to gain the victory, surely it should not be too difficult for present-day communities to make such arrangements in the interest of domestic tranquility in the home and in the state.

Perhaps the ideas expressed herein may be helpful to that endeavor and thus fulfill the hopes of the individuals who worked together to produce this book.

Contents

Comparative Studies in

COMMUNITY PROPERTY LAW

Development of Community Property Law in Arizona

*John D. Lyons**

If we date the community property system, in what is now Arizona, from the arrival of the first Spanish explorers in 1539, then it has existed there for 414 of the 415 ensuing years. The excluded year is 1865, when the Howell Code in its original form was in force.

This first code of the laws of Arizona was adopted by its first territorial legislature, taking effect, for the most part, on the first day of January, 1865.[1] It takes no notice of community property. On the contrary, it expressly repeals the laws of Mexico, Spain, and the Territory of New Mexico, theretofore existing in the territory,[2] adopts the common law of England as the rule of decision,[3] establishes dower and curtesy,[4] and provides that all property acquired by a married woman, whether by "grant" or "in any other manner" shall constitute her separate estate.[5] By an act of December 30, 1865,[6] however, the second territorial legislature repealed the two last-mentioned provisions and adopted a comprehensive community property statute.[7]

It has been suggested that the first legislature did not intend to abrogate the community property system, and that the later legislation was merely confirmatory of its already continuing existence.[8] Certainly the haste in which the original Howell Code was compiled and adopted,[9] and the expedition with which it was amended, support this view. Still, it is clear that the organizers of the territory, most of whom had recently arrived

---

* Dean and Professor of Law, University of Arizona College of Law.

1. Howell Code c. LXI, § 12 (1864).
2. *Id.* c. LXI, § 1.
3. *Id.* c. LXI, § 7.
4. *Id.* c. XXVII.
5. *Id.* c. XXXII, § 1.
6. Effective January 29, 1866. *Id.* c. I, § 2.
7. Ariz. Laws 1865, p. 58 *et seq.*
8. *See* 1 de Funiak, Principles of Community Property 4, n. 7 (1943).
9. It was compiled within six months after the organization of the territory. Territory of Arizona Legislative Journal 63 (1864). And its sixty chapters were adopted during a legislative session of forty-three days.

from common law jurisdictions, were no admirers of the existing laws.[10] And since their code was partly patterned upon the code of California,[11] they had before them the community property statutes of that state, had they wished to adopt them. Therefore, it seems equally reasonable to speculate that the community property statute of December 30, 1865, represented not the correction of an oversight, nor mere legislative confirmation of existing law, but, rather, a real change of heart, following an original intention to replace community property with a common law system. And if, in the absence of any satisfactory evidence of the true legislative intent, we apply the presumption that the legislature meant what it said, we must conclude that community property did not prevail in Arizona during 1865. This has been the view of the Arizona court.[12]

Nevertheless, and even though Arizona be taken to have "adopted," rather than "continued," the community system, its Supreme Court has said that the Spanish law, so far as it is consistent with the laws and customs of the state, may be applied to its interpretation.[13] The community property system is a creature of statute, to be sure, but it is also *sui generis*, and it is not governed by common law principles.[14]

In practice, however, these sound theories of interpretation have been largely honored in the breach. Direct citation of Spanish authority is almost unknown. The common law preference for case precedents is indulged as freely here as in other fields. And the system has undoubtedly been "molded to some extent by . . . common-law rules."[15]

---

10. *See* letter from Gov. Goodwin, dated November 9, 1864: "The laws and customs of Spain and Mexico had been clashing with the statute and common law of the United States. . . ." TERRITORY OF ARIZONA LEGISLATIVE JOURNAL 241-2 (1864); and letter of Judge Howell dated June 10, 1864: "[They] were so ill adapted to our condition that a complete organization of the Territorial Government could not be had until a code of laws was substituted for those now in force." *Id.* at 63.

11. TERRITORY OF ARIZONA LEGISLATIVE JOURNAL 35 (1865).

12. *See* Stiles v. Lord, 2 Ariz. 154, 158, 11 Pac. 314, 315 (1886): "[The act of December 30, 1865] must be held . . . to take the place of the act of 1864, and to repeal it by implication. This law enacted for this territory the community system . . ."; Blackman v. Blackman, 45 Ariz. 374, 382, 43 P.2d 1011, 1014 (1935): "In the original Howell Code of 1864 the common-law rule of marital property rights, somewhat liberalized, was adopted, but this rule was in effect abolished and the community property system was established by the act of December 30, 1865. . . ."

13. Pendleton v. Brown, 25 Ariz. 604, 610, 221 Pac. 213, 216 (1923). The statutory reception of the common law as the rule of decision has been amended so that it now applies only when consistent with our "established customs." HOWELL CODE c. LXI, § 7 (1864), as amended, Ariz. Laws 1907, c. 10, § 8.

14. Blackman v. Blackman, 45 Ariz. 374, 386, 43 P.2d 1011, 1015 (1935).

15. La Tourette v. La Tourette, 15 Ariz. 200, 207, 137 Pac. 426, 428 (1914).

This trend was manifested as early as 1876, in the first of the *Charauleau-Woffenden* cases.[16] The question in that case was whether the rents and profits derived from separate property were, themselves, separate or common. The act of December 30, 1865, said they were common.[17] This was also the Spanish law,[18] and coincided beautifully with its basic concept that since both spouses were primarily concerned with advancing the interests of the marital community, both would naturally wish to dedicate all of their acquests during coverture to that purpose.[19] But to the common-law-trained judges of the territorial court, the two ideas, that property could be the separate property of the wife, and that, at the same time, its fruits could be common, and, therefore, subject to the husband's control, seemed "antagonistic," and equivalent to "confiscation." It quoted with approval from a California decision:

> "The common law [sic] recognized no such solecism . . . . It would be to make the wife the trustee for the husband, holding the legal title, while he held the fruits of that title."[20]

On these common law grounds the court concluded that this provision of the community property statutes had been impliedly repealed by the Married Women's Property Act of 1871.[21]

This decision was followed in the second *Charauleau-Woffenden* case.[22] It was expressly overruled by the third.[23] At the end of ten years, in the fourth of these cases, the court returned to its original position, commenting that "It is time this vexed question were laid to rest."[24] How easily and how much better, that might have been done in the beginning, by referring to the applicable Spanish authorities! The Spanish rule, in this respect, could hardly be called inconsistent with our customs since it prevails in several states.[25] But instead of resorting to

---

16. Charauleau v. Woffenden, 1 Ariz. 243, 25 Pac. 652 (1876).
17. Ariz. Laws 1865, c. XXXI, § 9, p. 61.
18. 1 de Funiak, Principles of Community Property 180 (1943).
19. "Just as the salary of the husband contributes to defraying the expenses of matrimony, the interest and fruits borne by the property of each spouse are dedicated to the same purpose." 22 Scaevola, Código Civil 247 (1905), as quoted in De La Torre v. National City Bank of New York, 110 F.2d 976, 979, n. 2 (1st Cir. 1940).
20. Charauleau v. Woffenden, 1 Ariz. 243, 260, 25 Pac. 652, 657 (1876), quoting from George v. Ransom, 15 Cal. 322, 324 (1860).
21. Ariz. Laws 1871, p. 18.
22. Woffenden v. Charauleau, 1 Ariz. 346, 25 Pac. 662 (1876).
23. Woffenden v. Charouleau (sic), 2 Ariz. 44, 8 Pac. 302 (1885).
24. Woffenden v. Charouleau (sic), 2 Ariz. 91, 93, 11 Pac. 117, 118 (1886). The rule had in the meantime been adopted by statute. Ariz. Laws 1885, No. 5, p. 5, now Ariz. Code Ann. § 63-302 (1939).
25. 1 de Funiak, Principles of Community Property 181 (1943).

these basic sources the court struggled until the last to adapt the alien rules of the English common law to the community concept of marital property.

Such deviations from the classic community pattern tend to multiply by spontaneous generation. For example, once we have ruled that the fruits of separate property are separate we face a problem in the business whose profits are attributable in part to invested separate capital, and in part to the personal labor, skill, or management of a spouse. Under original community principles all of such profits would be community property. But the Arizona court, to be consistent, has had to rule that in such case the profits are separate to the extent that they are attributable to the separate capital, and community to the extent that they are attributable to the personal services of a spouse.[26]

This result is logical enough. It even bears a superficial resemblance to the sound community property doctrine that property purchased in part with community and in part with separate funds shall be deemed separate and community in the same proportions as the purchase price. But in practice it is wholly incapable of definite and certain application. For by what standard shall we determine what part of the profit is attributable to capital and what to personal services? Shall we allow legal interest on the investment and rule that the rest of the profit is community? Or shall we, on the other hand, allow the participating spouse a reasonable salary for his personal services and deem the rest to be the separate product of separate capital? Arizona has avoided both of these extremes in favor of the *ad hoc* approach to individual cases. Doubtless this is the fairest rule. But the standard of decision is so indefinite that one can seldom predict the result before the court has spoken. This illustrates rather graphically the secondary, generally unforeseen, and sometimes unfortunate, consequences which may follow an original deviation from a time-tried and integrated body of law.

In the application of common law rules to community property problems these early Arizona cases set a pattern which has persisted until the present. This was no doubt inevitable in a state where the law is administered by common law lawyers. And it must be conceded that since the "vexed" territorial courts

26. Barr v. Petzhold, 273 P.2d 161 (Ariz. 1954); *In re* Torrey's Estate, 54 Ariz. 369, 95 P.2d 990 (1939); Rundle v. Winters, 38 Ariz. 239, 298 Pac. 929 (1931).

have done the spade work in accommodating common law rules to this unaccustomed purpose, and as local precedents have multiplied, the resultant system has not worked too badly. Yet, Arizona lawyers can afford to remember that reliance upon Spanish authorities in community property cases is not a mere eccentricity. It can aid, upon occasion, in the sound resolution of basic problems, and is unobjectionable in either reason or authority.

Of course, the tendency to apply common law rules to community property cases is not peculiar to Arizona. Most, if not all, of the community states have evinced it to a considerable extent. And, together with frequent statutory amendments, it has resulted in some diversity in the details of the system amongst the states. We should not, however, overemphasize the importance of this diversity, for the common overriding fact of the existence of the conjugal partnership far outweighs these minor variances in its operation.

Arizona's first community property statute was apparently derived from California.[27] But, as the statutes of these states were amended and construed, their law grew apart, and in recent years the Arizona court has repeatedly said that its concept most closely resembles that of Washington.[28]

The foundation of the Arizona concept of community property is "equal rights,"[29] as laid down in the leading case of *La Tourette v. La Tourette:*[30]

> "The law makes no distinction between the husband and wife in respect to the right each has in the community property. It gives the husband no higher or better title than it gives the wife. It recognizes a marital community wherein

27. See Dunne, C. J., dissenting in Woffenden v. Charauleau, 1 Ariz. 346, 357, 25 Pac. 662, 665 (1876); Kirkwood, *Historical Background and Objectives of the Law of Community Property in the Pacific Coast States*, 11 WASH. L. REV. 1, 5 (1936).

28. See, *e.g.*, Cosper v. The Valley Bank, 28 Ariz. 373, 237 Pac. 175 (1925), in which the statement originated; Porter v. Porter, 67 Ariz. 273, 195 P.2d 132 (1948); Maricopa County v. Douglas, 69 Ariz. 35, 208 P.2d 646 (1949). After thirty years and important changes in the law of other states this frequently quoted observation might profitably be re-examined.

29. The term "entity theory," sometimes used particularly in connection with the similar Washington law, is unnecessarily misleading to common lawyers. The community is not a "legal entity" in their sense. And for the description of an "entity theory" Puerto Rico style, see De La Torre v. National City Bank of New York, 110 F.2d 976, 978 (1st Cir. 1940): "[A]s regards third parties, the [community] and the husband constitute a single entity. . . ."

30. 15 Ariz. 200, 205, 137 Pac. 426, 428 (1914).

both are equal. Its policy plainly expressed is to give the wife in this marital community an equal dignity, and make her an equal factor in the matrimonial gains . . . . It recognizes that the wife in her station is as much an agency in the acquisition as the husband, and is entitled to just as great an interest."

It follows that the wife's interest in the community property during coverture has never been regarded as inchoate, or a mere expectancy, but has always been recognized as a presently vested interest. The former disagreement over the nature of her interest, which "fed the flame of juridical controversy for many years,"[31] seems to have been finally resolved, in all of the community property states, in favor of a vested interest, partly from practical considerations originating with the federal income tax laws. But the Arizona emphasis on "equal rights" led inevitably to this conclusion from the beginning,[32] so that there has never been any other rule in that state.

It is highly significant that the early development of community property law in Arizona coincided with the nineteenth century trend toward the legal emancipation of women, which culminated in the Married Women's Property Acts. The sturdy chivalry (so insistent as to suggest a bad conscience) which characterized much judicial writing of this period is evident in the first two *Charauleau-Woffenden* cases.[33] It certainly had as much to do with the final result of those cases as the common law rules and community misconceptions on which it was ostensibly based. In a new jurisdiction, "whose institutions had not yet crystallized into form under archaic ideas of the subjection of the female sex,"[34] the spirit of the times could be freely indulged. This spirit, rather than any conscious reliance upon civil law concepts, seems to explain the emphasis upon "equal rights" and the wife's "vested interest." And as to several other questions, which were controversial during the early development of American community property in the west, it determined the course which Arizona was to follow.

The measure was equal rights, not merely equal title. To

31. Mr. Justice Holmes, in Arnett v. Reade, 220 U.S. 311, 319 (1911).

32. La Tourette v. La Tourette, 15 Ariz. 200, 208, 137 Pac. 426, 429 (1914); Goodell v. Koch, 282 U.S. 118 (1930).

33. Charauleau v. Woffenden, 1 Ariz. 243, 25 Pac. 652 (1876); Woffenden v. Charauleau, 1 Ariz. 346, 25 Pac. 662 (1876).

34. *See* Cosper v. The Valley Bank, 28 Ariz. 373, 376, 237 Pac. 175, 176 (1925).

early Arizona lawyers and lawmakers (and to their wives) the nice civil law distinction between *habere*, signifying ownership, and *tenere*, signifying the right to manage or administer, seemed as empty as it does to a modern Spanish feminist. Of how much satisfaction was it to an emancipated wife to possess equal title to the common property, if the power of disposition, so long, at least, as it was exercised for the "benefit" of the community, resided exclusively in the husband? This was in some respects less than the common law dower right, which could be released only with the wife's consent.

The first Arizona statute gave the husband "the entire management and control of the common property, *with the like absolute power of disposition as to his own separate estate . . . .*" (Italics supplied.)[35] This language, which seems to go even beyond the civil law, was broad enough to allow the husband to give away or waste the community property, since he could have done so with his separate estate; particularly since the same chapter gives the wife a specific remedy for mismanagement or waste of "her separate property."[36] As later modified the statute provided merely that the common property might "be disposed of by the husband only."[37] And by a 1901 amendment the wife's joinder was required in "all deeds and mortgages affecting [community] real estate, except unpatented mining claims."[38]

The husband's sole agency to dispose of the community property had rested upon the wife's presumed incompetence in business matters. It was as this presumption came to be regarded as less valid that his exclusive agency was withdrawn as to the relatively infrequent conveyance and encumbrance of real estate. For practical reasons it has been retained as to personal property.[39] But the court has been at pains to point out that:

> "The law, in giving this power to the husband during coverture to dispose of the personal property, does not do this in recognition of any higher or superior right that he has therein, but because the law considers it expedient and

---

35. Ariz. Laws 1865, c. XXXI, § 9, p. 61.
36. Ariz. Law 1865, c. XXXI, § 8, p. 60.
37. Ariz. Rev. Stat. ¶ 2102 (1887).
38. Ariz. Rev. Stat. ¶ 3104 (1901). This is still the law. Ariz. Code Ann. § 71-409 (1939).
39. Ariz. Code Ann. § 63-301 (1939).

> necessary in business transactions affecting the personalty to have an agent of the community with power to act."[40]

The next logical step is to make both the husband and the wife, like true partners, agents for the community in the disposition of its personalty. It remains to be seen whether female emancipation and legislative chivalry will go this far. At present the law deems the husband "best qualified for [this] purpose."[41]

As to the disposition of the wife's separate estate the Arizona statutes underwent a similar but more rapid evolution. They at first provided, contrary to the Spanish law,[42] that "the husband shall have the management and control of the separate property of the wife during the continuance of the marriage," although the wife was required to join in its sale or encumbrance.[43] But ever since the Married Women's Property Act of 1871,[44] married women of the age of twenty-one years, or upwards, have had the sole control and management of their separate property, as if unmarried.[45]

Another question which had to be settled was that of the liability of the separate and common property of the spouses for their separate debts. That the separate property of each was liable for the separate debts of its owner seems never to have been doubted.[46] And that the husband's separate property could not be charged with the antenuptial debts of the wife was provided in the first community property statute.[47] This exemption was soon applied mutually: "The separate property of the husband or wife shall not be liable for the debts of the other contracted before marriage."[48] That the same rule should apply to postnuptial separate debts appears logical,[49] and is generally assumed, although an argument to the contrary may be based on the maxim *expressio unius*.[50]

---

40. La Tourette v. La. Tourette, 15 Ariz. 200, 206, 137 Pac. 426, 428 (1914).
41. *Ibid.*
42. 1 DE FUNIAK, PRINCIPLES OF COMMUNITY PROPERTY 316 *et seq.* (1943).
43. Ariz. Laws 1865, c. XXXI, § 6, p. 60. There were some other exceptions, *e.g.*, when the husband did not reside in the territory.
44. Ariz. Laws 1871, p. 18.
45. ARIZ. CODE ANN. §§ 63-303, 71-409 (1939); Stiles v. Lord, 2 Ariz. 154, 11 Pac. 314 (1886); Miller v. Fisher, 1 Ariz. 232, 25 Pac. 651 (1875).
46. As to the wife's antenuptial debts this was specifically stated in the first community property statute, Ariz. Laws 1865, c. XXXI, § 13, p. 61.
47. *Ibid.*
48. ARIZ. REV. STAT. ¶ 2105 (1887); ARIZ. CODE ANN. § 63-304 (1939).
49. *See* 1 DE FUNIAK, PRINCIPLES OF COMMUNITY PROPERTY 452 (1943).
50. The grounds for rejection of the maxim in Forsythe v. Paschal, 34 Ariz. 380, 271 Pac. 865 (1928) are inapplicable to this situation.

Touching the more important problem of the liability of the common property for separate debts (generally the husband's) the Arizona rule is contrary to that of most community property states. The statute says only that "The community property of the husband and wife shall be liable for the community debts contracted by the husband during marriage . . . ."[51] Since only the husband can make contracts binding the common property,[52] and since there can be no such thing as a community debt contracted before the marriage or after its dissolution, this statute includes all community debts. But it is silent as to the community's liability for separate debts.

The first case involving this question was *Villescas v. The Arizona Copper Co.*[53] In a rather cursory opinion the court held the community chargeable with a criminal fine incurred by the husband quite apart from the community affairs. The court cites some authorities from other states, but seems to be chiefly influenced by the conviction that any other rule would be unfair to creditors, who must be protected from what it calls "secret contracts and agreements of the highly confidential relation of the spouses." Presumably this refers to agreements between husband and wife whereby separate property may be transmuted into community. Nothing is said about the unfairness to the marital partnership of having its assets applied to pay debts which are in no way connected with its affairs.

Later, in *Cosper v. The Valley Bank,*[54] involving an obligation which was held to be, in fact, a community debt, the court went out of its way to disapprove the holding in the *Villescas* case, and in a well-reasoned discussion to express the opinion that the common property is not chargeable with the separate debts of the spouses. This is now the settled rule in Arizona,[55] although, upon the dissolution of the community, separate debts are chargeable to the debtor's one-half.[56]

51. ARIZ. REV. STAT. ¶ 2106 (1887); ARIZ. CODE ANN. § 64-304 (1939).

52. ARIZ. REV. STAT. ¶ 2104 (1887); ARIZ. CODE ANN. § 63-303 (1939). An exception is the wife's right to contract debts for necessaries for herself and children. But even these are contracted upon the credit of the husband. ARIZ. REV. STAT. ¶ 2107, 2108 (1887); ARIZ. CODE ANN. § 63-305 (1939).

53. 20 Ariz. 268, 179 Pac. 963 (1919).

54. 28 Ariz. 373, 237 Pac. 175 (1925).

55. Barr v. Petzhold, 273 P.2d 161 (Ariz. 1954); Tway v. Payne, 55 Ariz. 343, 101 P.2d 455 (1940); McFadden v. Watson, 51 Ariz. 110, 74 P.2d 1181 (1938); Payne v. Williams, 47 Ariz. 396, 56 P.2d 186 (1936); Perkins v. First Nat. Bk. of Holbrook, 47 Ariz. 376, 56 P.2d 639 (1936); Jackson v. Griffin, 39 Ariz. 183, 4 P.2d 900 (1931); Forsythe v. Paschal, 34 Ariz. 380, 271 Pac. 865 (1928).

56. Tway v. Payne, 55 Ariz. 343, 101 P.2d 455 (1940); Jackson v. Griffin, 39 Ariz. 183, 4 P.2d 900 (1931).

In the *Cosper* case the court reasons that this result flows inevitably from what was, even then, the Arizona concept of each spouse's equal, undivided and vested interest in the community property. To charge the common property for an individual debt would be to make one's property liable for the debts of another. It holds, too, that the statutory subjection of the community property to community debts is to be construed as exclusive, and as stating "for what debts community property shall be liable."[57]

The result is good Spanish community property law. But to what extent, if at all, it is consciously based upon that authority, either directly or indirectly, is impossible to state. Its immediate reliance is upon *La Tourette v. La. Tourette.*[58] And the reflections in that case "upon the nature and character of this estate known as community property," so far as they concern the nature of the wife's present interest, were presented without specific reference to authority.

Once again, however, it is perfectly clear that the court, in the *Cosper* case, was greatly influenced by the modern view of women's rights, and the fact that the separate debt there involved was, as is usual, the husband's.

> "Development of the community property law of the western states has gone hand in hand with the general emancipation of women from the economic bonds which have so long burdened them. While under the common law the husband and wife were 'one,' and he was always the 'one,' the world has of recent years gone a long way toward recognizing that even a married woman was a human being, with most of the rights of such . . . ."[59]

The principle that community property is not answerable for the husband's separate debts has given rise to some modern problems not present in those community property states which hold to a contrary view. In *Oglesby v. Poage,*[60] for example, the court was concerned with a constitutional tax exemption for the property of military veterans. The particular case had to do with the taxability of certain real estate, the community property of a veteran husband and his non-veteran wife. While recognizing that the wife's tax liability is her separate obliga-

57. Cosper v. The Valley Bank, 28 Ariz. 373, 382, 237 Pac. 175, 178 (1925).
58. 15 Ariz. 200, 137 Pac. 426 (1914).
59. 28 Ariz. 373, 375, 237 Pac. 175, 176 (1925).
60. 45 Ariz. 23, 40 P.2d 90 (1935).

tion, the court concluded that the rule against the collection of separate debts out of community property is a legislative policy which must yield to the constitutional exemption of the veteran's property only. The wife's property must, therefore, pay its share of taxes, regardless of the fact that the enforcement of the payment would result in a sale of her interest. This enforcement procedure is possible because the interests of the spouses "are separate for the purpose of taxation," citing the authority to file separate returns of community income taxes.

Then, there is the problem of the divorced man who remarries. Is the property of the second community chargeable with the alimony and child support decreed to the wife and children of the first? It is his separate obligation. To charge it to the community is contrary to the rule, and unfair, by community property standards, to the wife and children of the second marriage. Yet, to exempt the community property may put him beyond the reach of his legal and moral obligations. This question has not been decided by the Arizona Supreme Court at this writing, and the trial courts of the state have reached conflicting conclusions.

Some of the trial courts have followed, and others have refused to follow, the Washington rule. In Washington, as in Arizona, community property is not liable for the husband's separate debts. But in *Fisch v. Marler*,[61] the Supreme Court of Washington held that the husband's earnings could be garnished for accrued installments of alimony due to his former wife. The claim of the divorced wife upon the earnings of her former husband is said to be a "fixed and prior" one. Her claim is not in all cases to be enforced to the point of exhaustion of such earnings, for the present wife also has a claim thereon. Therefore, the court may exercise its discretion in allocating the husband's earnings according to the necessities of the parties.

This decision could not be followed in Arizona without doing violence to community property principles which have been thoroughly settled in that state for many years. It is, in effect, a common law decision, for it treats the husband's earnings as his own. But it is a basic principle of Arizona community property law that no distinction in the character of the common property can be based upon its source as between the spouses. Each has an equal, present and existing interest therein, whether

---

61. 1 Wash.2d 698, 97 P.2d 147 (1939).

it originates entirely from the earnings of the husband, entirely from the earnings of the wife, or partly from each.[62] In *Payne v. Williams*,[63] for example, it was held that the husband's salary could not be garnished for his separate debt. This is so basic to the community property concept that to deny it is to strike at the roots of the system.

Some indication of the thinking of the Washington court is contained in the case of *Stafford v. Stafford*,[64] in which it refused to apply the rule of *Fisch v. Marler* to community real estate. In distinguishing the latter case the court says: "The husband has much broader control over community personal property than he has over community real estate."[65] But it is emphasized in the Arizona case of *La Tourette v. La Tourette*,[66] that this power of control is only as agent for the community and not in recognition of any higher right or title. Despite the husband's broader control over it, community personal property is as much community property, and the wife's vested interest therein is as genuine, as in the case of community real estate.

The Washington court has pointed out that alimony and support money payments are not a debt in the ordinary sense, as, for example, within the meaning of the exemption statutes.[67] That is true. They are public obligations. But for our present purposes this appears to be a distinction without a difference. There would seem to be no principle of community property law under which community property, as such, is free from liability for separate ordinary debts, yet answerable for separate public obligations. Certainly no such principle prevails in Arizona where the community has been held not answerable for a separate criminal penalty assessed against the husband,[68] nor upon the wife's separate statutory obligation to support her aged mother.[69]

Yet this distinction between separate debts contracted by the spouse and his separate obligations which are imposed by

62. ARIZ. CODE ANN. § 63-301 (1939). See also 1 DE FUNIAK, PRINCIPLES OF COMMUNITY PROPERTY 166-68 (1943).

63. 47 Ariz. 396, 56 P.2d 186 (1936).

64. 10 Wash.2d 649, 117 P.2d 753 (1941).

65. *Ibid.*, 117 P.2d at 754.

66. 15 Ariz. 200, 206, 137 Pac. 426, 428 (1914).

67. Fisch v. Marler, 1 Wash.2d 698, 715, 97 P.2d 147, 154 (1939); Stafford v. Stafford, 18 Wash.2d 775, 788, 140 P.2d 545, 551 (1943).

68. Cosper v. The Valley Bank, 28 Ariz. 373, 237 Pac. 175 (1925), overruling Villescas v. Arizona Copper Co., 20 Ariz. 268, 179 Pac. 963 (1919).

69. Maricopa County v. Douglas, 69 Ariz. 35, 208 P.2d 646 (1949).

law does suggest a solution to the problem which is fair and equitable for the wife and children of the first marriage, and avoids the emasculation of the community property principle. Under the Spanish law of community property, according to de Funiak,

> "It is undoubted . . . that where a spouse having a duty or obligation imposed by law had insufficient separate funds at the moment to meet such duty or obligation, it might be met from the *spouse's share* in the community property, provided that the other spouse suffered no detriment therefrom and that expenditures by one spouse from the common fund were properly charged against that spouse's share . . . . In the case of the ordinary separate creditor, his rights to reach his debtor's properties were subordinated to the well-being and interests of the family which required that the community property be kept intact for its benefit during the marriage. But obligations imposed by the state itself took priority over everything else."[70] (Italics supplied.)

This is quite different from holding the community property, as such, answerable for these obligations. And it avoids the community heresy of treating the husband's earnings as his own, as at common law. It is simply to say that for the collection of public obligations the community may be treated as divisible. The rule is derived from basic community property sources and is consistent with our laws and customs. As to the separate tax liability of a spouse, this solution has already been adopted, in principle, by the Arizona Supreme Court, in *Oglesby v. Poage*.[71] And it seems to offer the soundest solution, under Arizona law, for the enforcement of the remarried man's obligations to the wife and children of a former marriage.

Summary

The most important influence in shaping the development of community property law in Arizona has been, of course, the community property system of Spain and Mexico. It was the law of the region for more than three hundred years, and in broad outline it is still the law of Arizona.

The common law, also, has exercised an influence. That was, perhaps, inevitable, because of the common law training of the Arizona bench and bar, and because of the former inaccessibility

---

70. 1 DE FUNIAK, PRINCIPLES OF COMMUNITY PROPERTY 468-69 (1943).
71. 45 Ariz. 23, 40 P.2d 90 (1935).

of community property materials. But it is a dangerous influence. The concepts are fundamentally divergent, and their mixing can lead to unfortunate results.

Finally, there has been the influence of the nationwide trend toward the legal emancipation of married women. This movement has coincided, in point of time, with the history of the territory and state of Arizona. It seems to explain the characteristic Arizona doctrine of equal rights, which includes the Spanish doctrine of equal title, and adds a large share of management and control in the wife. The result is a system which, from the woman's point of view, must be the most satisfactory since the days of the Amazons.

Personal Injuries Under the California Community Property Law

*William Q. de Funiak**

The prevalence of personal injury actions with an accompanying, and to some an alarming, increase in the amount of recoveries, not only in California but throughout the country, may well warrant some review of the legal rules governing where spouses are involved. In this respect, we may consider the matter from three standpoints. First, where the personal injury is inflicted by a spouse or by both spouses on a third person; second, where the personal injury is inflicted upon a spouse by some third person; and third, where one spouse inflicts the injury upon the other spouse or is at least in some measure responsible therefor.

Where the injury is inflicted upon a third person by a spouse or by both spouses, the important concern relates to the personal responsibility of the spouses and what property or properties, separate and community, are liable at the suit of the third person. Little difficulty presents itself where both spouses join in the commission of the tort so that they are in the position of joint tortfeasors. The separate property of both as well as all the community property, regardless of by which spouse acquired, becomes liable.[1] And certainly the same result would ensue where the husband directs or ratifies such a tort committed by the wife. While the courts would probably not be inclined to consider from a legal standpoint that a wife could "direct" the commission of a personal injury by the husband so as to render her personally liable, and would require strong evidence of any so-called "ratification" by her of his tort, nevertheless conceiv-

---

* Professor of Law, University of San Francisco; author, *Principles of Community Property* and *Cases and Materials on Community Property*.

1. Although an action of waste, an illustration is Bonneau v. Galeazi, 215 Cal. 27, 8 P.2d 133 (1932), where the action for damages was against husband and wife. Judgment against both was sustained on appeal and particularly as to the wife on the ground the evidence showed that she participated in the tort.

ably either situation might arise so as to impose liability upon the wife.[2]

The more common case is that in which the personal injury is inflicted upon some third person by one spouse alone. In California, recapitulation of the Civil Code and the recent cases show that the husband is not liable for civil injuries committed by the wife and that damages are recoverable from her alone[3] (in the absence, of course, of "direction" or "ratification" by the husband). Thus, neither the separate property of the husband nor community property acquired by the husband can be subjected to liability for torts of the wife.[4] However, the separate property of the wife and her earnings are liable for her tort.[5] It is immaterial whether these earnings of the wife are community property, which ordinarily they legally are,[6] or whether they are her separate property pursuant to antenuptial or postnuptial agreement between the spouses; either agreement is legally permissible in California.[7] Some areas of doubt exist as to the liability of these earnings where their form changes or they are commingled with other property, such as with community property acquired by the husband. So long as they are still traceable in other forms, they should still be liable, but it would seem that if so commingled with exempt properties as to be unidentifiable or untraceable they would no longer be reachable.

Where the physical injury of a third person is inflicted by the husband alone, his separate property is subject to liability and the community property in its entirety,[8] except that so much of the community property as is represented by earnings of the wife is not liable.[9] But if these earnings of the wife are commingled with community property acquired by the husband beyond identification, the whole commingled fund or property

2. Common law influences on the courts of most community property states must be considered here. See 1 de Funiak, Principles of Community Property § 182 (1943).

3. McClain v. Tufts, 83 Cal. App.2d 140, 187 P.2d 818 (1947), 21 So. Calif. L. Rev. 388 (1948).

4. Cal. Civ. Code § 171a (Deering, 1949); McClain v. Tufts, 83 Cal. App.2d 140, 187 P.2d 818 (1947).

5. Cal. Civ. Code §§ 167, 171a (Deering, 1949).

6. Cal. Civ. Code § 171c (Deering, 1953), enacted in 1951, in providing for management by the wife of her earnings expressly states that the section shall not be construed as making such money the separate property of the wife nor as changing the respective interests of the spouses therein.

7. Cal. Civ. Code §§ 159, 177 *et seq.* (Deering, 1949).

8. Grolemund v. Cafferata, 17 Cal.2d 679, 111 P.2d 641 (1941).

9. Cal. Civ. Code § 168 (Deering, 1949).

may be subjected to such liability.[10] The separate property of the wife is not liable for the husband's tort.[11]

While the foregoing rules apply to most situations, an exception must be recognized by reason of the application of the California Vehicle Code.[12] While the extent of this liability of an owner of a motor vehicle is limited by Section 403 of this Code, it is important to notice that Section 402 imputes to an owner liability for the negligence of the operator if such operation is by permission, express or implied, of the owner. This section has been applied to one co-owner where another co-owner is operating the vehicle and is negligent. Thus, the question has arisen as to whether a wife, as co-owner of a family automobile, is subject to liability when the husband injures someone while operating the vehicle. Bearing in mind that in California spouses may own property in community or as joint tenants or tenants in common,[13] it may be noticed that the California Supreme Court has pointed out that where the vehicle is owned as community property, the entire management and control of it is by law completely in the husband and so the wife has no consent to give which could add anything to his control. Accordingly, no liability would be imposed on her or subject her separate property or her earnings to liability for the husband's tort. On the other hand, if the spouses own the vehicle as joint tenants or tenants in common, the court points out that her voice in its use is equal to that of the husband and it becomes a question of fact whether he used it with her consent, express or implied, so as to subject her to liability under Section 402.[14] Under whatever form of ownership the vehicle is held, within the limits set by Section 403, the husband may become liable for a tort committed by the wife while driving the vehicle, if he has expressly or impliedly consented to her driving it.[15]

With respect to the foregoing situation, it may be pointed out that a plaintiff who wishes to hold an owner or co-owner liable must establish ownership at the time of the injury and

10. See, *e.g.*, Truelsen; Porter, Executor v. Nelson, 42 Cal. App.2d 750, 109 P.2d 996 (1941).

11. CAL. CIV. CODE § 171 (Deering, 1949).

12. Generally, see Miller, *Community Function and Automobile Owners' Responsibilities*, 6 LOYOLA L. REV. 43 (1951).

13. See CAL. CIV. CODE §§ 682, 683 (Deering, 1949).

14. Wilcox v. Berry, 32 Cal.2d 189, 195 P.2d 414 (1948); similarly, Cox v. Kaufman, 77 Cal. App.2d 449, 175 P.2d 260 (1946).

15. Formerly, under the *California Vehicle Code*, this was not true, as in Hill v. Jacquemart, 55 Cal. App. 498, 203 Pac. 1021 (1921); but as indicated the situation is now otherwise.

the permission, express or implied, of such owner or co-owner to the operation. Such plaintiff, wishing to establish liability on the part of a wife as co-owner of an automobile driven by the husband, has the additional burden of proving that her ownership is of a separate property nature as a tenant and not that of a community property nature.[16] Of course, it might be considered that the title evidence, such as a bill of sale or the registration certificate, might show the form of ownership, and, if showing a tenancy, that the burden is then on the wife to prove that despite such form the automobile is nevertheless community property.[17] As anyone owning an automobile in California knows, there is scarcely room on a registration certificate for two names, let alone any statement as to the form of ownership.[18] There is authority that there is nothing in the provisions of the Vehicle Code requiring anything beyond the listing of the owner or owners and the mere fact that the names of husband and wife (*e.g.*, "John and Jane Doe") are listed does not indicate the character of ownership.[19] Actually, such a listing should raise a presumption of community property, but it may be noticed that the California Supreme Court has pointed out that a registration of "John Doe and/or Jane Doe" rebuts any presumption of community property and indicates a joint tenancy.[20] Of course, as already indicated above, a form of title showing joint tenancy is rebuttable to show that the property is actually community property.

With respect to the situation in which a third person inflicts personal injury upon a spouse, we enter the realm in which there is a split among the community property states as to whether the cause of action and the recovery thereon is the separate property of the injured spouse or is community property. The more reasonable view, it seems to me, is that followed

---

16. Pacific Tel. & Tel. Co. v. Wellman, 98 Cal. App.2d 151, 219 P.2d 506 (1950).

17. While an instrument of title stating a tenancy raises a presumption that such is the ownership, this is rebuttable to show that actually the property is held by the spouses in community. This is usually accomplished by showing that the property was purchased with community funds and that it was not intended to be other than community property. A leading case is Tomaier v. Tomaier, 23 Cal.2d 754, 146 P.2d 905 (1944).

18. See my comments in 3 SURVEY OF CALIFORNIA LAW 160 (1950-1951).

19. Pacific Tel. & Tel. Co. v. Wellman, 98 Cal. App.2d 151, 219 P.2d 506 (1950), distinguishing Caccamo v. Swanston, 94 Cal. App.2d 957, 212 P.2d 246 (1949).

20. Wilcox v. Berry, 32 Cal.2d 189, 195 P.2d 414 (1948).

in Louisiana,[21] and evidently also in Nevada[22] and New Mexico,[23] that there are or may be two causes of action, one in the injured spouse for pain, suffering and disfigurement which is the separate property of that spouse, and one in the community for loss to the community in expenses, loss of services and earnings, and the like. Certainly, the foregoing states recognize such a rule where the wife is the spouse injured.

While the other community property states, including California, follow the view that the cause of action to an injured spouse and the recovery therefor are community property,[24] California has a somewhat peculiar view developed as to this, where the wife is injured, which up to a point follows the view in the first group of states. While there is apparently only one cause of action, two actions would seem to be required, although these may be consolidated. One action must be brought by the wife to recover for her pain and suffering, although the recovery will represent community funds.[25] The other action, for what are called the "consequential damages," for loss to the community, must be brought by the husband, although it appears that he may delegate this authority to the wife.[26] It will be seen, accordingly, that there is some recognition that two different matters are involved, although the conclusion is that everything is community property. Naturally, the contributory negligence of the husband will defeat his recovery for the consequential damages and likewise will defeat the wife's action for damages for her pain and suffering.[27] If she sues later, the judgment against the husband in his prior action is res judicata as to his contributory negligence and accordingly defeats the wife's action.[28] The effect of the contributory negligence rule to defeat the wife's recovery seems somewhat unpopular at present

21. See, *e.g.*, Arts 2334, 2402, LA. CIVIL CODE of 1870; Simon v. Harrison, 200 So. 476 (La. App. 1941).

22. Fredrickson & Watson Const. Co. v. Boyd, 60 Nev. 117, 102 P.2d 627 (1940), followed in King v. Yancey, 147 F.2d 379 (9th Cir. 1945); Underhill v. Anciaux, 68 Nev. 69, 226 P.2d 794 (1951).

23. Soto v. Vandeventer, 56 N. Mex. 483, 245 P.2d 826 (1952).

24. 1 DE FUNIAK, PRINCIPLES OF COMMUNITY PROPERTY § 82 *et seq.* (1943).

25. Sanderson v. Niemann, 17 Cal.2d 563, 110 P.2d 1025 (1941), describing the wife as an indispensable party plaintiff, although husband may join with her. Right of wife to sue was conferred by CAL. CODE CIV. PROC. ANN. § 370 (Deering, 1949), which is held, however, not to change rule that damages recovered are community property. See Gioretti v. Wollaston, 83 Cal. App. 358, 257 Pac. 109 (1927).

26. See Louie v. Hagstorm's Food Stores, Inc., 81 Cal. App.2d 601, 184 P.2d 708 (1947).

27. McFadden v. Santa Ana, O. & T. St. Ry., 87 Cal. 464, 25 Pac. 681 (1891).

28. Zaragosa v. Craven, 33 Cal.2d 315, 202 P.2d 73 (1949).

and there is agitation to enact legislation abolishing contributory negligence in favor of the comparative negligence doctrine. It may also be noted that in a recent case the California Supreme Court has held that where the wife sues after the death of the husband, his contributory negligence should not defeat her recovery, since he can no longer profit from his own contributory negligence.[29]

Another facet of this situation is that in California the spouses may contract between them that what either acquires, although it would otherwise be community property, shall be the separate property of the spouse acquiring it.[30] Dictum of the California Supreme Court indicates that the spouses may contract that a cause of action for personal injury shall be the separate property of the injured spouse.[31] However, recently, in an action by the wife to recover damages for personal injuries to her, wherein the defendant answered alleging contributory negligence of the husband, and the spouses then entered into a contract whereby the husband relinquished any interest in the cause of action, this was not recognized by the court as effective to remove the husband's contributory negligence as a defensive factor and to enable the wife to recover.[32]

One other matter may be commented upon in connection with a personal injury to a spouse during marriage. In the so-called *Franklin* case,[33] a district court of appeal held that although personal injury to a husband during the marriage gave rise to a cause of action which was community property, nevertheless if the injured husband did not effect a recovery until after termination of the marriage by divorce, the recovery was his separate property. Fairly recently, although the same question was not involved in the case before it, the California Supreme Court took occasion to overrule expressly the view expressed in the *Franklin* case and to declare that both the cause of action and the proceeds of the recovery thereon, no matter when recovered, are community property.[34]

By virtue of California Civil Code Section 169, earnings and accumulations of the wife, while living separate and apart from the husband, are her separate property. Living separate and

29. Flores v. Brown, 39 Cal.2d 622, 248 P.2d 922 (1952).
30. Right to contract, see CAL. CIV. CODE §§ 158-160 (Deering, 1949).
31. Zaragosa v. Craven, 33 Cal.2d 315, 202 P.2d 73 (1949).
32. Kesler v. Pabst, 273 P.2d 257 (Cal. 1954).
33. Franklin v. Franklin, 67 Cal. App.2d 717, 155 P.2d 637 (1945).
34. Zaragosa v. Craven, 33 Cal.2d 315, 202 P.2d 73 (1949).

apart, in this respect, does not mean that the spouses must have been divorced or separated by a decree of court, but merely that the wife is living apart with no intention of resuming cohabitation.[35] A cause of action for personal injury to the wife, inflicted during this period of separation, is considered an "accumulation" within this code section and is the separate property of the wife.[36] It would be otherwise, of course, if the recovery was made by the wife during this separation, but for an injury inflicted while she was living with her husband. This seems clear in view of the language of the Supreme Court in overruling the *Franklin* case.[37] Likewise, in view of that language and other authorities, a recovery by a spouse during marriage for injury inflicted prior to marriage would be the separate property of the injured spouse.[38] The fact that at the time of the injury, the man who is now her husband was contributorily negligent will not defeat her recovery, since he has no interest in it.[39]

The situation of one spouse inflicting personal injury on the other spouse during the marriage presents no unusual difficulties of solution in its ordinary aspects. In California,[40] as in other states, whether community or non-community property states, one spouse may not sue another for personal injury inflicted during the marriage.[41] Foregoing any discussion of this, we may merely recognize that it represents a presently established matter of public policy. However, a handful of cases have presented an interesting offshoot of this matter. Many years ago, in Texas, a wife separated from her husband. While so separated and prior to any decree of divorce or separation, the husband with the aid of a friend seized and forcibly detained the wife

35. See discussion in Makeig v. United Security Bank & Trust Co., 112 Cal. App. 138, 296 Pac. 673 (1931).

36. See Christiana v. Rose, 100 Cal. App.2d 46, 222 P.2d 891 (1950), reviewing authorities to this effect from other states.

37. Zaragosa v. Craven, 33 Cal.2d 315, 202 P.2d 73 (1949).

38. See Morrissey v. Kirkelie, 5 Cal. App.2d 183, 42 P.2d 361 (1935); Finley v. Winkler, 99 Cal. App.2d 887, 222 P.2d 345 (1950).

39. Finley v. Winkler, 99 Cal. App.2d 887, 222 P.2d 345 (1950).

40. Peters v. Peters, 156 Cal. 32, 103 Pac. 219 (1909). And see Cubbison v. Cubbison, 73 Cal. App.2d 437, 166 P.2d 387 (1946).

41. See 1 DE FUNIAK, PRINCIPLES OF COMMUNITY PROPERTY § 153 (1943). It must be recognized that there may be qualifications of this rule, as in Louisiana where it appears that although the wife may not sue the husband she does have a cause of action which she may prosecute against his insurer. See Burke v. Massachusetts Bonding & Ins. Co., 19 So.2d 647 (La. App. 1944), *aff'd*, 209 La. 495, 24 So.2d 875 (1946); McHenry v. American Employers Ins. Co., 18 So.2d 840 (La. App. 1944), conforming to answer to certified question in 206 La. 70, 18 So.2d 656 (1944).

while he attempted to persuade her to live with him again. After effecting her escape or release, the wife sued both the husband and his friend for damages for false imprisonment. Upon the trial she obtained a judgment against both, but upon appeal the judgment against the husband was reversed on the ground that the injury was inflicted during coverture and so gave no cause of action. However, the judgment against the other defendant was sustained, it being said that there could be no enforced contribution between the defendants and the judgment was several.[42] A very similar factual situation arose more recently in Idaho and the Supreme Court of that state adopted a different view as to the right to sue the husband and recover from him, despite the fact that the tort occurred during coverture. Among other things, the court placed this right of action on the ground that the wife had a status of her own and that no difficulty arose as to the recovery, since it would come within the statute relating to accumulations of a married woman while living separate and apart from her husband.[43] In California, also recently, has arisen the question of whether a wife could sue her husband for a tort inflicted by him while they were separated, specifically during the period between the interlocutory decree of divorce and the final decree of divorce. Upon the ground that the tort was committed prior to the final decree and while the parties were still legally married, the court held that the wife, although suing after final divorce, could not maintain the action.[44]

Another case of recent origin involved a man who, knowing that he did not have a valid decree of divorce from a former marriage, entered into an attempted marriage with a woman who believed in good faith that they were married. Subsequently, he sued her for a tort, attempting to allege that since they were not legally married, there was no bar to his suing her in tort. However, as might be anticipated, the court held that he was estopped to deny the validity of the marriage and was thus, in effect, in the same position as a legal spouse attempting to sue the other spouse for a tort inflicted during marriage.[45]

While not involving a tort inflicted during marriage by one spouse against the other, brief notice may be given to the mat-

---

42. Nickerson and Matson v. Nickerson, 65 Tex. 281 (1886).
43. Lorang v. Hays, 69 Idaho 440, 209 P.2d 733 (1949).
44. Paulus v. Bauder, 106 Cal. App.2d 589, 235 P.2d 422 (1951).
45. Watson v. Watson, 39 Cal.2d 305, 246 P.2d 19 (1952).

ter of one spouse suing the other during marriage to recover for personal injury allegedly inflicted by the defendant upon the plaintiff prior to marriage. Admittedly an unusual situation, it has arisen, obviously in the effort to effect a payment by an insurer of the defendant. In California, we have had the case of an engaged couple riding in a car driven by the man and colliding with another car. After the engaged couple were married, the wife sued the husband on the ground that his negligence contributed to her injury. It was held that she had a separate property cause of action which she could enforce by action against him during the marriage and the fact that he carried insurance did not deprive her of this right.[46]

In conclusion, it may be said the foregoing discussion of the three situations is not intended to constitute a complete coverage of all aspects or possibilities concerning these situations, but rather to consider the present state of the California law, in the light of the more recent cases.

46. Carver v. Ferguson, 254 P.2d 44 (Cal. App. 1953).

The Creditor and the Community In Idaho

*W. J. Brockelbank**

A great deal has been written on the assets of the community, but much less on its liabilities. In this article it is proposed to have a look at the community from the point of view of the outsider who has to do business with one or the other of its owners, the husband and wife. Since, nowadays, nearly everybody is married, this look at the outsider and the community will necessarily cover nearly every problem of collection of the average creditor.

Community property exists in only eight states.[1] No recent converts have been made. When the income tax increased to a point where it became a serious burden on the taxpayer, certain states adopted the community system as a measure of tax relief.[2]

But when Congress provided for the system of split income of husband and wife,[3] so that the community system no longer gave a tax advantage, the states that had adopted the community system as a measure of tax relief stumbled over each other in the rush to repeal.[4] This was probably all for the best. Those states never understood community property and if it could not be used for the intended purpose it was better not to use it at all.

Yet it is rather significant that, in the brief period when it was in force, not one of those states was convinced of any in-

---

* Professor of Law, University of Idaho.

1. Arizona, California, Idaho, Louisiana, Nevada, New Mexico, Texas, and Washington.

2. Oregon, Oklahoma, Michigan, Pennsylvania, Nebraska, and Hawaii.

3. Revenue Act of 1948, § 301, 62 STAT. 114 (1948). See Rubin & Champagne, *Some Community Property Aspects of the 1948 Revenue Act*, 9 LOUISIANA LAW REVIEW 1 (1948).

4. Michigan repealed her community property statute thirty-eight days after Congress passed the Revenue Act of 1948. Mich. Pub. Acts 1948(E.S.), No. 39, p. 95; MICH. COMP. LAWS §§ 26:216(21)—26:216(25). The Pennsylvania act had been held unconstitutional in Willcox v. Penn Mutual Life Insurance Co., 357 Pa. 581, 55 A.2d 521 (1947). The Oregon, Nebraska, Oklahoma and Hawaii acts were repealed in 1949. Moshofsky, *Repeal of the Community-Property Law*, 28 ORE. L. REV. 311 (1949); Note, *Epilogue to the Community Property Scramble: Problems of Repeal*, 50 COL. L. REV. 332-51 (1950); Legislation, *Community Property Laws—Repeal*, 28 NEB. L. REV. 142 (1948).

trinsic merit of the system as a solution of marital property problems. It is believed that one of the stumbling blocks to the adoption of the community system anywhere is the inadequacy of its dealing with the rights of creditors. The common law states, in the brief look they were afforded at the community system, sought a simple answer to the question: how will it operate for the ordinary creditor who must do business with one or both spouses? First, they found eight different answers and, second, each of them was complex and uncertain.

The object of the present study is not to hold up the Idaho solution of the creditor's difficulties as the ideal solution. Nor is it expected that any converts will be made. The purpose is rather to point out the inadequacies of the system as it now exists in order that other community property states may have some basis for comparison and especially in order that we, in Idaho, may fill in some of the gaps and thus improve the situation for use by ourselves.

I

The community system comes to us from the civil law.[5] One of the characteristics of the civil law is codification.[6] A civilian expects and usually gets an answer to every question from the code. The common law lawyer is beginning to adopt this idea. In recent years many important subjects of the law have been codified[7] and much that remains is covered by the *Restatements*.[8] So when the merchant, who has done business with and extended credit to a married person, asks, "Where do I stand and what

5. 1 DE FUNIAK, PRINCIPLES OF COMMUNITY PROPERTY c. 1 (1943); Kirkwood, *Historical Background and Objectives of the Law of Community Property in the Pacific Coast States*, 11 WASH. L. REV. 1 (1936); Lobinger, *The Marital Community: Its Origin and Diffusion*, 14 A.B.A.J. 211 (1928); Loewy, *Spanish Community of Acquests and Gains and its Adoption and Modification by State of California*, 1 CALIF. L. REV. 32 (1912).

6. In studying French law we "pass into a world governed by codes. . . . [A] code is supposed . . . to provide a fresh start in all those parts of the law with which it deals. . . . [I]t should be interpreted only in the light of its own provisions and definitions." AMOS & WALTON, INTRODUCTION TO FRENCH LAW 4 (1935); BUCKLAND, ROMAN LAW AND COMMON LAW 6-14 (1936).

7. Important segments of our law have been codified. As examples one may cite the Uniform Sales Act, the Uniform Conditional Sales Act, the Negotiable Instruments Law, the Warehouse Receipts Act, the Bills of Lading Act, the Stock Transfer Act, the Partnership Act, the Limited Partnership Act, the Model Business Corporation Act, and a host of other uniform acts on particular subjects. "The center of gravity of the legal system has been shifting to legislation." Roscoe Pound, *Cacoethes Dissentiendi: The Heated Judicial Dissent*, 39 A.B.A.J. 794, 795 (1953).

8. Restatements cover the subjects of Agency, Conflict of Laws, Contracts, Judgments, Property, Restitution, Security, Torts, Trusts, the Code of Criminal Procedure and the Model Code of Evidence.

property is available for the payment of my claim?" he is entitled to a simple straightforward answer. Any system of law that cannot give him a simple answer is not only unsuitable for export, it is unsuitable for use at home.

To begin, we may eliminate, with a word, the consideration of the creditor's rights against the single person. These rights in Idaho do not differ materially from the rights of creditors against single persons elsewhere. Section 11-201 of the Idaho Code of 1947 provides that "all goods, chattels, moneys and other property, both real and personal, or any interest therein of the judgment debtor, not exempt by law, and all property and rights of property, seized and held under attachment in the action, are liable to execution." Particular provision is made for corporate shares and gold dust[9] and debts owing to the debtor.[10] The general exemption law in Idaho[11] is similar to that in most states and of course the creditor expects to be subject to the statute of limitations,[12] the homestead laws[13] and the law of bankruptcy.[14] All these provisions apply not only to single persons, but also to married persons whenever the debt is a separate debt.

But what of the community and community debts?

Before proceeding it may be well to clarify and simplify our problem by asking what are the different kinds of debts and what are the different kinds of property that may be subjected to their payment?

First, all debts are incurred either before or after marriage. Of course, antenuptial debts are subject to the above provisions concerning the debts of single persons, but the division is worthy of notice in its relation to the community because the question must be asked, how far is community property available for the satisfaction of antenuptial debts? May a person who has no property beyond what is covered by the exemption laws avoid payment by getting married? Is this escape mechanism the same for both men and women?

From another point of view, debts may be classified as arising out of contracts, torts or other obligations imposed by law. This

9. IDAHO CODE § 11-201 (1947).
10. *Ibid.*
11. *Id.* § 11-205
12. *Id.* §§ 5-201—5-240.
13. *Id.* §§ 55-1001—55-1304.
14. 30 STAT. 544 (1898), *as amended,* 11 U.S.C. §§ 1-1103 (1952).

classification is desirable, for while the capacity of a man and woman to incur debts in each of these subdivisions is the same prior to marriage, there may be marked differences between the male and female capacity after marriage.

The contract container and the tort container are simple enough. They bring into play the whole law of contracts and torts. No elaboration is necessary. By "other obligations imposed by law" is meant a broad catch-all subdivision that will include not only the obligation to pay taxes, family support, fines and criminal penalties, but also every other obligation and especially those growing out of the field which used to be called quasi-contracts and constructive trusts, but which today, in most law schools, travels under the vocable "restitution."[15]

Finally we must divide antenuptial debts into the two classes: those incurred by the man and those incurred by the woman. There will be no difference between these two classes of debts so far as the availability of the *separate* property of each debtor is concerned, but each class may very well involve different treatment when it comes to the availability of community property for their satisfaction.

The above classification of antenuptial debts will hold good for the postnuptial debt, except to observe that postnuptial debts should first of all be classified as community debts and separate debts. Beyond that, we must notice again that each may grow out of a contract, a tort or other obligation imposed by law and may be incurred either by husband or the wife.

Coming now to a classification of the different kinds of property that may be subjected to the payment of each class of debt, we must first isolate the separate property of the wife and the separate property of the husband. Then comes community property. Is it necessary to subdivide further? It would greatly simplify both the learning and the practice of law if it were not. However, simplification of learning or practice is and should be of little persuasive effect in the realm of social values. The Idaho legislature of 1881 set up a special kind of community property, *viz.*, "rents, issues and profits" of the wife's separate property and "all compensation due or owing for her personal

15. The term "restitution" has been given greater currency by its use in the *Restatement of the Law of Restitution, Quasi Contracts and Constructive Trusts.* Two valuable casebooks on the subject by Professors Patterson and Thurston are in current use in the law schools.

TABLE I

Classification of Debts and Property That May Be Used to Satisfy Them

				Separate Property of W	Separate Property of H	Community Property within 11-204	Community Property outside 11-204
Antenuptial Debts	Incurred by H		Contract				
			Tort				
			Other Obligations imposed by law				
	Incurred by W		Contract				
			Tort				
			Other Obligations imposed by law				
Postnuptial Debts	Community Debts	Incurred by H	Contract				
			Tort				
			Other Obligations imposed by law				
		Incurred by W	Contract				
			Tort				
			Other Obligations imposed by law				
	Seperate Debts	Incurred by H	Contract				
			Tort				
			Other Obligations imposed by law				
		Incurred by W	Contract				
			Tort				
			Other Obligations imposed by law				

services" (both of which are community property in Idaho)[16] and provided that this special kind of community property should be "exempt from execution against her husband."[17] Thus the property available for the payments of debts must be divided into four classes: The separate property of the wife, the separate property of the husband, the special kind of community property covered by Section 11-204 and finally community property outside of Section 11-204. The above scheme of classification is set up in Table I.

Since this table gives a complete list of debts and the kinds of property available for their satisfaction, its use makes possible the testing of a given system of law for completeness and the appraisal of its over-all effectiveness. It is the purpose of this article thus to test the law of Idaho.

II

We shall attempt to fill in the pigeonholes of the table by answers contained in the statutes and decisions. Let us begin with the statutes. They are meager indeed.

For purpose of reference they are set out in a footnote.[18] It will be noticed that all three sections state explicitly what property is *not* liable. The creditor of the husband must touch neither the separate property of the wife nor the "rents, issues and profits" of the separate property of the wife nor the "compensation due or owing for her personal services."[19] Neither must the antenuptial creditor of the wife touch the separate property of the husband. But as to what property *is* liable, there is only one statement. Section 32-911 says that the separate property of the wife *is* liable for "her own debts contracted before or after marriage." Beyond this there is silence.

It will be noticed that silence encompasses nearly all of the community property and nearly all of the separate property of

---

16. IDAHO CODE § 32-906 (1947).

17. *Id.* § 11-204

18. *Ibid.*: "Exemption in favor of married woman. All real and personal estate belonging to any married woman at the time of her marriage, or to which she subsequently becomes entitled in her own right, and all the rents, issues and profits thereof, and all compensation due or owing for her personal services, is exempt from execution against her husband."

Id. § 32-910: "Liability for antenuptial debts. The separate property of the husband is not liable for the debts of the wife contracted before the marriage."

Id. § 32-911: "Wife's liability for personal debts. The separate property of the wife is not liable for the debts of her husband, but is liable for her own debts contracted before or after marriage."

19. *Id.* § 11-204.

the husband. Yet the separate property of the husband and the community property together will constitute just about all of the property that is owned by the average couple. This means that the creditor who seeks an answer in the statutes as to what property is available to the payment of his claim will find a statement concerning only a negligible part of the family property and this statement, so far as it goes, will tell him, not what property he may attach, but what property he may not attach.

He must conclude that as a practical matter the statutes have failed to give information as to what he can do.

III

In view of the incompleteness of the statutes, the creditor must seek to fill in the gap from the cases. What will he find?

The Supreme Court, unlike the legislature, cannot make law *ad libitum.* Even to make law by the slow glacier-like process, which has given us the common law, the court must await a case. In Idaho, on the question of the availability of the different elements of property classified in Table I for the payment of the debts of the spouses, the Supreme Court has done a lot of waiting. In fact in only a very few cases has the court had an opportunity to make a decision.

First, it is not surprising to find that the cases hold that the separate property of the wife is liable for her separate debts. These may be independent decisions or cases simply enforcing Section 32-911 that "the separate property of the wife . . . is liable for her own debts contracted before or after marriage."[20]

That the separate property of the husband is liable for his own debts may be taken for granted. No case before the Supreme Court has ever raised the point and the legislator considered it unnecessary to state the principle in the section where for reasons of symmetry one would expect to find it (Section 32-910).

Evans v. Kroutinger and *McCarthy v. Paris*[21] held that the separate property of the wife could not be taken by the creditors of the husband.

As to the liability of community property the simplest case

20. Boise Association of Credit Men Ltd. v. Glenn Ferry Meat Co., 48 Idaho 600, 283 Pac. 1038 (1930); Briggs v. Mason, 44 Idaho 283, 256 Pac. 368 (1927); Sassaman v. Root, 37 Idaho 588, 218 Pac. 374 (1923); Dernham and Kaufmann v. Rowley, 4 Idaho 753, 44 Pac. 643 (1896); Bassett v. Beam, 4 Idaho 106, 36 Pac. 501 (1894).

21. 9 Idaho 153, 72 Pac. 882 (1903) and 46 Idaho 165, 267 Pac. 232 (1928).

is one holding that it is available for the payment of community debts. While no case on so simple an issue has ever been appealed to the Supreme Court, *Gustin v. Byam*[22] held that a wife did not make out a case of fraud when she proved that a husband, shortly before divorce, allowed what was presumably a community creditor to satisfy his claim from community personalty.

While the rule that community property is liable for community debts needs no belaboring, what about its availability for the payment of the separate debts of the spouses? Idaho has arrived at the position that it *is* liable for the separate debts of the husband but is *not* liable for the separate debts of the wife. In the important case of *Holt v. Empey*[23] a creditor for the separate debt of the husband was allowed to satisfy his claim from the community. The court did not inquire whether the separate debt in question was antenuptial or postnuptial. It simply held that "community real estate is liable to attachment and execution for the debts of the husband whether incurred for his own use or for the benefit of the community." The basis of the decision was that there was no reason to depart from the general rule announced in 5 Ruling Case Law 858 that community property is liable for the separate debts, obligations and liabilities of the husband.

In the important decision of *Hall v. Johns*[24] in 1909, the wife had borrowed money for her own use and benefit, and the surety on her obligation, having been compelled to pay, sought reimbursement. The trial court's opinion that her husband was not liable and that the judgment against the wife could not be satisfied out of the common property was affirmed. The decision, in itself, probably states present law; but several dicta of the court would be of questionable authority today. For instance, the court states that title to community property is in the husband and, during the existence of the community, the wife's interest is a mere expectancy. The contrary was held in *Kohny v. Dunbar* in 1912.[25]

It is uncertain whether the court in *Hall v. Johns* was of the

---

22. 41 Idaho 538, 240 Pac. 600 (1925). But a wife may make out a case of fraud if she proves that her husband connives with another to bring a collusive suit in order to defeat the interest of the divorce-seeking wife in the community. Pittock v. Pittock, 15 Idaho 47, 96 Pac. 212 (1908).

23. 32 Idaho 106, 178 Pac. 703 (1919).

24. 17 Idaho 224, 105 Pac. 71 (1909).

25. 21 Idaho 258, 121 Pac. 544 (1912).

opinion that the wife did not validly contract for want of capacity or whether having contracted, the husband and so the community was not liable therefor. In any case the court stated that the community property cannot be bound by postnuptial contracts of the wife made for the use and benefit of her own separate property and for this proposition it seemed appropriate to the court to cite a Michigan case holding that a husband is not liable for money lent to a wife. The same sort of reference to the common law to fill up gaps left by the statutes is employed in an early California case.[26] This method ignores the whole history of community property. It may be all right to take over bodily a principle from the common law if, after an examination of the background of Spanish law from which we took the law of community property, no principle is found, but to do so unconsciously, as if a case in community property is "just another case" like those in contracts or torts or other common law subjects, is to demonstrate an ignorance of the wrench of historical continuity involved. One modern scholar has characterized this method as one of "startling obtuseness"[27] and "erroneous"[28] and another as "unfortunate."[29]

The most recent case involving the possible liability of community property is *Great American Indemnity Co. of New York v. Garrison.*[30] In that case a husband who was a bonded treasurer of Clearwater County, Idaho, misappropriated state funds which his surety was later obliged to pay. The suit for reimbursement was heard in the federal court on grounds of diversity of citizenship. The court sitting in Washington purported, under the *Erie* decision, to follow the Washington conflicts of laws rule, making Idaho law applicable as being the place where the debt arose or the place where the tort was committed. Finding no Idaho law the court said that there was no reason to suppose that the Idaho Supreme Court would apply the rule of contract debts, which makes the community liable, to the husband's torts in the face of the almost universally accepted principle that the marital community is not liable for the husband's torts. For this proposition, cases from Washington and the current encyclopedias are cited. The encyclopedias repeat the citations from Washington and all the cases from other states. The latter are

26. Van Maren v. Johnson, 15 Cal. 308 (1860).
27. 1 DE FUNIAK, PRINCIPLES OF COMMUNITY PROPERTY 111 (1943).
28. *Id.* at 439.
29. Jacob, *The Law of Community Property in Idaho*, 1 IDAHO L.J. 1, 5 (1931).
30. 75 F. Supp. 811 (E.D. Wash. 1948).

not uniformly in favor of immunity from liability. So one can just about say that the court, instead of applying "a universally accepted principle," is in reality applying Washington law to an Idaho tort. It is well to notice that this case, unlike the ordinary case, does not add the reasoned conviction of an additional court, for under the *Erie* decision the federal court does not express its own convictions but only those of the state court it happens to be following. Since the case is not binding on the Supreme Court of Idaho, it should not be taken too seriously as a monument to the eternal law of Idaho. So far as it goes and looking only at its exact holding, we can say that there is no community liability for the tort of a married man committed in connection with his function as a public officer.

In regard to the question whether the separate property of the wife is available to satisfy a community debt, a preliminary question arises in Idaho as to the capacity of a married woman to contract. An ancient territorial statute (still in force as Section 29-101 of the Idaho Code of 1947) provided that "All persons are capable of contracting, except minors, persons of unsound mind, and persons deprived of their civil rights." The court has decided that this statute cannot be taken "to confer upon married women the right to make any and all contracts . . . and this is evident from the fact that the act with relation to the wife becoming a sole trader remains upon the statute book."[31] The sole trader law, passed in 1875,[32] regulated and restricted the right of a wife to do business for herself and its repeal in 1917[33] does not seem to have restored her general contractual capacity, if any she ever had. While her capacity is not general she has been specifically enabled to make contracts relating to her separate property,[34] to manage and control the rents and profits thereof[35] and the earnings for her personal services.[36] She has general capacity to make marriage settlements[37] and a contract entered into in a state where her common law disabilities have been removed will be enforced.[38] The court has finally arrived at the formula that a married woman can contract in relation to her

31. Dernham and Kaufmann v. Rowley, 4 Idaho 753, 44 Pac. 643 (1896).
32. Territory of Idaho Acts, approved Jan. 17, 1875; Idaho Rev. Stat. §§ 5850-5860 (1887).
33. Idaho Sess. Laws 1917, c. 158, p. 483.
34. Idaho Code § 32-904 (1947).
35. *Id.* §§ 32-906, 32-913.
36. *Id.* § 32-913.
37. *Id.* § 32-905.
38. Meier & Frank Co. v. Bruce, 30 Idaho 732, 168 Pac. 5 (1917).

separate property, her personal services and for her own use and benefit.[39]

The above limitations create a situation where it is unusual for a community debt to be incurred by the wife. However, since compensation for her personal services and the rents and profits of her separate estate fall into community, since contracts concluded in other states where her common law disabilities have been removed are enforced in Idaho and since conceivably contracts made for her own use and benefit may also be for the benefit of the community, the point may arise.

Supposing that the obstacle of the wife's incapacity is surmounted, what is the liability of the wife's separate property for a community debt? The court has erected another obstacle—this one a requirement of pleading and proof. The court has uniformly held that no recovery can be had unless it is pleaded and proved that the contract is for the use and benefit of the wife. Two cases refused, because of this lack of pleading and proof, to hold the wife liable on what very well may have been community obligations.[40] But when, as in *Briggs v. Mason*,[41] the complaint properly alleged that the wife specially promised to pay a certain grocery bill and that the groceries were sold for her use and benefit, the court allowed execution against the wife's separate property. Here was a contract which was indeed for her own use and benefit—for undoubtedly she consumed part of the groceries and had an interest in providing for the family—but it was also a contract that creates perhaps the most typical of community debts. The court insists on the point of pleading,

39. The statement made is about as far as it is safe to go. The whole question merits a separate study. It is in crying need of legislative clarification. More detailed information may be obtained from the following cases: Vanderpool v. Bank of Hansen, 2 F.2d 877 (S.D. Idaho 1924); State *ex rel.* Robins v. Clinger, 72 Idaho 222, 238 P.2d 1145 (1951); Loomis v. Gray, 60 Idaho 193, 90 P.2d 529 (1939); Craig v. Lane, 60 Idaho 178, 89 P.2d 1008 (1939); Beckstead v. Gee, 58 Idaho 758, 79 P.2d 293 (1938); Pacific Acceptance Corp. v. Myers, 49 Idaho 585, 290 Pac. 404 (1930); Farnworth v. Viet, 39 Idaho 40, 225 Pac. 1023 (1924); Howell v. Martin, 36 Idaho 468, 211 Pac. 528 (1922); Overland National Bank v. Halveston, 33 Idaho 489, 196 Pac. 217 (1921); Humbird Lumber Co. v. Doran, 24 Idaho 507, 135 Pac. 66 (1913); Tipton v. Ellsworth, 18 Idaho 207, 109 Pac. 134 (1910); Bank of Commerce v. Baldwin, 14 Idaho 75, 93 Pac. 504 (1908); Edminston v. Smith, 13 Idaho 645, 92 Pac. 842 (1907); Holt v. Gridley, 7 Idaho 416, 63 Pac. 188 (1900); Strode v. Miller, 7 Idaho 16, 59 Pac. 893 (1900); Jaeckel v. Pease, 6 Idaho 131, 53 Pac. 399 (1898); Dernham and Kaufmann v. Rowley, 4 Idaho 753, 44 Pac. 643 (1896); Bassett v. Beam, 4 Idaho 106, 36 Pac. 501 (1894).

40. Pacific Acceptance Corp. v. Myers, 49 Idaho 585, 290 Pac. 404 (1930); Ness v. Coffer, 42 Idaho 78, 244 Pac. 145 (1925).

41. 44 Idaho 283, 256 Pac. 368 (1927).

but the question of whether separate property is liable for a community debt is, for it, unworthy of notice.

Two other cases may have some bearing on the question. In *Booth Mercantile Co. v. Murphy*[42] the wife placed a mortgage on her separate realty in Idaho to secure payment for furniture and supplies purchased in Utah for a hotel business she was operating in Utah. The court, in allowing the creditor to foreclose, was indifferent to whether her domicile was in Utah or Idaho and whether this was a Utah or Idaho contract since a mortgage on her separate property had direct reference to her separate property. The court concluded: "In a sense it would be difficult to name a contract a married woman might make that would not in some respects inure to the benefit of the community, but that fact alone does not lessen her obligation thereon." Had this suit been for a deficiency judgment, the above language might indicate that either "her own debts contracted . . . after marriage" for which Section 32-911 renders her liable or "contracts for her own use and benefit" within the formula so constantly used by the court might be broad enough to include a community debt. However the court was careful to confine itself to the lien created by the mortgage and the statement quoted rises no further than a dictum in regard to her personal obligation or the availability of her separate property not covered by the mortgage.

In *Overland National Bank v. Halveston*[43] the bank sued to recover on three promissory notes made by a wife, one for an assessment on corporate stock which she claimed to be community property, a second for money borrowed from the bank to cover an overdraft on the bank by her son, and a third for the same purpose plus medical attendance for herself. The first note according to the wife was a community obligation and the third one was certainly a community obligation in part (for medical attendance) and unless the bank dealt on the faith of her separate credit the second note and the remainder of the third note may also have been community obligations. The court gave judgment against her on all three notes. The court is concerned almost exclusively with her capacity to contract and at one point says "she is capable of making contracts . . . to the same extent as if she were unmarried."[44] The court is indifferent

42. 14 Idaho 212, 93 Pac. 777 (1908).
43. 33 Idaho 489, 196 Pac. 217 (1921).
44. *Id.* at 500, 196 Pac. at 221. This may have been a slip.

to the availability of her separate property for the satisfaction of a community obligation and holds with reference to the wife's claim that the stock is community property that she is estopped to deny that it is her separate property—this, not on the basis of representations made but simply in the sense that she is barred. Of course, if she is never allowed to avoid liability by showing that the debt is a community debt, this means to the realist that her separate property is liable for community debts. In reality this case allows the separate property of the wife to be liable for a community debt but the court clouds its holding in the language of estoppel and is unwilling to face the problem and give a clear statement of what it is really doing.

It is difficult to draw any conclusion with confidence. While it is possible to cite cases where the separate property of the wife has been taken to satisfy a community debt, the court does not think in these terms. The most that can be said is that a contract which the wife has capacity to make, if properly pleaded and proved to be for her own use and benefit, may bind her separate property; for in such a case the court is willing to give personal judgment against her. The court's interest is not in the availability of the separate property but in pleading and proof that the contract is for her own use and benefit.

This being the situation, it is certain that if the community debt is not incurred by her but by her husband, her separate property is not liable.[45]

There are few other cases of importance. One case decides only a procedural point that the community is bound only if the husband, having been served with process, is a party to the action. The case is for the wife's slander.[46] The court is careful to exclude any indication of what the result might have been had the husband been joined. Other cases merely enforce, for the benefit of creditors, the provisions of the statutes before noted.[47]

---

45. Thomas v. Young, 42 Idaho 240, 245 Pac. 75 (1926).

46. First National Bank of Sandpoint v. Samuels, 53 Idaho 780, 27 P.2d 959 (1933).

47. Section 32-911 to the effect that the separate property of the wife is liable for her own debts was enforced in Sassaman v. Root, 37 Idaho 588, 218 Pac. 374 (1923), and Boise Ass'n of Credit Men, Ltd. v. Glenns Ferry Meat Co., 48 Idaho 600, 283 Pac. 1038 (1930). Section 32-911 to the effect that the separate property of the wife is not liable for the debts of the husband was enforced in McKeehan v. Vollmer-Clearwater Co., 30 Idaho 505, 166 Pac. 256 (1917); Bank of Orofino v. Wellman, 26 Idaho 425, 143 Pac. 1169 (1914); Baldwin v. McFarland, 26 Idaho 85, 141 Pac. 76 (1914); Holt v. Gridley, 7 Idaho 416, 63 Pac. 188 (1900); Young v. First National Bank of Hailey, 4

We set out in Table II the liabilities of the different kinds of separate and community property.

IV

This table includes only the bare bones of the statutes and the cases. It is appropriate to complete it by a few propositions that may be taken for granted and others resulting from inferences and *a fortiori* reasoning. For instance, it may be taken for granted that the separate property of the husband is liable for all his antenuptial debts arising not only out of contract but arising as well from his torts or other obligations imposed by law. The same may be said of his postnuptial separate debts.

Idaho 323, 39 Pac. 557 (1895). This result was taken for granted in Feltham v. Blunck, 34 Idaho 1, 198 Pac. 763 (1921). Section 11-204 to the effect that the "rents, issues and profits" of the separate property of the wife are "exempt from execution against her husband" was enforced in McCarthy v. Paris, 46 Idaho 165, 267 Pac. 232 (1928); Evans v. Kroutinger, 9 Idaho 153, 72 Pac. 882 (1903); Thorn v. Anderson, 7 Idaho 421, 63 Pac. 592 (1900), and Humbird Lumber Co. v. Doran, 24 Idaho 507, 135 Pac. 66 (1913) *dictum.* The provision of Section 11-204 that "all compensation due and owing [the wife] for her personal services is exempt from execution against her husband" came before the court for interpretation in McMillan v. United States Fire Ins. Co., 48 Idaho 163, 280 Pac. 220 (1929). It was held that the privilege of exemption is lost when the compensation is paid to the wife and she uses it in the purchase of other property. Edminston v. Smith, 13 Idaho 645, 92 Pac. 842 (1907), held that the wife was personally liable on her contract to pay for her own bed and board.

48. IDAHO CODE § 32-911 (1947) as applied in the cases set out in notes 46 and 47 *supra.*

49. IDAHO CODE § 32-910 (1947).

50. *Id.* § 11-204 as applied in the cases set out in note 47 *supra.*

51. This is the result of Holt v. Empey, 32 Idaho 106, 178 Pac. 703 (1919). The court made no distinction as to whether the debt was antenuptial or postnuptial or whether incurred for his own use or for the benefit of the community. This result may be inferred also as to community debts from Gustin v. Byam, 41 Idaho 538, 240 Pac. 600 (1925), and Pittock v. Pittock, 15 Idaho 47, 96 Pac. 212 (1908), and the court clearly so held in McMillan v. United States Fire Insurance Co., 48 Idaho 163, 280 Pac. 220 (1929).

52. It was taken for granted in Holt v. Empey, 32 Idaho 106, 178 Pac. 703 (1919), that the separate property of the husband would be liable for his debts—all his debts both antenuptial and postnuptial, and both community and separate. Such is also the understanding of Jacob, *The Law of Community Property in Idaho,* 1 IDAHO L.J. 1 (1931).

53. This is the result of Hall v. Johns, 17 Idaho 224, 105 Pac. 71 (1909).

54. With some misgivings the word "no" is placed here for both community and separate debts resulting from the husband's tort. It results from Great American Indemnity Co. of New York v. Garrison, 75 F. Supp. 811 (E.D. Wash. 1948). It is hard to believe that this was not a community tort. It was committed while the husband was on a job (treasurer of Clearwater County), the wages from which certainly would be community property, and the moneys misappropriated probably were spent for family expenses.

55. This is probably a safe conclusion from the fact that the court in First National Bank of Sandpoint v. Samuels, 53 Idaho 780, 27 P.2d 959 (1933) affirmed the trial court decision that a judgment for the wife's slander was not a lien on community realty.

TABLE II

Liabilities of the Different Kinds of Separate and Community Property Resulting Alone From the Statutes and the Decisions

				Separate Property of W	Separate Property of H	Community Property within 11-204	Community Property outside 11-204
Antenuptial Debts	Incurred by H		Contract	No[48]	Yes[52]	No[50]	Yes[51]
			Tort	No[48]		No[50]	
			Other Obligations imposed by law	No[48]		No[50]	
	Incurred by W		Contract	Yes[48]	No[49]		
			Tort	Yes[48]			
			Other Obligations imposed by law	Yes[48]			
Postnuptial Debts	Community Debts	Incurred by H	Contract	No[48]	Yes[52]	No[50]	Yes[51]
			Tort	No[48]		No[50]	No ?[54]
			Other Obligations imposed by law	No[48]		No[50]	
		Incurred by W	Contract	Yes[48]			
			Tort	Yes[48]			No[55]
			Other Obligations imposed by law	Yes[48]			
	Separate Debts	Incurred by H	Contract	No[48]	Yes[52]	No[50]	Yes[51]
			Tort	No[48]		No[50]	No ?[54]
			Other Obligations imposed by law	No[48]		No[50]	
		Incurred by W	Contract	Yes[48]			No[53]
			Tort	Yes[48]			
			Other Obligations imposed by law	Yes[48]			

When Section 32-910 provides that the separate property of the husband is not liable for the debts of the wife *contracted* before marriage, it is safe to say that the draftsman meant *incurred* before marriage. If the husband is not to be liable for his wife's antenuptial contracts *a fortiori*, he is not to be liable for her torts or other obligations imposed by law. In the same vein the husband's separate property should not be available for the payment of the wife's postnuptial separate debts.

The lawyer in Idaho is pretty safe in assuming that the general community property (that is, that part of it outside of the special exemption provided for by Section 11-204) is liable for all debts of the husband both antenuptial and postnuptial, and both community and separate. This is certainly the spirit of *Holt v. Empey*.[56] It is the assumption of Jacob[57] and of the bench and bar of my acquaintance. If there is any exception, it is that of a separate tort of the husband incurred while a public officer as held in the Federal District Court decision in *Great American Indemnity Co. of New York v. Garrison*.[58] It is believed that this case would not be followed by the Supreme Court of Idaho. This position is strengthened by inferences from the case of *McMillan v. United States Fire Insurance Co.*[59] There community property, bought with the wife's wages, was held available for the payment of a community contract debt of the husband. It was argued that this was within the exemption provided for by Section 11-204. The court rejected the argument because, as required by Section 11-204, once the wages are paid they are no longer "due and owing." So community property, about which no exemption argument exists, *is* liable for the debt of the husband. Nothing is predicated on the fact that the particular kind of debt involved arose out of contract and it is believed therefore that the general community property is liable for *all* debts incurred by the husband whether arising out of contract, tort or other obligations imposed by law.

This is about as far as it is safe to go on propositions that may be taken for granted and others resulting from inferences and *a fortiori* reasoning. The result is set out in Table III.

---

56. See note 51 *supra*.
57. Jacob, *The Law of Community Property in Idaho*, 1 IDAHO L.J. 1, 37 (1931).
58. 75 F. Supp. 811 (E.D. Wash. 1948).
59. 48 Idaho 163, 280 Pac. 220 (1929).

TABLE III

LIABILITIES RESULTING FROM STATUTES
DECISIONS AND INFERENCES THAT MAY SAFELY BE MADE

				Separate Property of W	Separate Property of H	Community Property within 11-204	Community Property outside 11-204
Antenuptial Debts	Incurred by H		Contract	No	Yes	No	Yes
			Tort	No	Yes	No	Yes
			Other Obligations imposed by law	No	Yes	No	Yes
	Incurred by W		Contract	Yes	No		
			Tort	Yes	No		
			Other Obligations imposed by law	Yes	No		
Postnuptial Debts	Community Debts	Incurred by H	Contract	No	Yes	No	Yes
			Tort	No	Yes	No	No? Yes
			Other Obligations imposed by law	No	Yes	No	Yes
		Incurred by W	Contract	Yes			
			Tort	Yes			No
			Other Obligations imposed by law	Yes			
	Seperate Debts	Incurred by H	Contract	No	Yes	No	Yes
			Tort	No	Yes	No	No? Yes
			Other Obligations imposed by law	No	Yes	No	Yes
		Incurred by W	Contract	Yes	No		No
			Tort	Yes	No		
			Other Obligations imposed by law	Yes	No		

V

It will be noticed that there are some gaps. It is believed that, as the matter now stands, no one can safely fill in any of the gaps. There is neither statute, decision nor a safe inference on which to rely.

At this point it may be well to make the observation that altogether too much of the law of Idaho as revealed in Tables II and III comes from the cases and from mere inference.

A serious burden is placed on business dealings when the creditor is asked to deal under the threat of a law suit to make his position certain. Adequate and precise answers should be supplied by the statutes, and the time is ripe for a committee of lawyers, bankers and businessmen to study the inadequacies of the law and, after careful study, formulate a clearly expressed policy. The proposed policy should be given wide publicity and remain for some time a target for further study and criticism. After all questions have been threshed out, then a text should be presented to the legislature for enactment.

It is not the purpose of this paper to draft such a text. That is beyond the ken of any one man. Rather it is proposed to take up and discuss the principal gaps as revealed by Table III and make some observations that might be useful in any further study undertaken. When a gap appears, it has long been the habit of both lawyers in their briefs and the court in its decisions to follow "the weight of authority." He who can count the most cases in his favor or the most states has a pretty good chance of prevailing. It is even an exaggeration, in many suits, to say that the cases are counted. What is counted is the number of *citations* of cases in American Jurisprudence, Corpus Juris and Corpus Juris Secundum, for outside of three or four of the larger centers there is a lack of adequate library coverage of both law reports and statutes.[60] When it is realized that the encyclopedias cite cases for about everything they *say* as well as what they *hold* and that cases will be cited from both common law and community property states, one begins to see on what a slender thread many a case in the trial courts must hang. If this is a true description of how cases are decided, it highlights the desirability of a legislative solution.

60. Professor Jacob deplored the "want of library resources" in Idaho in his article on *The Law of Community Property in Idaho*, 1 IDAHO L.J. 1, 121 (1931).

The first gap is the question: is community property available to the creditor for the payment of antenuptial debts incurred by the wife? We already know from the statutes that the separate property of the husband is not available for their payment[61] and that the separate property of the wife is available.[62] What of the availability of community property?

No Idaho case answers this question. But the Supreme Court of Idaho has decided that the separate debts of the wife contracted *after* marriage cannot be satisfied out of community property.[63] Section 32-911 renders the separate property of the wife liable for debts contracted both before and after marriage, and if this fund is the only one liable for debts contracted *after* marriage, by the same reasoning it must be the only fund liable for debts contracted *before* marriage since both are equally within the section. If *Hall v. Johns* is to be followed, we may then expect that the Supreme Court will decide that the community is not liable.

Is this a correct interpretation of Section 32-911? The inference that, because the wife's separate property *is* liable, the community is *not* liable does not necessarily follow. In reality there is a gap. The section says the separate property is liable and says nothing about the community one way or the other. An early California court faced with this question of a gap said it must be solved "by considerations arising from the rule of the common law"[64] and since by the common law the husband is liable for the debts of the wife contracted *dum sola*, he is still to be liable.[65] But community property comes from the Spanish law and when a gap appears, reference should first be made to it under the principle that when a legislature adopts a statute from another law it impliedly adopts that other law's interpretation along with the statute.

Looking at the Spanish law we find that neither spouse is liable for the antenuptial debts of the other, but all the property of each is liable for his or her own debts. Since the wife owns a one-half interest in the community, that half is to be liable for

---

61. IDAHO CODE § 32-910 (1947).
62. *Id.* § 11-204 as applied in the cases set out in note 47 *supra.*
63. Hall v. Johns, 17 Idaho 224, 105 Pac. 71 (1909).
64. Van Maren v. Johnson, 15 Cal. 308 (1860).
65. At this time in California the husband was the owner of the community and the wife had a mere expectancy. The California statute said the husband's separate property was not liable and so the community was liable as the only property of the husband not expressly exempted.

her debts, but since her share cannot be determined until dissolution of the community, the community is not liable during coverture.[66] Thus the decision that the community is not, during coverture, to be liable for the antenuptial debts of the wife follows the Spanish law and is presumably what the legislature meant to adopt when the community system was taken over.

Admitting the above interpretation, is this solution one which we must accept as part of our law or should it be changed by legislative action? The reason given for the non-liability of the community for antenuptial debts is that the community property system has considered the well being and interests of the family of more importance than the rights of creditors.[67] But this looks like outlawing the creditor just because he is a creditor. After all, ours is a credit economy and before we write the creditor off let us consider his position. In favor of a contrary rule Judge Speer of Texas has said that unmarried persons who were debt-ridden could escape into marriage knowing that their future earnings and acquisitions thenceforth could not be reached by their antenuptial creditors.[68] This reasoning is particularly forceful in states like Idaho, Louisiana and Texas where rents and profits of separate property fall into community. It is less so in the other community property states where they remain separate. Consider the case of the modern young woman earning a good salary as a lawyers' stenographer. She rents an apartment and buys $1000 worth of electrical equipment on credit. Her marriage marketability in Idaho will be high. All unwittingly her trusting creditor has supplied her with a $1000 dowry. If, like most young women, she has no separate property, he will have to wait for the dissolution of the community before he can collect. In the meantime the couple has used the equipment and worn it out. And during coverture the community is being enriched by her earnings.

Here is a proper place for the legislature to act. We should neither worship history just because it is history nor look with hostility upon the creditor just because he is a modern phenomenon. Even in states where rents and profits of separate property remain separate, the ancient rule might be considered inadequate for the wife may have no separate property at the time of marriage and the couple can thus sponge on the creditor to the

---

66. 1 de Funiak, Principles of Community Property § 165 (1943).
67. *Id.* § 158.
68. Speer, Law of Marital Rights in Texas § 385 (3d ed. 1929).

extent of the rental value of the property sold. But the case of the creditor is stronger in Idaho, Louisiana and Texas where rents and profits of separate property fall into community. In those states two solutions might seriously be considered by the legislature. First, make the entire community property available for the payment of the debt on the principle that the community, having profited from both the use of the property and the work and labor of the wife, should shoulder the burden of paying the bill or second, the community should be reachable to the extent of one-half. The second solution involves difficulties of appraisal and accounting which might render it impractical. Whatever the solution adopted, certainly this is a situation for legislative action.

VI

Another gap, which poses a number of problems, is the question of what property is available for satisfaction of community debts incurred by the wife. We have already seen that Section 32-911 makes her liable "for her own debts contracted before or after marriage," that, as to capacity, she may contract in relation to her separate property, her personal services and for her own use and benefit. Such of these contracts as create community obligations have received scant attention from the court and rather haltingly has it allowed her separate property to be liable. The whole matter should be clarified by statute.

There seems to be little reason why the wife should not be given complete contractual capacity. She already has enough for most practical purposes, but the existence of any limitation at all leads to expensive litigation. There is no evidence that the power to contract without limitation, that a wave of legislation in the early part of this century carried to women in twenty-seven jurisdictions,[69] has led to untoward results. If the wife must keep her promise when she goes surety for a member of her family or signs an appeal bond for a friend,[70] it may teach her a wholesome lesson of responsibility. With complete contractual capacity her separate property would be available to satisfy both separate and community debts incurred by her, and she would take her place in the marital partnership as an equal of her husband.

---

69. The count of jurisdictions is that of Vernier in 3 AMERICAN FAMILY LAWS 35 (1935). Probably since 1935 many other jurisdictions have joined the list.

70. She is not now liable. Craig v. Lane, 60 Idaho 178, 89 P.2d 1008 (1939); Beckstead v. Gee, 58 Idaho 758, 79 P.2d 293 (1938).

There is also no adequate reason why debts arising from tort and other obligations imposed by law should not bind her separate property. This is true under present law if we are willing to interpret the word "contracted" in Section 32-911 to mean "incurred" so that it will read "the separate property of the wife . . . is liable for her own debts *incurred* before and after marriage." Whatever may be thought of the above propositions as a matter of policy, they should be discussed by the bar and the public and clarified by positive legislative enactment.

A more difficult question concerns the availability of *community property* for the payment of community debts incurred by the wife. The wife has been given the management and control of "the earnings for her personal services and the rents and profits of her separate estate."[71] Both of these fall into community in Idaho,[72] and both of these are declared to be "exempt from execution against her husband."[73] By argument *e contrario* does this mean that these two elements of community property are *not* exempt from execution against the *wife?* Probably. This is the least that could be expected. But the matter should not be left to guesswork. The statutes should expressly so state. The question may attain considerable practical importance. Suppose a woman with some fortune and excellent earning capacity marries a man with no fortune who from incompetency is unable to earn after marriage. If the wife retains her job and invests her fortune wisely, the two elements mentioned will constitute about all the community property available to creditors. It would seem clear then that the community within Section 11-204 should be available for the satisfaction of community debts incurred by the wife.

The problem of whether community outside of Section 11-204 (that is community property generally) should be liable for community debts incurred by the wife raises questions of fundamental policy about which opinion is sure to be divided. At present our law splits the community down the middle and puts one part (the rents and profits of the wife's separate estate and earnings for her personal services) under her management and control and all the rest under his. It gives her in addition a veto power in transactions relating to community realty and the

---

71. Idaho Code § 32-913 (1947).
72. *Id.* § 32-906.
73. *Id.* § 11-204.

mortgaging of exempt property by requiring her signature.[74] The fact that *her* part is exempt from execution against her husband under Section 11-204 would, by symmetry of reasoning, lead us to conclude that *his* part (that outside Section 11-204) is exempt from execution against *her*. This is probably the law in Idaho, although no statute or case says so.

Whether it should be the law, that is, whether the legislature in attempting to enact what is an ideal policy should alter it, presents a very difficult question. It raises the fundamental issue of whether the present division of control resulting from Sections 11-204, 32-912 and 32-913 is wise. As the law stands each spouse controls what he or she can earn and the rents and profits of his or her separate property. Whether the common kitty, which we call community property, should be under joint control[75] and the debts created by one spouse be payable out of the money earned by the other depends on how much pooling marriage entails. Does the union of two hearts require the union of two purses? That it does, in all the successful marriages, is a fact of everyday life. But it is precisely in the successful marriage where rules are not needed and will not be followed. The rules are made for the moments of stress and strain[76] and must exist in order that the creditor too may not be sacrificed on the altar of marital discord. Perhaps a case may clarify the problem. An outsider views *H* and *W* as an ideal and united couple. He seels one of them a bill of goods. When the bill is not paid, a second look reveals *H* and *W*, battling with fang and claw, for a divorce. In picking up the pieces, for the purpose of satisfying his claim, must the creditor be careful to attach only items of property earned by the spouse who purchased or may he attach anything that is community property without regard to which spouse earned it? It comes down to this: Is he creditor entitled to say to the wife who complains that the creditor is attaching some property she has bought with her earnings or her income: "When I sold the goods to your husband you were happily married and I supposed you would allow your earnings

74. *Id.* §§ 32-912, 45-1102.

75. It has been suggested that measures for joint control might take over *some* of the rules (but not all) of the commercial partnership. Daggett, *Is Joint Control of Community Property Possible?*, 10 TULANE L. REV. 589 (1936).

76. Llewellyn, *Behind the Law of Divorce*, 32 COL. L. REV. 1281, 1304 (1932), states Erlich's view to the effect that "rules for courts regarding husband and wife should be built in terms not of marriage, but of separation and divorce."

and income to be used to pay for the goods. All the good wives I know do that." And, is the wife entitled to reply: "You ought to grow up. You know any marriage may go on the rocks and when you sell to my husband you had better look at *his* income and not at *mine.*" The first policy favors the sale of goods and discourages divorce; the second favors cautious extension of credit, jittery marriages and easier divorce. May a wise God give wisdom to his legislature to make a wise decision.

Policy Questions on Marital Property Law in Louisiana

*Harriet S. Daggett**

Purpose

The purpose of this discussion is to emphasize the confusion, inequities, and maladjustments to social and economic realities presently existing in the marital property law of Louisiana. The belief of the writer in the community system is strong because its basic pattern is designed to stabilize and protect the family. It envisions an ultimate equal sharing in the financial gains of two people working for a mutual interest. This object is protected, as is any well organized business, by provision for a sinking fund to sustain the endeavor in case of loss by an unsuccessful venture of one partner. The fact that this fund was labelled separate property of the wife was not to favor her unduly but because, in the setting of an earlier day, that was the safest method of protection for all concerned. Re-examination of the community property system has been thought necessary for quite some time because its adherents fear that, without adjustment to present conditions, dissatisfactions may become sufficiently acute to result in its abandonment.[1] Its complexities[2] are so great that its acceptability can be maintained only by clear demonstration of achievement of its worthy basic objects, those best strengthening the ties and economic basis of the family.

---

* Professor of Law, Louisiana State University.

1. For reasons similar to those advanced here, France in 1945 engaged in a revision of her Civil Code. Marital property laws have been examined. In his article, *The Revision of the French Civil Code*, 25 TULANE L. REV. 435, 444 (1951), Dr. Marc Ancel states ". . . the old community property system . . . now receives little support in France." A compromise appears to have been reached between the old community law and a system of entire separation of property, according to Dr. Ancel. Definite action to allay apparent dissatisfactions is being taken in the State of New Mexico. See N.M. Laws 1953, 21st Sess., Sen. Res. No. 3, p. 636. See also Professor R. E. Clark's excellent study, *Management and Control of Community Property in New Mexico*, 26 TULANE L. REV. 324 (1952).

2. See Huie, *Separate Claims to Reimbursement from Community Property in Louisiana*, 27 TULANE L. REV. 143 (1953). See Professor de Funiak's statements regarding abandonment of the system, 1 DE FUNIAK, PRINCIPLES OF COMMUNITY PROPERTY 20, nn. 18, 19 (1943).

Before a presentation of legislative enactments and judicial decisions, may it be said that the writer has no interest in what is "his" and "hers" as such except insofar as these ownerships may affect the stability and tranquility of the family, which a majority still believes to be the best institution for society. This paper does not purport to present *Wife versus Husband* with a brief for the "rights" of women or men. Its spirit is in the interest of the earnings of a man or woman by labor, profession, or small business whose failure may presently drag down the married partner and thus wreck the entire financial structure of the family and perhaps the marriage.

Stress is placed here on the small business because large concerns ordinarily have constant access to legal advice and are made aware of dangers and pitfalls and hence seek protection through the corporate device or otherwise. Professor de Funiak stresses the fact that loyal, hard-working couples even of primitive times evolved the system out of recognition of fair dealing and ordinary justice and for individual satisfaction as a democratic concept. Not the great property owners but couples struggling to attain some degree of financial security are those for whom these suggested changes are today worst needed.

The community has been consistently held not to be a business partnership or the marriage partner entitled to the legal reliefs established therefor.[3] Yet, under present property laws it would appear that many liabilities of a partnership are present without the assets enjoyed by that device.[4] To aver that irritations and strains, frustrations and dissatisfactions arise when property which one believes to be his own is interfered with is to concur with a majority in North America. Dogs and many other animals will defend their property lines, their bed and their bone. Thus the idea of ownership must be deeply ingrained in the animal world of which man is thought to be the apex, and hence it would not appear to be illogical to suppose that marital property laws as other property laws of men and women may produce those factors which tend to lead to the disruption of their associations in business and, far more importantly, in marriage.

---

3. DAGGETT, THE COMMUNITY PROPERTY SYSTEM OF LOUISIANA 23 *et seq.* (1945).

4. Art. 2807, LA. CIVIL CODE of 1870; Heatwole v. Stansbury, 212 La. 685, 33 So.2d 196 (1947); Mackenroth v. Pelke, 171 La. 842, 132 So. 365 (1931); Frierson v. Frierson, 164 La. 687, 114 So. 594 (1927); Succession of Boyer, 36 La. Ann. 506 (1884); City Insurance Co. v. Steamboat Lizzie Simmons, 19 La. Ann. 249 (1867); Squire v. Belden, 2 La. 268 (1831).

The community property pattern was designed by those well versed in the intricacies and imponderables of that unique association known as marriage. It still obtains in many of the so-called civilized countries of the world, though Professor de Funiak points out that economic causes and not "civilization" produced the plan.[5] The major thoughts of Louisiana formulators had to do with protection of the family and its economy of the times before the days of easy and frequent divorce which indeed may settle property questions, a minor matter in comparison to problems of the mind and spirit, which seem to be even more confused after the parties leave the divorce court.

The community property system was not only in the day of its inception (as previously stated) but is even *now* in the writer's judgment the fairest, most thoughtfully designed plan for marital property law yet devised. To weaken the confidence of its adherents by failure to adjust it to economic and social conditions revolutionized since the pattern was first adopted for Louisiana would seem to be most unwise, and would perhaps result in irreparable loss to the state as well as to its individual citizens. The philosophy of Louisiana's Civil Code clearly bespeaks the family unit idea and attempts to protect the institution.[6] It was not in the minds of the law makers of that day that, if the spouses could not get along because of difference of opinion on financial matters, they should be encouraged to get a divorce. The consideration of such a step was not in contemplation due to social and other taboos—nor was it considered good family law or business practice to have all of the eggs in one basket so that a financial slip of the husband would leave the whole family, including him, with nothing.[7]

Legislation and its Judicial Interpretations

In the early part of this century, law makers were anxious to recognize women's contributions and the country's need of them in business and industry and a little later they may have been attempting to reward their services in the first world war.[8] Mechanization, generally, produced tools for war and peace, many of which could be handled as well or better by women

5. 1 DE FUNIAK, PRINCIPLES OF COMMUNITY PROPERTY 27 (1943).
6. Note elaborate provisions for collation and forced heirship.
7. Provisions for dotal and paraphernal property of wife, marital portion, protection when separate regime contracted for.
8. WOMEN'S BUREAU BULL. No. 249, THE STATUS OF WOMEN IN THE UNITED STATES (U.S. Dep't Labor 1953).

than men, and realization of the existence of this great dormant labor force came quickly to the country's leaders.

As an integral part of this movement a series of Louisiana statutes popularly called married women's emancipatory acts appeared.[9] These provisions cleared away old limitations and protective devices and granted full power to married women in the way of privileges and responsibilities that were available to any person *sui juris* in regard to his property, or in regard to his ability to act in various civil capacities.

However, to prevent confusion in connection with the existing legal fabric of community property law, a statement was carried through this series of acts that they did not purport to affect the provisions dealing with this type of property.[10] During the period previously alluded to, and a forerunner and preconcomitant to the series and again in recognition of the increasing part that women were taking in the world of business and industry, what later seemed to be a companion piece of legislation was passed in 1912, reading as follows:

> "The earnings of the wife when living apart from her husband although not separated by judgment of court, her earnings when carrying on a business, trade, occupation or industry separate from her husband, actions for damages resulting from offenses and quasi offenses and the property purchased with all funds thus derived, are her separate property."[11]

The amendment was properly placed in the article of the Code dealing with the separate property of the spouses and was generally understood to complement the so-called emancipatory series.[12]

Twenty-one years later, interpretation of this amendment was directly asked of the Supreme Court of Louisiana.[13] The high mood of gratitude for services performed in the first world war had passed for everyone: a terrible economic depression was being suffered; jobs were scarce for all; creditors were desperately trying to collect; and it was normal in the general avenues of thought to find reversals of position. Moreover, the

---

9. U.S. Const. Amend. XIX; La. Acts 1916, No. 94, p. 212; La. Acts 1918, No. 244, p. 435; La. Acts 1920, No. 219, p. 364; La. Acts 1921, No. 34, p. 38; La. Acts 1926, No. 132, p. 207; La. Acts 1928, No. 283, p. 548.

10. *Ibid.*

11. La. Acts 1912, No. 170, p. 310.

12. Art. 2334, La. Civil Code of 1870.

13. Houghton v. Hall, 177 La. 237, 148 So. 37 (1933).

Justices readily perceived that, regardless of the legislature's best intentions to recognize the place that married women were taking in business and industry, the method employed would weaken the community structure as well as producing greater inequities between spouses.[14] Hence, chivalrous tongued judges who had spoken of married women as being most favored in the law became silent and the Supreme Court decided[15] that the wife was not able to earn any separate property unless she was living separate and apart from her husband, presumably under conditions which would warrant a judicial separation or divorce.[16] Moreover, a wife could not sue on a contract the benefits of which would accrue to the community.[17] Though she was perfectly capable under the emancipatory acts of entering unassisted into the contract and her husband was a stranger to it, he, as master of the community, must sue. Again, the theory of a "public merchant"[18] was expanded to cover manufacturing and the husband and community held solidarily with the wife for unfortunate ventures of the wife in this type of business.[19] Presumably, if all earnings or profits of the wife in a separate business, profession, or industry are community, losses also, even in a tort rising out of a contract, would be community, under some indeterminate form of agency doctrine,[20] perhaps ratification by acceptance of benefits *if* there have been any benefits!

Thus began the march of the one basket theory with a veiled concomitant of invitation to divorce or judicial separation as the only suggested means of relief.[21] Neither spouse today has legal[22] control over the other and even under the best adjusted marital

14. 177 La. 237, 265, 148 So. 37, 45 (1933).
15. Houghton v. Hall, 177 La. 237, 148 So. 37 (1933).
16. See concurring opinion by Chief Justice O'Niell, 177 La. 237, 266, 148 So. 37, 45 (1933). "I believe that all that the Legislature intended to do by the act of 1912 was to allow a wife who is living separate and apart from her husband to retain her earnings as her separate property. Whenever the husband tires of such a situation, he may put an end to it by service of the necessary summons upon his wife to return to the matrimonial domicile, or suffer the consequence."
17. Succession of Howell, 177 La. 276, 148 So. 48 (1933).
18. Art. 131, La. Civil Code of 1870.
19. Charles Lob's Sons v. Karnofsky, 177 La. 229, 148 So. 34 (1933).
20. Adams v. Golson, 187 La. 363, 174 So. 876 (1937); McClure v. McMartin, 104 La. 496, 29 So. 227 (1901); Art. 2985, La. Civil Code of 1870; Note, 20 Tulane L. Rev. 279 (1945). See reversal of policy re automobiles: Brantley v. Clarkson, 217 La. 425, 46 So.2d 614 (1950), 12 Louisiana Law Review 94 (1951).
21. See statement of Chief Justice O'Niell reproduced in note 16 *supra*.
22. No authorization required under so-called emancipation acts. See note 9 *supra*. For physical control, see State v. Priest, 210 La. 389, 27 So.2d 173 (1946).

relations, where each spouse is working hard for the financial interests of the family, if bad fortune falls upon the efforts of the one, the other will fall. As a spiritual postulate, this may be acceptable; but as an economic and social one, it would appear to be of doubtful value. The growth in numbers of small businesses, as, for example, shoppes, notably tea, beauty, gift, hobby, and the like, is valuable to society economically and otherwise, and is encouraged even by national legislation.[23] They are often run by married women. Financially responsible husbands under our present legislation must watch the balance sheets, if any, with extreme care.

It will be recalled that legislation in 1855[24] was passed in the interest of commerce and not just to free the wife dealing with separate property of legal limitations. It resulted in shifting the burden of proof from creditors who had formerly had to show that money and supplies *had inured* to the benefit of the wife's property to the wife, who had to show that they had *not*.[25] Thus, dealing with married women, many of them owning the great inherited plantations of that day, was made safer. It is submitted again, not necessarily in the interest of the *wife* but of the economics of the state, particularly the small business, as well as for the family welfare and unity, a more valuable asset of the state, that thoughtful legislation is needed. The two-income family increases purchasing power and tax collections. A United States labor report for 1953 indicates agreement that this development is accompanied by an increase in homeowners, thus "having a profound effect on family life: more stability, more sense of property, more feeling of 'belonging' to economic society."[26]

Referring again to the legislative mood of empowering married women, another attempt provided that, if community property stood in the name of the wife, the husband could not sell or mortgage it without the wife's written authority or consent.[27]

---

23. Exec. Order No. 10493, 18 FED. REG. 6583 (1953); Exec. Order No. 10504, 18 FED. REG. 7667 (1953). An "Institute on Small Business Planning and Loans" was held at the University of North Carolina Law School, January 15 and 16, under the joint sponsorship of the North Carolina Bar Association and the law schools of Duke University, the University of North Carolina, and Wake Forest College.

24. La. Acts 1855, No. 200, p. 254.

25. Berwick v. Sheriff, 49 La. Ann. 201, 21 So. 692 (1896); Dougherty v. Hibernia Ins. Co., 35 La. Ann. 629 (1883); Rice v. Alexander, 15 La. Ann. 54 (1860); Arts. 127, 128, 129, LA. CIVIL CODE of 1870.

26. WOMEN'S BUREAU BULL. No. 249, THE STATUS OF WOMEN IN THE UNITED STATES 13 (U.S. Dep't of Labor 1953).

27. La. Acts 1912, No. 170, p. 310.

Our Supreme Court, quickly stepping to what they must have thought to be the rescue of the community property system, held that neither could the wife sell or mortgage the property without the husband's written consent.[28] To go further, the court also held that property standing in the joint names of husband and wife could be dealt with solely by the husband.[29]

Two decisions of the Supreme Court of Louisiana declared cancellation of mineral leases upon community property because payments were made to the joint bank accounts of husband and wife rather than to the account of the husband alone, as the wife could have drawn the money, though she made no attempt to do so.[30] The harshness of these decisions may have later been softened somewhat as to effect upon a lessee,[31] but nonetheless stand as illustrations of the extreme need for care when a wife enters even indirectly into a contract concerning community property.

Purchasers from a married woman purporting to deal with her separate property are naturally loath to accept title unless the husband's signature appears, since her recitation that the property is separate is subject to proof;[32] and if it fails, under a commingling doctrine or otherwise,[33] title falls. Thus, the so-called married women's emancipatory acts with their limitation as to dealing with community property result, practically, in making it perhaps more rather than less difficult than before their advent for a married woman to deal even with her separate property though the need for assistance by her husband was stated in the provisions to have been eliminated.

If the wife recites in a deed of transfer that she is selling her separate property and it is proved to be community property, the husband's signature "authorizing" his wife will estop him to claim later that the property is community,[34] but will not estop

28. Bywater v. Enderle, 175 La. 1098, 145 So. 118 (1932).

29. Otwell v. Vaughan, 186 La. 911, 173 So. 527 (1937); Young v. Arkansas-Louisiana Gas Co., 184 La. 460, 166 So. 139 (1936).

30. Clingman v. Devonian Oil Co., 188 La. 310, 177 So. 59 (1937); LeRosen v. North Central Texas Oil Co., 169 La. 973, 126 So. 442 (1930). See La. Acts 1896, No. 63, p. 96.

31. Jones v. Southern Natural Gas Co., 213 La. 1051, 36 So.2d 34 (1948), 23 Tulane L. Rev. 418 (1949).

32. Johnson v. Johnson, 213 La. 1092, 36 So.2d 396 (1948); Daggett, The Community Property System of Louisiana 34, n. 12 (1945).

33. De Maupassant v. Clayton, 214 La. 812, 38 So.2d 791 (1949); Johnson v. Johnson, 213 La. 1092, 36 So.2d 396 (1948); Marlatt v. Citizens' State Bank & Trust Co., 180 La. 387, 156 So. 426 (1934).

34. Rousseau v. Rousseau, 209 La. 428, 24 So.2d 676 (1946); Normand v. Davis, 202 La. 565, 12 So.2d 273 (1943); Succession of Hostetter, 128 La. 468, 54 So. 961 (1911); Kerwin v. Hibernia Ins. Co., 35 La. Ann. 33 (1883).

the forced heirs who have accepted with benefit of inventory nor will it affect the rights of creditors of the husband and the community.[35] Again, if the husband authorizes the wife to sell, and her proof of separate property fails, title has been held good under an agency theory, namely, that the community for which she is acting is selling.[36] Under this analysis the husband's authorizing signature would appear to be more than a mere estoppel against him to claim that the property is community and not the wife's separate property if her recitation is untrue, and will validate the title. An application of this view would seem to protect the purchaser not only against the husband by estoppel but also after his death against forced heirs of the husband, who might accept his succession under benefit of inventory and thus not be bound by his estoppel. Conveyancers rightly fear, however, to rely on this theory, as agency of the wife is an uncertain doctrine.[37]

If the husband recites an appearance and signs the deed as joint seller, a practice used in some offices, doubtless the vendee is nicely protected whether the property is community or separate. But what of the family, if indeed the property is the wife's separate property? Could either the husband or wife upon dissolution of the community successfully maintain even that a debt was owed by the community for the whole or the half of the value received to the separate estate of the wife for her benefit or that of her heirs?[38]

Even the "faith of the public record" doctrine works to the detriment of the wife's commercial standing in the line of cases not comprehended in the doctrine. The general rule was purportedly settled for all time and everybody in 1910 by the landmark case of *McDuffie v. Walker*,[39] said to have been followed ever since in unbroken line of judicial decisions.[40] Those cases where faith alone does not save the relying purchaser are said to be those where property vests "by operation of law."[41] When does

---

35. Chevalley v. Pettit, 115 La. 407, 39 So. 113 (1905); McKenzie v. Bacon, 40 La. Ann. 157, 4 So. 65 (1888). *Cf.* Berry v. Wagner, 151 La. 456, 91 So. 837 (1922).

36. Garlick v. Dalbey, 147 La. 18, 84 So. 441 (1920).

37. See Dimmer v. Davis Bros. Lumber Co., 135 So. 684 (La. App. 1931); DAGGETT, THE COMMUNITY PROPERTY SYSTEM OF LOUISIANA 20 *et seq.* (1945).

38. See Huie, *Separate Claims to Reimbursement from Community Property in Louisiana*, 27 TULANE L. REV. 143 (1953).

39. 125 La. 152, 51 So. 100 (1910).

40. *Cf.* Thompson v. Thompson, 211 La. 468, 30 So.2d 321 (1947); Knoblock & Rainold v. Posey, 126 La. 610, 52 So. 847 (1910).

41. Bishop v. Copeland, 222 La. 284, 62 So.2d 486 (1953).

the law "operate" is obviously the question, puzzling occasionally even to the learned in the great science. When a person dies, his forced heirs and indeed his legal heirs are vested by operation of law with their proper share of inheritance; and the purchaser, even relying on a recorded judgment placing the vendor in possession of property belonging to these heirs and not to the seller, will not be protected, though there is nothing in the record to give notice of the right of the heirs.[42] Upon dissolution of the community by death of one of the spouses, the heirs of the deceased are vested by operation of law with his half of the community property.[43]

Those cases dealing with the latter "operation" obviously may be distinguished on law, fact, procedural approach and otherwise as may perhaps too many cases, it would sometimes seem; but in stark reality the result is that on occasion a married man swearing to a lie of singleness passed a good title under the record doctrine, his divorce not having been recorded, to the wife's half of the community;[44] under similar facts, however, the wife,[45] as usurper of the husband's power during marriage was not able to deal validly regardless of "operation of law," which presumably vests shares of community property upon dissolution of the community by divorce,[46] because of the power of the husband concept. The soundness of the several decisions is not in issue—only the effect upon those who would deal with a married woman. Their fears would appear to be well justified.

Retail merchants are hounded by the spectre of that elastic word "necessities"[47] with which a husband must furnish his wife. This responsibility would seem to result chiefly from responsibilities of a husband as such, in or out of a community régime, and hence may be less troublesome than community use ratification by the husband of articles not in the necessity group, purchased by the wife.[48] There is little chance for the creditor if the husband proves adamant in his refusal to ratify after being

42. *Ibid.* But see Sun Oil Co. v. Tarver, 219 La. 103, 52 So.2d 437 (1951). See also Lee v. Jones, 69 So.2d 26 (La. 1953); *but see* Thompson v. Thompson, 211 La. 468, 30 So.2d 321 (1947).

43. Allen v. Anderson, 55 So.2d 596 (La. App. 1951).

44. Humphreys v. Royal, 215 La. 567, 41 So.2d 220 (1949).

45. Succession of James, 147 La. 943, 86 So. 403 (1920).

46. Art. 2406, LA. CIVIL CODE of 1870; Daggett, *Division of Property Upon Dissolution of Marriage*, 6 LAW & CONTEMP. PROB. 225 (1939).

47. Art. 1786, LA. CIVIL CODE of 1870; D. H. Holmes Co. v. Morris, 188 La. 431, 177 So. 417 (1937).

48. For an excellent record illustration, see Montgomery v. Gremillion, 69 So.2d 618 (La. App. 1953).

apprised of the purchase. On the other hand there is little chance for the husband's escape from liability unless he can promptly capture the articles and send them back, which may result in serious impairment of his personal domestic felicity. A merchant may well desire the custom of women with good jobs or successful professions. The woman may retain her maiden name, which she has a legal right[49] to do, if recognition in her field of endeavor has come before marriage. The unsuspecting merchant may ultimately find this apparently excellent risk a poor one, indeed, by virtue of an unknown marriage and the *Houghton-Hall* edict.[50]

Garnishment[51] would seem to lie for debts of the husband and community against the wages of a wife who is trying to aid and comfort a husband failing in health, finance, or otherwise and unwilling to desert him. Question has been raised regarding the right of creditors of a discharged bankrupt to continue collections against an employed wife, not personally discharged. A very sound theory of the community as an ideal being, likened unto a succession, has been established by the Supreme Court[52] and is certainly well supported by the theory of community property in its entirety. This concept should negate the idea of holding a wife for community debts after the husband head of the community has been discharged in bankruptcy. However, these situations as items on this list for discussion certainly add to the apparently increasing dissatisfaction with the present state of the laws of marital property.

In the old basic law of community property appears elaborate machinery for a separation of property to be instigated only by a wife.[53] As a practical matter, and for the great majority of families, this recourse is of little value. The wife must have separate property or the hope of it, and the husband's financial affairs must be in such "disorder" that her estate will be endangered. The husband whose separate or community business may be endangered by the wife's financial "disorder" does not have the right to such an action. Since the wife's earnings from a business occupation or industry are community property, it would not appear that she could bring the action to protect those earnings, if the husband's ventures were tottering. The

49. Succession of Kneipp, 172 La. 411, 134 So. 376 (1931).
50. Houghton v. Hall, 177 La. 237, 148 So. 37 (1933).
51. La. R.S. § 13:3911 *et seq.* (1950).
52. Demoruelle v. Allen, 218 La. 603, 50 So.2d 208 (1950).
53. Art. 2425 *et seq.*, La. Civil Code of 1870.

device always smacked of a garage-locking after the car was stolen, anyway, and is of little value except as the one means of dissolving the community after marriage without disturbing the personal relationship.[54] Loyal wives have always furnished money if they had it to husbands in financial stress, if they wanted it, even when pledging for their husbands' debts was prohibited.[55] The law makers knew that, as witness the devices for protection of this family sinking fund in the separation of property idea,[56] the wife's legal mortgage,[57] and other less obvious provisions.

Separate property of the spouses is that which is received by inheritance or by particular gift, *inter vivos* or *mortis causa.*[58] Separate earnings of the wife while living separate from her husband apparently with cause for judicial separation or divorce, are her separate property.[59] The first square decision[60] was that the wife gained a separate estate from earnings in a house of prostitution to which her husband brought his custom but not as her exclusive client and where he was treated according to the testimony as was any other person, and was ejected "when his money ran out." What a platform of vulgarity upon which the court was forced to rest the first direct application of the doctrine!

A recent case has stated the test of the phrase "living separate and apart" with effect of making the wife's earnings separate property to be the same as that applied for divorce under the two-year act. The parties must so live that there can be no doubt in the minds of citizens as to the breakdown of all personal relationships. Thus, a wife who had sheltered her sick husband in a building upon the grounds of her adjacent boarding house could not label her earnings as separate.[61]

It is indeed unfortunate that the private lives of persons who have not seen fit to expose to public view in court the innermost secrets of their personal relationships should have these matters

---

54. DAGGETT, THE COMMUNITY PROPERTY SYSTEM OF LOUISIANA 57 *et seq.* (1945).

55. Art. 2398 *et seq.*, LA. CIVIL CODE of 1870, negated by emancipatory acts. See note 9 *supra.*

56. Art. 2425 *et seq.*, LA. CIVIL CODE of 1870; DAGGETT, THE COMMUNITY PROPERTY SYSTEM OF LOUISIANA 57 *et seq.* (1945).

57. DAGGETT, THE COMMUNITY PROPERTY SYSTEM OF LOUISIANA, 44 *et seq.* (1945).

58. Art. 2334, LA. CIVIL CODE of 1870.

59. Houghton v. Hall, 177 La. 237, 148 So. 37 (1933).

60. Small v. McNeely, 195 So. 649 (La. App. 1940).

61. Succession of Le Jeune, 221 La. 437, 59 So.2d 446 (1952).

reviewed on a property question.[62] This reward by the state particularly to a wife who instead of seeking divorce and alimony has gone to work in either the oldest or the newest profession for women seems peculiarly unfitting.

It is far from clear whether a wife living separate and apart having one of the many causes for *judicial separation* will be able to accumulate separate property; whether the matter of whose "fault" it is will be made a factor; whether under the two-year act test earnings will become separate immediately upon the beginning of separate living or after two years. Perhaps the whole impossible situation will fall with the weight of its own stupidity and thus one item of unbalance will be cleared away without legislation. Despite the best efforts of the court, however, but minor successes can be achieved within the present legislative pattern to cure what the writer believes to be major ills at the present time.

Recovery by the husband for injuries are his separate property, if he is living separate and apart from his wife by reason of her behavior.[63] Previous to the *Houghton-Hall*[64] analysis of part of the 1912 statute[65] discussed above, it was clear that recoveries for personal injuries to the wife were her separate property in any case.[66] Since that decision it seems doubtful, if put at issue, whether under a later statute and the court's interpretation of it the wife could insist successfully on the classification as separate property without proving her living separate and apart. Unless the court decides on an inconsistent interpretation of the latter part of the same paragraph, dealing with recoveries for "offenses and quasi offenses" to the wife, a living separate and apart would be a requisite.[67]

Preservation of property as separate during the existence of the community is another problem. In the case of the husband, it is well settled that in order to retain the separate character in a purchase of realty with separate funds he must give a double recitation in the deed to the effect that he is buying

62. See Daggett, *What Future for Community Property Law in Louisiana*, 4 SOUTHWESTERN L.J. 20, 23, 24 (1950). See also Malone v. Cannon, 215 La. 939, 41 So.2d 837 (1949) (marital portion).

63. La. Acts 1920, No. 186, p. 304, amending and re-enacting Art. 2334, LA. CIVIL CODE of 1870.

64. Houghton v. Hall, 177 La. 237, 148 So. 37 (1933).

65. La. Acts 1912, No. 170, p. 310.

66. La. Acts 1902, No. 68, p. 95, amending Art. 2402, LA. CIVIL CODE of 1870.

67. La. Acts 1912, No. 170, p. 310.

with his separate funds for his separate benefit.[68] It is suggested that in purchasing stocks, bonds, or other movables that this recitation might be solemnly made before a notary and proper witnesses concurrently with the purchase of movables and a copy of the instrument attached to the evidence of title of the movables. It is possible that this device might be effective in a settlement between the spouses or their heirs at the termination of the community. No test case can be cited at the moment. Obviously it would not affect creditors as all of the husband's property, separate or community, is available to separate and community creditors.[69]

Whatever the recitation by the wife to preserve title in her separate estate, she must prove[70] it although the time-honored rule is that she may introduce evidence outside of the instrument to prove that the property is her separate property while the husband may not do so.[71] The question of uncertainty regardless of recitation has been previously discussed. Also, it has been demonstrated that a wife investing her separate property in a business in which she labors, would seem not to be able to preserve the earnings therefrom as they go into the community and if the venture is unsuccessful will lose not only her original investment of separate funds but reduce the community as well under the public merchant theory coupled with the *Houghton-Hall* decision.

Moreover, the wife apparently cannot maintain as separate the earnings of her separate property under mere factual administration by herself because of the latest legislative edict unless she files an instrument containing a double declaration of reservation and intention.[72] This legislation is said to have been passed for tax reasons and to simplify proof. The tax reason, if ever a sound one for family protective purposes, no longer exists under modified tax rules regarding marital property.[73] So far

68. DAGGETT, THE COMMUNITY PROPERTY SYSTEM OF LOUISIANA 29 *et seq.* (1945).

69. *Id.* at 50.

70. See note 32 *supra.*

71. Staunton v. Vinterella, 223 La. 958, 67 So.2d 550 (1953).

72. La. Acts 1944, No. 286, p. 836, amending Art. 2386, LA. CIVIL CODE of 1870; Matthews v. Hansberry, 71 So.2d 232 (La. App. 1954) [citing K. & M. Store, Inc. v. Lewis, 22 So.2d 769, 771 (La. App. 1945); United States v. Burglass, 172 F.2d 960, 963 (5th Cir. 1949); and Trorlicht v. Collector of Revenue, 25 So.2d 547, 551 (La. App. 1946)]. The Supreme Court thus far does not seem to have applied the amended article 2386. *Cf.* Guilbeau v. Guilbeau, 224 La. 837, 71 So.2d 129 (1954).

73. Revenue Act of 1948, 62 STAT. 110 (1948). See § 351 (eliminating community property provisions of § 811(e) of the Internal Revenue Code); § 361 (adding the marital deduction provision to § 812(a) of the Internal Revenue

as the simplification of proof purpose is concerned, it might be asked, simplification for whose benefit? Again, the answer would be for those attacking on all fronts any and all family reserves when the husband meets financial ill fortune.

Moreover, what is administration? It has been indicated that the husband's administrative powers over the wife's property include investment of funds, coming to his hands with consequent result of shifting title to the community, an apparent deviation from the accepted and legally protected theory of mere administration found in dealing with minors and interdicts, decedents' estates, absentees and other areas clearly distinguishing administration from converted ownership.[74]

Suppose the wife does file the instrument required to preserve her separate administration, where does administration leave off and making her capital work as a business begin? The line would seem to be quite hazy and, with what appears to be fast becoming an irrebuttable presumption of community, it is easy to predict with some degree of assurance which answer will prevail.

Previously, with thought of encouraging small investors in homestead associations, moneys deposited by a wife would become her separate property regardless of the source of the funds.[75] No longer is this the case.[76] This situation may not present as strong a case as previously cited examples but is another illustration of the trend to prevent the segregation of a fund to protect the family from the ill winds of depressions, regressions, running readjustments, economic dips, levelings off or whatever be the current term for these unhappy events.

Thus, it would seem that we have legally gone "Onward to Yesterday"[77] or beyond while the world has continued ever toward tomorrow with its tremendous changes, presumably an advance in our social and economic life. Married women are in general legally incapable of dealing with community property and materially hampered in either acquiring or dealing with

---

Code); and §§ 104(c) and 301 (providing for the splitting of income between spouses by amending § 12(d) of the Internal Revenue Code). Rubin & Champagne, *Some Community Property Aspects of the 1948 Revenue Act*, 9 Louisiana Law Review 1 (1948).

74. Succession of Schnitter, 220 La. 323, 56 So.2d 563 (1951).

75. La. Acts 1902, No. 120, p. 195; La. Acts 1932, No. 140, p. 455.

76. Cameron v. Rowland, 215 La. 177, 40 So.2d 1 (1949); La. Acts 1938, No. 337, p. 828; La. Acts 1940, No. 95, p. 443.

77. Said to be a favorite slogan of Wm. J. Nichols. Saturday Review of Literature, Dec. 19, 1953, p. 9.

their separate property. The trend of court decisions and recent legislation is to place all marital property in the community classification. The results are submitted to be:

1. Deleterious to dealing with immovables because of the uncertainty of title when property stands in the name of a married woman and to commerce in movables purchased by the wife under her mandate.

2. Deleterious to business growth because of the fear of each spouse to venture lest all family assets may be lost.

3. Deleterious to family security as no protection is available to segregate the earnings of one spouse if the other is unsuccessful.

4. Deleterious to marital tranquility because of lack of control of earned property and formalities and insecurity of separate property.

5. Deleterious to the state because of effect on marital relations leading to separation and divorce.

6. Deleterious to the state as it principally affects the middle class, financially speaking, understood to be the foundation stone of the state's prosperity and stability.

7. Deleterious psychologically to an intelligent and industrious wife to be classified on legal capacity with children and mental defectives.

Possible Adjustments

It should be constantly borne in mind that the community property idea is one of a sharing as equally as possible by the spouses of the material accumulations of the period of the marriage dimly reflecting the spiritual concept of the sharing of the joys and sorrows of life itself. The enfolding of children within the unit perfects the whole and protection of all types is contemplated for each and every member of the group termed the family.

(a) *Control.* Certainly the basic policy of the court in the *Houghton-Hall*[78] case was sound for, regardless of legislative intent, devotion of all the energies of a spouse to building a separate estate as the expense of the other would destroy the community ideal as surely as any other method. Framers of the Code foresaw the danger and provided the marital portion,[79] which,

78. Houghton, v. Hall, 177 La. 237, 148 So. 37 (1933).
79. Art. 2382, La. Civil Code of 1870.

if interpreted in the light of its purpose and not with injection of the "fault" theory, which is another invitation to divorce, serves as some protection against a selfish spouse.[80]

Equal division of accumulations as between the spouses or their heirs must be maintained or the community plan abandoned. In all types of business association, settlement is contemplated for occurrence at the completion of the joint enterprise or dissolution of the business association. Management or control of the business while in operation is indeed another matter. The oversimplified answer is sometimes given by presumably thoughtful persons that "every business has to have a head," which apparently again indicates confusion between marital relations and marital property. The precept is doubtless sound for business enterprises and one thesis of this discussion is indeed to urge its incorporation as one element of adjustment of community property problems. When husband and wife are each running a separate business or attempting to hold separate jobs, the good management, thrift, luck, or what have you, of the one, cannot save the other but both businesses must stand or fall together. Thus, there is no real head to either. Moreover, short of disturbance of the marital relationship, there is no way to get one. There is no machinery for getting a new manager in time to prevent disaster. Enterprise is discouraged. Lending agencies are wary. Conveyancers are uneasy. Spouses become frustrated and dissatisfied and not only may the business associations fall but they may take the marital association with them.

Simple legislative curatives may be found. Oklahoma's plan for control by the wife earning separately from the husband seems feasible and certainly had nothing to do with the state's apparent distaste for any and all community property systems.[81] This plan provided for completely separate control and management of the two endeavors when both spouses were separately engaged in ventures for material gains.[82] Creditors reliance was upon but the one business which they had furnished unless other voluntary arrangements were made. Obviously, proper recordation for their protection was necessary. While Oklahoma apparently instituted the system for tax purposes

---

80. Malone v. Cannon, 215 La. 939, 41 So.2d 837 (1949).

81. See discussion of repeal and its aftermath by Trice, *Community Property in Oklahoma*, 4 SOUTHWESTERN L.J. 38 (1950).

82. See Daggett, *The Oklahoma Community Property Act—A Comparative Study*, 2 LOUISIANA LAW REVIEW 575 (1940).

only and abandoned it after the tax need had passed,[83] they nonetheless were aware of conditions prevailing when they sought to institute the system and made proper provision to avoid the situation presently prevailing in Louisiana. It is of particular present interest that the French commissioners engaged in preparing a revision of the French Civil Code for possible adoption have decided upon split control provisions similar to those outlined in this article, evidencing the existence of the same dissatisfactions presently manifested in Louisiana.[84]

If the Oklahoma or a similar plan were adopted, provision could be made within the pattern for title certainty when property stands in the wife's name. Obviously, that item might be cared for without adoption of a comprehensive control plan and is being presently urged by some thoughtful persons who are particularly interested in that phase of the confusion.

(b) *Balance and Equality.* Certainly sources of community and separate property whatever they may be should be the same for both spouses that equitable division might be made at the dissolution of the community. Obligations to each other should be the same and the Code so states.[85] Support of the wife by the husband rises from the relationship,[86] and is recognized by the necessity doctrine[87] and by alimony provisions even after divorce.[88] Proper emphasis would not seem to have been placed upon the wife's assumption of similar responsibilities to the husband specifically provided by the Code during marriage at least.[89] Redistribution of wealth by the tax method materially reduces the monetary importance of separate property acquired by inheritance and gift of great fortunes and small, thus increasing the need for balance and equity in community regulations.

(c) *Marriage Contract.* Spouses should be able to organize their business affairs as financial advantage or security dictates. They should be able to reorganize their business affairs if their marital happiness tends to be affected by them. Permission to make a marriage contract during marriage would be a very simple change in the law.[90] The machinery governing marriage

83. See note 73 *supra.*
84. See note 94 *infra.*
85. Art. 119, LA. CIVIL CODE of 1870.
86. Art. 120, LA. CIVIL CODE of 1870. See also LA. R.S. § 14:74 (1950).
87. Art. 1786, LA. CIVIL CODE of 1870.
88. Art. 160, LA. CIVIL CODE of 1870.
89. Arts. 2389, 2435, LA. CIVIL CODE of 1870.
90. Art. 2329, LA. CIVIL CODE of 1870.

contracts is still intact.[91] Sufficient modification of the action for separation of property to make the device effective would not be unduly complicated.

A traditional fear seems to be that domestic felicity might be disturbed if such contracts were allowed. The present fear is that much disturbance will result if the relief continues to be disallowed. Moreover, marriage contracts of the past were really made by parents in the interest of their children. This stage of economic and social life has passed in Louisiana for better or worse. The hard realities of life fortunately do not cloud the proper bliss of courtship, thus few contracts at all are made. If permitted later when time, thought and experience might dictate a need for rearrangement in the interest of the marriage, and with present day participation by the wife in business, much good might be accomplished. It seems uniquely Victorian that the most interested of all parties may not contract with each other.

Another fear seems to be that the greedy, jealous, dominant spouse might browbeat the amiable or timid one into signing a bad contract. Obviously, dictators in homes and out of them probably will always exist regardless of preventive legislation and can do little if any more harm to a marriage with right of contract than without it. Moreover, the law presently contains the protection of the marital portion,[92] the provision for sharing of marital establishment expenses by those separate in property[93] and other wise provisions to meet obvious contingencies.

Little change may be needed but it is needed badly if the community property system is to survive and survive as a protector of family finance and a binder and promoter of emotional security and satisfaction rather than a wedge for disintegration of all of these elements. These pages are not to say with D. H. Lawrence "Let there be a parliament of men and women for the careful and gradual unmaking of laws" but to urge the repair of these laws at the earliest possible date that their original purpose and usefulness may be retained. The mail shirt of indifference is a poor shield against the effects of maladjusted provisions of marital property law.

When the thoughts of the fine minds of the leaders of Lou-

---

91. Art. 2325 *et seq.*, La. Civil Code of 1870.
92. Art. 2382, La. Civil Code of 1870.
93. Art. 2435, La. Civil Code of 1870.

isiana come to be turned to a recognition and solution of these problems, doubtless most equitable and satisfactory measures may be devised without reference to suggestions most humbly suggested here as mere possibilities.[94]

94. See Ancel, *The Revision of the French Civil Code*, 25 TULANE L. REV. 435, 444 (1951); Clark, *Management and Control of Community Property in New Mexico*, 26 TULANE L. REV. 234 *et seq.* (1952); Daggett, *Is Joint Control of Community Property Possible?*, 10 TULANE L. REV. 589 *et seq.* (1936).

Nevada Community Property Law

*Annette R. Shermack**

A case unique in Nevada, and probably elsewhere, *Anderson v. McGill Club*,[1] illustrates the substantive force of the community property concept. There Gladys Anderson brought an action against the defendant corporation which maintained a gambling room. Her complaint alleged that for several months the defendant had "knowingly, willfully, maliciously, and unlawfully in a spirit of recklessness, and from wanton and malicious motives"[2] procured, permitted and tempted divers persons, including the husband of the plaintiff, Chet Anderson, to "frequent said room and habitually engage in playing poker and stud horse poker, from which games the defendant received a share of the money played."[3] It was further alleged that Chet was of such nature he could not resist the temptation to gamble, and being so tempted, and without Gladys' consent, he spent many hours apart from her engaged in gambling and losing portions of his salary as a clerk, the only source of income for himself, his wife and children. For her suffering, the loss of her husband's companionship and the money upon which she relied for support, Gladys sought $5,000 damages.

The lower court held the complaint did not state a cause of action, and this decision was affirmed, the majority of the court taking the view the complaint was defective in that Gladys did not allege the defendant knew her husband was a married man, or make other allegation showing a direct and intentional invasion of the marital relation existing between Gladys and Chet.

It is easy to sympathize with the author of the opinion for the court, Chief Justice Sanders, who said:

> "The complaint is a novelty, both in form and substance. No appeal for redress by a wife for a like grievance has ever found its way into court, and I am apprehensive that in their just indignation against the nefarious nuisance maintained by the defendant and in their commendable zeal for

---

* Member, New Mexico Bar.

1. 51 Nev. 16, 266 Pac. 913 (1928).
2. *Id.* at 19, 266 Pac. at 913.
3. *Ibid.*

the protection of the home and the innocent members of the family my associates have been led to affirm a proposition of law which cannot be sustained."[4]

While the complaint alleged some of the elements of both loss of consortium and alienation of affection, the court felt it could not be "pegged" as stating either of these actions, but viewed it as one for the tort of intentional invasion of the marital relation. Whatever the cause of action was, the significance of the case lies in its indication of the very real and direct interest a wife has in community property, the extent to which the courts will go in the protection of that interest and the great divergence of concepts in the philosophy of the civil law from that of the common law.

This case also serves as overture to what might be termed the "purity" of treatment of community property law in Nevada.

Nevada was originally part of the Utah Territory and previous to statehood its law of marital ownership was that of the Spanish and Mexican community property system. The constitution of 1848 rceognized the existence of community property and directed that laws be enacted defining the rights of the wife in both separate and community property.[5] The adoption of common law as the rule of practice and procedure in 1861[6] was thought to govern property rights between husband and wife prior to the first statutory definition of community property in 1864,[7] in some of the early cases;[8] however, the denial of continuity of community property law in these cases is of only academic interest today, as the statutes of 1864 adopted community of property almost as it was administered in Mexico.[9] The statutes of 1864 were modeled after those existing in Cali-

4. *Id.* at 20, 266 Pac. at 913.

5. NEV. CONST. Art. IV, § 31 (1848): "All property, both real and personal, of the wife owned or claimed by her before marriage, and that acquired afterward by gift, devise or descent, shall be her separate property; and laws shall be passed, more clearly defining the rights of the wife in relation, as well to her separate property, as to that held in common with her husband. Laws shall also be passed providing for the registration of the wife's separate property."

6. Nev. Laws 1861, c. 1, p. 1.

7. Lev. Laws 1864-5, c. 76, p. 239.

8. Johnson v. Garner, 233 Fed. 756 (D.Nev. 1916); Winters v. Winters, 34 Nev. 323, 123 Pac. 17 (1912); Lake v. Bender, 18 Nev. 361, 7 Pac. 74 (1884); Darrenberger v. Haupt, 10 Nev. 43 (1875); 1 DE FUNIAK, PRINCIPLES OF COMMUNITY PROPERTY 112, § 52 (1943).

9. Nixon v. Brown, 46 Nev. 439, 214 Pac. 524 (1923).

fornia.[10] New legislation in 1873[11] superseded the act of 1864, and with changes and amendments remains the law today.[12]

Community property is defined as all property acquired after marriage by husband or wife or both, except such property as comes within the definition of separate property.[13] Separate property of the spouses is that owned by him or her prior to marriage, or acquired thereafter by gift, bequest, devise or descent, together with the rents, issues and profits therefrom.[14]

The husband has the entire management and control of the community property, both real and personal, and may dispose of it as absolutely as he would his separate estate, subject to the exception that any conveyance of the homestead must be joined in execution and acknowledgment by both husband and wife.[15] This exception has been held to refer to the homestead "in fact."[16] However, the wife may be constituted agent for the husband and he will be bound by her contracts of purchase if such agency can be established either by a showing of actual authorization, or of ostensible agency by course of conduct.[17] The general principles of agency apply.[18] The wife is given control of her earnings and accumulations and those of her minor children living with her, when such earnings and accumulations are used for the care and maintenance of the family.[19] It is provided where the husband has allowed the wife to appropriate her earnings to her own use, such earnings, together with their rents and profits, are deemed given to the wife by the husband and are her separate property.[20] The husband's power of management of the community property includes the right to make gifts of it to third persons without the consent of the wife where it does not appear there was any fraudulent intent to defeat the claims of the wife in such property and where the gift is reasonable with reference to the value of the whole amount of community property.[21]

---

10. 1 de Funiak, Principles of Community Property 112, § 52 (1943).
11. Nev. Laws 1873, c. 119, p. 193.
12. See Nev. Comp. Laws (1929) (Supps. 1931-41 and 1943-9).
13. Nev. Comp. Laws § 3356 (1929).
14. *Id.* § 3355.
15. *Id.* § 3360.
16. First Nat. Bank of Ely v. Meyers, 39 Nev. 235, 150 Pac. 308 (1916).
17. Harrah v. Specialty Shops, 67 Nev. 493, 221 P.2d 398 (1950); Travers v. Barrett, 30 Nev. 402, 97 Pac. 126 (1908).
18. Harrah v. Home Furniture, 67 Nev. 114, 214 P.2d 1016 (1950).
19. Nev. Comp. Laws § 3360 (1929).
20. *Id.* § 3369; Goldsworthy v. Johnson, 45 Nev. 355, 204 Pac. 505 (1922).
21. Nixon v. Brown, 46 Nev. 439, 214 Pac. 524 (1923).

Neither husband nor wife is liable for antenuptial debts of the other[22] and the husband is not liable for the wife's antenuptial torts.[23] The separate property of the wife is not liable for the debts of her husband, but is liable for her own debts.[24] But, the wife must support her husband out of her separate property when he has no separate property, and when there is no community property and the husband due to infirmity is unable to support himself.[25] Where a husband neglects to provide necessaries for his wife, any person may so provide them and recover their value from the husband.[26] The husband is not liable for the wife's support if she has unjustifiedly abandoned him.[27] The wife's interest in the community property is not subject to attachment in an action against the wife on an alleged guaranty contract.[28]

Husband and wife may hold property as "joint tenants, tenants in common, or as community property,"[29] and they are free to make any contract with one another, or with any other person, respecting property, as if they were unmarried, subject to the general rules governing persons in relations of confidence and trust.[30] Except as limited by this right of contract, neither husband nor wife has any interest in the separate property of the other.[31] Aside from the power given husbands and wives to alter their relations as to property, they may not alter their legal relations by agreement,[32] except that they may enter into separation agreements and may provide for the support of either of them and of their children during separation.[33] If a divorce is contemplated by the parties, they may provide that such agreement is made for the purpose of removing the subject matter from the field of litigation and that the agreement shall be-

---

22. Nev. Comp. Laws § 3371.01 (Supp. 1931-41).
23. Slack v. Schwartz, 63 Nev. 47, 161 P.2d 345 (1945).
24. Nev. Comp. Laws § 3371 (1929).
25. *Id* § 3378.
26. *Id.* § 3376.
27. *Id.* § 3377. Apparently no cases have arisen under this section and it is subject to conjecture whether this provision makes any change in the character of the husband's earnings and acquisitions during such period of unjustified abandonment. However, as the courts' powers over division of both community and separate property upon divorce are very broad, Nev. Comp. Laws § 9463 (Supp. 1931-41), the question could arise only in unusual instances.
28. Peterson v. Wiesner, 62 Nev. 184, 146 P.2d 789 (1944).
29. Nev. Comp. Laws § 3362 (1929).
30. *Id.* § 3373.
31. *Id.* § 3372. But see Nev. Comp. Laws § 9463 (Supp. 1931-41).
32. Nev. Comp. Laws § 3374 (1929).
33. *Ibid.*

come effective only in event a divorce is granted.[34] The mutual consent of the parties is sufficient consideration for such agreement.[35]

Husband and wife are free to enter into marriage contracts or settlements.[36] Property rights shall be governed by the community property law unless a marriage contract or settlement contains contrary stipulations.[37] Such contracts must be executed in writing with the formalities required for conveyances of land, and when recorded in any county wherein real estate affected is located, they constitute full notice of their contents.[38] Unless so recorded, marriage contracts or settlements are valid only as between the parties.[39] A minor capable of contracting marriage may make a valid marriage contract or settlement.[40]

The wife is given complete power over her separate property.[41] She may convey, charge, encumber, or in any manner dispose of it.

Where a wife suffers personal injuries due to the negligence of another, suit may be brought by the husband and wife jointly or separately at their option. When they sue jointly, the damages must be segregated; the damages assessed by reason of personal injuries and pain and suffering are awarded to and belong to the wife, while damages assessed for loss of services, hospital and medical expenses and other care are awarded to the husband. Where the wife sues separately, all damages sustained by her are awarded to and belong to her.[42]

Upon divorce, it is provided the court shall make such disposition of the community and separate property as shall appear just and equitable, giving consideration to the respective merits of the parties and the condition in which they will be left by the divorce, the party through whom the property was acquired,

---

34. *Ibid.*
35. *Id.* § 3375.
36. *Id.* § 3380.
37. *Ibid.*
38. *Id.* §§ 3381, 3382, 3383.
39. *Id.* § 3384.
40. *Id.* § 3385.
41. *Id.* § 3363.
42. Nev. Comp. Laws § 3389.01 (Supp. 1943-9). This section passed in 1949 incorporated in the statutes the previous holding in Fredrickson & Watson Const. Co. v. Boyd, 60 Nev. 117, 102 P.2d 627 (1940), with added provision it is optional for husband and wife to sue jointly or separately. See also Underhill v. Anciaux, 68 Nev. 69, 226 P.2d 794 (1951).

and the burdens, if any, imposed upon it for the benefit of the children.[43]

Upon the death of the wife, the entire community property vests without administration in the surviving husband, except for the case where the husband has abandoned the wife without such cause as would entitle him to a divorce, when the wife's half of the community property, subject to the payment of the equal proportion of community debts, is subject to her testamentary disposition in the same manner as her separate property.[44]

Upon the husband's death, one-half of the community property vests in the surviving wife and the other half is subject to testamentary disposition by the husband. If he dies intestate, the property goes equally to his surviving wife and children; if there are no children, the entire community estate goes to the wife, subject to the payment of debts.[45] It is also required that the homestead and other property exempt from execution be set apart for the use of the widow and minor heirs, if any.[46] Even though a homestead has not been declared during the life of the decedent, the court must set aside a homestead in community property on the widow's request.[47]

Estates in dower and curtesy are abolished.[48]

Nevada law incorporates provision for the filing of an inventory of the separate property of the wife.[49] Unfortunately, no information is available as to the frequency of use of the inventory. However, as will be noted hereafter, the presence or

---

43. NEV. COMP. LAWS § 9463 (Supp. 1931-41) expressly amending NEV. COMP. LAWS § 3366 (1929). The earlier section provided the community property must be equally divided between the parties except that where the decree of divorce was rendered on the ground of adultery or extreme cruelty, the guilty spouse should only be entitled to such portion of the community property as the court in its discretion might deem just to allow. See Johnson v. Garner, 233 Fed. 756 (D.Nev. 1916), for discussion of a conflicting statute adopted in 1861, NEV. COMP. LAWS § 9465 (1929), and amended in Nev. Laws 1939, c. 25, § 2, p. 18.

44. NEV. COMP. LAWS § 3395.01 (Supp. 1931-41).

45. *Id.* § 3395.02.

46. *Ibid.* In Nevada a homestead of the value of $10,000 may be declared, and after filing such declaration husband and wife shall be deemed to hold the homestead as joint tenants. NEV. COMP. LAWS § 3315 (Supp. 1943-9). See *In re* Cook's Estate, 34 Nev. 217, 117 Pac. 27 (1911), for discussion of homestead on separate property.

47. *In re* Cook's Estate, 34 Nev. 217, 117 Pac. 27 (1911).

48. NEV. COMP. LAWS § 3361 (1929).

49. *Id.* § 3357. *Id.* §§ 3358, 3359, provide for the filing of inventory for record to serve as notice of the wife's title to the property and the effect of failure to so file.

absence of inventory has considerabe probative value in establishing the character of property as the separate property of the wife or as community property.[50]

Nevada has no statutory presumptions respecting the character of ownership of property as community or separate according to the manner in which title is taken by one or the other or both of the spouses.[51]

Under the general statutory framework outlined above, Nevada's courts have been called upon chiefly to interpret the definitions of community and separate property with reference to initial acquisition and transmutation from one form of ownership to another, and to declare the rights of husband and wife under contracts executed between them, both as to the character of the property in transactions involving creditors and between the parties upon divorce.

Another, and a most enlightened, segment of Nevada law concerns its holding as to the character of ownership of compensation awarded for injuries sustained by the spouses due to the negligence of third parties and the allied problem of imputing the negligence of one spouse to the other.

The following paragraphs are intended to give only a very general summary of the principles of Nevada law with reference to these matters.

The courts of Nevada never experimented with the idea that the wife's interest in the community property is only a mere expectancy, but from the beginning viewed it as a present, vested interest.[52] In a very eary case the husband's interest in the community property was described as a moiety.[53] In a later case where it was urged that the wife's interest in the community was subject to the payment of an inheritance tax upon the death of her husband, the much criticized distinction between the term "goes to" and "belongs to" which appear in the earlier

---

50. See Petition of Fuller, 63 Nev. 26, 159 P.2d 579 (1945), where it is held failure to file inventory is a circumstance to be considered on question of proof of character of ownership. To the same effect is Thomas v. Nevans, 67 Nev. 122, 215 P.2d 244 (1950).

51. Such provisions are present in New Mexico and California: N.M. STAT. ANN. § 65-401 (Supp. 1953); CAL. CIV. CODE § 164 (Deering, 1949). See Clark, *Presumptions in New Mexico Community Property Law: The Cali-*

52. 1 DE FUNIAK, PRINCIPLES OF COMMUNITY PROPERTY 312, § 110 (1943).

53. Crow v. Van Sickle, 6 Nev. 146 (1870).

Nevada statutes[54] in describing the interest of the wife and husband respectively in the community property upon the death of the other spouse, utilized to urge a difference in the character of their ownership, was flatly rejected and it was held the wife's interest in the community did not pass to her under the laws of inheritance.[55]

Parallel in importance with the recognition of the wife's vested interest in community property is the general presumption recognized in Nevada, as it is believed under all community property systems, that property acquired after marriage by husband and wife is community property,[56] unless the time and manner of its acquisition establish it as separate property of one or the other of the spouses under the statutory definition.[57] If property, or an equitable interest in it, is acquired before marriage, it is presumed to be separate property.[58] In each instance these presumptions may be rebutted by a showing of clear and convincing evidence in proof of the contrary.

The general test of whether property is community or separate is whether it was purchased with or acquired in exchange for community or separate funds or property.[59] The character of ownership does not depend on who may have record title to the property, or, indeed, upon how the parties regard it as being held, but upon the circumstances of its acquisition, and the character of ownership is determined as of such time.[60]

A husband may make a valid gift of community funds or property to his wife to be held as her separate property,[61] but

---

54. *In re* Williams' Estate, 40 Nev. 241, 161 Pac. 741, L.R.A. 1917C 602 (1916); NEV. REV. LAWS §§ 2164, 2165 (1912). California formerly had the same provision, CAL. CIV. CODE §§ 1401, 1402, prior to amendment, 1923; and such is the present provision in New Mexico, N.M. STAT. ANN. §§ 31-108, 31-109 (1941).

55. *In re* Williams' Estate, 40 Nev. 241, 161 Pac. 741 (1916).

56. *In re* Wilson's Estate, 56 Nev. 353, 53 P.2d 339 (1936); Lake v. Bender, 18 Nev. 361, 7 Pac. 74 (1884).

57. NEV. COMP. LAWS § 3355 (1929); Barrett v. Franke, 46 Nev. 170, 208 Pac. 435 (1922).

58. *In re* Wilson's Estate, 56 Nev. 353, 53 P.2d 339 (1936); Barrett v. Franke, 46 Nev. 170, 208 Pac. 435 (1922); Laws v. Ross, 44 Nev. 405, 194 Pac. 465 (1921); Lake v. Bender, 18 Nev. 361, 7 Pac. 74 (1884).

59. Petition of Fuller, 63 Nev. 26, 159 P.2d 579 (1945); *In re* Wilson's Estate, 56 Nev. 353, 53 P.2d 339 (1936); Malmstrom v. People's Drain Ditch Co., 32 Nev. 246, 107 Pac. 98 (1910).

60. *In re* Wilson's Estate, 56 Nev. 353, 53 P.2d 339 (1936); Hill v. Du Pratt, 51 Nev. 242, 274 Pac. 2 (1929); Milisich v. Hillhouse, 48 Nev. 166, 288 Pac. 307 (1924); Barrett v. Franke, 46 Nev. 170, 208 Pac. 435 (1922). See Edmonds v. Perry, 62 Nev. 41, 140 P.2d 566 (1943), for interesting related joint bank account case.

61. Petition of Fuller, 63 Nev. 26, 159 P.2d 579 (1945); Stockgrowers & Ranchers Bank of Reno v. Milisich, 52 Nev. 178, 283 Pac. 913 (1930).

proof to establish such gift must be clear and convincing. Ordinarily a mere verbal assertion of gift, or the recording of a conveyance in the wife's name is insufficient to establish a gift where the property was acquired with community funds.[62] Nevertheless, it should be noted that at least one Nevada case unequivocally invokes the presumption of gift to the wife where property has been transferred or conveyed to her by her husband.[63] This case asserted that the presumption could be overcome only by clear and convincing evidence to the contrary, saying this meant more than a preponderance of the evidence, as if the evidence were in conflict the presumption would prevail. The authorities relied upon in this case are from common law jurisdictions and it is submitted that this presumption of gift is not logically a strong one, as its substantive basis, that is, a limited interest of the wife in marital gains, is not present in Nevada.[64] It is also doubtful if the presumption has any force in actions where creditors or other third parties are involved.

With respect to the character of particular acquisitions, it has been held that the earnings of either the husband or the wife are community property.[65] Compensation for injuries to the person arising from violation of the right of personal security is not community property, but separate; the character of a judgment obtained by one spouse as separate or community property depends on the right violated.[66] Thus, where the wife sustains injuries as the result of negligence of third parties, her physical pain and suffering are not the loss of the husband or the community, but are a loss personal to the wife, and contributory negligence of the husband may not be imputed to the wife

62. *In re* Condos' Estate, 266 P.2d 404 (Nev. 1954); Petition of Fuller, 63 Nev. 26, 159 P.2d 579 (1945); *In re* Wilson's Estate, 56 Nev. 353, 53 P.2d 339 (1936); Milisich v. Hillhouse, 48 Nev. 166, 228 Pac. 307 (1924).

63. Peardon v. Peardon, 65 Nev. 717, 201 P.2d 309 (1948).

64. See discussion of the case of Lombardi v. Lombardi, 44 Nev. 314, 195 Pac. 93 (1921), in 1 DE FUNIAK, PRINCIPLES OF COMMUNITY PROPERTY 190, § 73 (1943), adverse to the holding that when either community or separate funds are devoted by the husband to the improvement of the wife's separate property, the title to the property is not changed, but as between the spouses, in the absence of an agreement, the husband is presumed to have intended a gift to the wife. The burden of the criticism is there is no reason to presume a gift. In any case, it is submitted such rule is certainly at loggerheads with the rule of Lake v. Bender, 18 Nev. 361, 7 Pac. 74 (1884), and Ormachea v. Ormachea, 67 Nev. 273, 217 P.2d 355 (1950), to the effect the community owns so much of the increase from separate property as is due to the labor or management of the spouses.

65. Ormachea v. Ormachea, 67 Nev. 273, 217 P.2d 355 (1950); Jones v. Edwards, 49 Nev. 299, 245 Pac. 292 (1926). See, however, NEV. COMP. LAWS § 3369 (1929); Goldsworthy v. Johnson, 45 Nev. 355, 204 Pac. 505 (1922).

66. Frederickson & Watson Const. Co. v. Boyd, 60 Nev. 117, 102 P.2d 627 (1940).

to defeat her recovery.[67] Similarly, the proceeds from a mother's exercise of her statutory right to maintain an action for the death of a minor adopted child are not community property, and the contributory negligence of the father cannot be imputed to the mother to defeat recovery.[68] The increase, fruits and profits from separate property remain separate property where the additional acquisition comes mainly from the property itself; but where such acquisitions are due mainly to the efforts or skill of the parties, they are community property.[69]

It has been seen that in Nevada husband and wife have great latitude to determine their relations as to their property by contract. The extent to which they may do so is seen in the recent case of *Woods v. Bromley*,[70] where a separation agreement recited that the husband and wife held certain property as joint tenants and they agreed that it was their intent to thereby vest title in themselves as tenants in common. It was held the contract itself vested title in them in common as opposed to the contention of the wife that such change could be accomplished only by formal conveyances as the contract contained a provision that such would be executed. The decision was based upon the fact that the agreement clearly disclosed the intention of the parties to execute an immediate severance of the unities of joint tenancy and create tenancy in common.

Due to the relation of husband and wife as one of "confidence and trust,"[71] the rules respecting fiduciaries apply to them with regard to constructive fraud and Nevada has held that the law implies one of the parties has a superiority over the other and a contract between them is to the advantage of the one presumptively superior—the husband.[72] Upon the husband, then, is cast the burden of overcoming such presumption by showing compliance with the equitable requisites of good faith, full knowledge, independent consent and action.[73] Yet it has been recognized that the wife may in fact be the superior spouse, as under statutes emancipating women the relationship of superiority is easily interchangeable.[74]

---

67. *Ibid.*
68. Los Angeles & S.L.R.R. v. Umbaugh, 61 Nev. 214, 123 P.2d 224 (1942).
69. Ormachea v. Ormachea, 67 Nev. 273, 217 P.2d 355 (1950); Lake v. Bender, 18 Nev. 361, 7 Pac. 74 (1884).
70. 241 P.2d 1103 (Nev. 1952).
71. NEV. COMP. LAWS § 3373 (1929).
72. Crawford v. Crawford, 24 Nev. 410, 56 Pac. 94 (1899).
73. *Ibid.*
74. Peardon v. Peardon, 65 Nev. 717, 201 P.2d 309 (1948).

The most frequent examples of litigation regarding contracts between the spouses occur in divorce cases. When property settlements are incorporated in a divorce decree they are to be construed fairly and reasonably, not too strictly or technically.[75] Before a property settlement incorporated in a divorce decree may be set aside on the ground of fraud, the fraud must be established as extrinsic,[76] that is, such fraud as prevents a party from having his day in court.

Reference has already been made to the wide discretionary powers of the courts in Nevada in respect to the division of property upon divorce.[77] However, if property rights are not in issue in a divorce action and the decree is limited to dissolution of the marriage, rights of the spouses in the property are not prejudiced thereby, but each party may thereafter enforce them in a separate action for such purpose.[78] Each spouse's former separate property remains his or her individual property, and former community property is held by the parties as tenants in common in such case.[79] It has been held the Nevada courts have power in divorce actions where the parties are within the jurisdiction of the court to pass indirectly upon title to land located in another state, though it is recognized the judgment is effective only *in personam*.[80]

In conclusion it is submitted Nevada has been singularly fortunate in avoiding some of the perplexing and troublesome

---

75. Murphy v. Murphy, 64 Nev. 440, 183 P.2d 632 (1947).

76. Mazour v. Mazour, 64 Nev. 245, 180 P.2d 103 (1947); Calvert v. Calvert, 61 Nev. 168, 122 P.2d 426 (1942).

77. See, generally, Ormachea v. Ormachea, 67 Nev. 273, 217 P.2d 355 (1950); Herzog v. Herzog, 249 P.2d 533 (Nev. 1952); Cunningham v. Cunningham, 61 Nev. 93, 116 P.2d 188 (1941); Walker v. Walker, 41 Nev. 4, 164 Pac. 653 (1917). The last cited case involves an unusual marriage settlement agreement and is exemplary of the powers of the Nevada courts upon divorce in division of property.

78. First Nat. Bank of Nevada v. Wolff, 66 Nev. 51, 202 P.2d 878 (1949).

79. First Nat. Bank of Nevada v. Wolff, 66 Nev. 51, 202 P.2d 878 (1949) overruled *sub silentio* the earlier holding in Keenan v. Keenan, 40 Nev. 351, 164 Pac. 351 (1917), where it was ruled a wife who had left her residence in Nevada and secured a divorce elsewhere, then returned to Nevada and in a separate action for such purpose tried to assert her rights in the former community property of the spouses, could not do so, the court basing its decision on the language of NEV. COMP. LAWS § 3366 (1929), and declaring only the court on divorce had power to divide community property. In this connection, however, probably only the court granting the divorce would have jurisdiction to divide the property of either spouse or the community according to the merits of the issue and the circumstances of the parties as provided in NEV. COMP. LAWS § 9463 (1929), as amended, Nev. Laws 1939, c. 25, § 1, p. 18. Therefore, if such issue were not litigated, in the divorce action, it is questionable if action could thereafter be brought for more than equal division of the community and for separate property.

80. Buass v. Buass (sic), 62 Nev. 232, 147 P.2d 495 (1944).

rules adopted in other community property jurisdictions. (1) Nevada from the beginning saw the wife's interest in community property as a present, vested interest. (2) The power of the spouses to transmute their holdings from community to separate property and vice versa has never been questioned. (3) Without the aid of statute, Nevada determined that the proceeds of a judgment for personal injury to one of the spouses for pain and suffering or other personal loss is the separate property of such spouse, and such right to compensation cannot be defeated by the imputation of negligence of the other spouse.

It is believed that Nevada has been able to steer such a clear course by virtue of the fact her courts have generally resorted to the fundamental civil law concept of community property and have not been misled by too great a concern for what other community property states have held. Many of the decisions of this state stand as fine examples of the way in which community property principles may be applied in the just and equitable solution of modern problems.

New Mexico Community Property Law: The Senate Interim Committee Report

*Robert Emmet Clark**

A 1953 New Mexico Senate Resolution[1] called for a study of the community property laws of the state. The Senate Judiciary Committee was constituted an Interim Committee "to study, and to recommend to the Twenty-Second Legislature (1955), legislation which will equalize the rights and obligations of women under the community property law. . . ." Also to be examined were "the problems of taxation, probate procedure, disposing of community property by will, the economic effect upon family businesses and other related problems involved in any change of the community property laws."

As indicated in a Report[2] to the Committee, the terms "equalize" and "equal rights" are not accurate or fortunate expressions in this context. If the words were accepted literally with respect to the economic status of women, the result would be the impairment of important rights and advantages. It is believed that the actual point of focus of the resolution is the problem of concurrent ownership, between husband and wife, of the family resources. It is also believed that suggestions are desired for improved legal techniques which will facilitate this type of ownership while at the same time respecting the spouses' rights of individual ownership.

The purpose of, as distinguished from the motive for,[3] the study was to review the community property method in New

---

* Associate Professor of Law, University of New Mexico.

1. Sen. Res. 3, 21st Legislature, State of New Mexico, 1953.

2. The term *Report* cited hereafter refers to THE COMMUNITY PROPERTY LAW OF NEW MEXICO: A REPORT TO THE SENATE INTERIM COMMITTEE ON COMMUNITY PROPERTY PURSUANT TO SENATE RESOLUTION No. 3, by Joe W. Wood, Assistant Director, New Mexico Legislative Council Service (21st Legislature, State of New Mexico, 1954).

3. The motive for this study is found in a legislative compromise. Senate Bill 6 which would have granted the wife testamentary power over her interest in the community property was introduced but its future was uncertain. The resolution authorizing a study was proposed, then the bill was withdrawn. The resolution passed unanimously.

Mexico with the intention of determining what specific inadequacies have developed since the present statutes were enacted in 1907. That some complexities have arisen in nearly half a century is not surprising. Nor is that fact in itself an unfavorable comment on this form of marital property ownership. Although it cannot be attempted here, it would be worthwhile, perhaps, to compare the changes made in systems prevailing in other states during the same period. It may be that the absence of substantial changes in the New Mexico system since 1907 is some evidence of its soundness and its adaptability. However, complexities have developed. They parallel those in other areas of law. And they are largely the result of economic expansion and its accompanying changes in attitudes toward family security. The marked transition from a rural, individual-conscious society to an urban, group-conscience social order probably accounts for much general dissatisfaction in the United States with marital property laws. The movement of populations, inspired in part by cheap transportation and communication, is another factor. New incentives for easy acquisition and quick transfers of property augmented marital property problems. Wage and salary schedules and employment opportunities have been drastically altered. The whole taxation system has been changed in the last generation. Divorce and mortality statistics cannot be discounted. Life, liability and other forms of public and private insurance are now standard security equipment of perhaps a majority of families. These factors should not be overlooked.

Dissatisfaction with existing forms of marital property ownership is not confined to the community states. The inadequacies of separation of property regimes in the so-called common law states are receiving attention.[4] This is not strange when it is remembered that the origins of those systems are mainly feudal and, in spite of the Married Women's Acts,[5] are essentially unrealistic in modern times. No philosophy of family economic unity underlies those systems. No legal co-ownership of family

4. Kahn-Freund, *Inconsistencies and Injustices in the Law of Husband and Wife*, 15 MOD. L. REV. 133 (1952), 16 MOD. L. REV. 34, 148 (1953); Kepner, *The Joint and Survivorship Bank Account—A Concept Without a Name*, 41 CALIF. L. REV. 596 (1954); Townsend, *Creation of Joint Rights Between Husband and Wife in Personal Property*, 52 MICH. L. REV. 779, 957 (1954).

5. The expression Married Women's Acts is used to cover the emancipatory legislation, passed in the nineteenth and early twentieth centuries, which granted women the right to appear in court, make contracts, conveyances and manage their own property. See 3 VERNIER, AMERICAN FAMILY LAWS § 167 *et seq.* (1935). New Mexico's principal acts were passed in 1897. See N.M. STAT. ANN. § 21-6-6(1953).

resources exists although there apparently always have been attitudes and actual practices of co-ownership between husband and wife. Nevertheless, *in law* the family wherewithal was or is either "his" or "hers" except where the parties—usually only those with enough property to warrant seeking legal advice—have arranged otherwise. In contrast, the community property method is based on the philosophy that all marital gains are "theirs."

The stated scope of the Report is the New Mexico law as it exists today.[6] No attention is given to departures from traditional community property principles. Nor is comment made on the merit of such departures. The author of the Report quite honestly does not attempt to cover the entire field of community property law. "Rights and obligations arising from the family relationship irrespective of ownership of property" are not discussed.[7] Conflict of laws problems, few of which appear in the reported New Mexico cases, are omitted. References to decisions in other states and to legal commentators are held to a minimum.

Despite the author's modest claim that the Report does not cover Family Law,[8] it is submitted that the Report might be appropriately described as a review of one of the most important areas of Family Law, the economic basis and solidarity of the family.

Space limitations prevent a complete description of the New Mexico system. It is sufficient to state that the community property method has existed continuously in this region under Spanish, Mexican and American rule. As part of the civil law not "repugnant to or inconsistent with"[9] the United States Constitution and laws passed under its authority, the community system was protected by the Kearny Code. The Organic Act did not alter it. Except for a few statutes on inheritances and conveyances which, because they introduced the common law theory of merger of husband and wife, caused some confusion in the nineteenth century, the law of marital property, it was believed until 1919,[10] continued for over half a century after

6. REPORT, p. 11.

7. *Id.* at 12.

8. *Ibid.*

9. KEARNEY CODE, LAWS, § 1 (1846), in 1 N.M. STAT. ANN. p. 340 (1953).

10. See Beals v. Ares, 25 N.M. 459, 185 Pac. 780 (1919), wherein the Supreme Court decided that a statute of 1876 that declares: "In all the courts in this territory the common law as recognized in the United States of America shall be the rule of practice and decision. . . ." had abrogated the civil law, including the community property system, except to the extent that it was preserved by statute. N.M. Laws 1876, c. 2, § 2; N.M. STAT. ANN. § 21-3-3 (1953).

the American conquest to be the civil law of Spain and Mexico as it existed at the time of the Treaty of Guadalupe.[11] In 1901 a comprehensive community property law was enacted.[12] It was repealed and replaced by the statutes of 1907,[13] which were affirmed upon statehood in 1912.[14] Except for a few changes[15] the 1907 statutes are the present community property law.

These statutes were patterned after California's.[16] They contain the essentials of community property policy as found in the other community states; for example, separate property is recognized and defined as property owned by either spouse before marriage and acquired afterward by gift or inheritance together with "the rents, issues and profits thereof."[17] All other property acquired by either or both spouses after marriage is presumed to be community.[18] The husband is charged with the management and control of the marital property,[19] except where he is incapacitated and the wife has been judicially appointed head of the community.[20] With respect to the community realty, the husband's powers are limited.[21] Upon dissolution of the community by divorce or separation[22] there must be an equal division of the marital gains.[23] The husband has testamentary

---

11. See 1 DE FUNIAK, PRINCIPLES OF COMMUNITY PROPERTY § 53 (1943); Laughlin v. Laughlin, 49 N.M. 20, 26, 155 P.2d 1010 (1944): "Our community property system is statutory, and with some exceptions, was adopted from the laws of Mexico and Spain as it existed at the time of the signing of the treaty of Guadalupe Hidalgo."

12. N.M. Laws 1901, c. 62, p. 112.

13. N.M. Laws 1907, c. 37, p. 46.

14. N.M. CONST. Art. 22, § 4.

15. See, *e.g.*, N.M. Laws 1915, c. 84 § 1, p. 123, doing away with the requirement of the wife's written consent for the disposal of community personalty by the husband; N.M. Laws 1927, c. 84, § 1, p. 259, providing for direct conveyances between husband and wife; N.M. Laws 1947, c. 191, p. 393, providing that a conveyance to husband and wife *described as such* in the instrument is presumed to be community property and changing part of the effect of August v. Tillian, 51 N.M. 74, 178 P.2d 590 (1947).

16. See McDonald v. Lambert, 43 N.M. 27, 85 P.2d 78, 120 A.L.R. 250 (1938), overruled in Chavez v. Chavez, 56 N.M. 393, 244 P.2d 781, 30 A.L.R.2d 1236 (1952).

17. N.M. STAT. ANN. §§ 57-3-4, 57-3-5(1953).

18. *Id.* § 57-4-1.

19. *Id.* § 57-4-3. See Clark, *Management and Control of Community Property in New Mexico*, 26 TULANE L. REV. 324 (1952).

20. *Id.* §§ 57-4-5—57-4-9; Frkovich v. Petranovich, 48 N.M. 382, 151 P.2d 337, 155 A.L.R. 395 (1944).

21. See Frkovich v. Petranovich, 48 N.M. 382, 389, 151 P.2d 337, 342, 155 A.L.R. 295, 301 (1944): "[W]hether the husband has, notwithstanding the 1915 amendment, some power of *management* of the community real property superior to the power of the wife, we do not consider nor decide. . . ."

22. N.M. STAT. ANN. ANN. § 22-7-2(1953) provides for separation and division of property without stating any ground for divorce.

23. Sands v. Sands, 48 N.M. 458, 152 P.2d 399 (1944); Beals v. Ares, 25 N.M. 459, 185 Pac. 780 (1919).

power over one-half of the community estate, but the wife has none.[24] If she predeceases her husband all the community property "belongs to" him without administration.[25] Nevada is the only other state with the same limitation on the wife's testamentary power.[26] As to their separate property, the New Mexico spouses have full and exclusive powers of control and disposition.[27]

This is an outline of the New Mexico system. Although the system is entirely statutory, the courts still look to the civil law of Spain and Mexico for interpretations.[28]

The Report to the Committee reviews carefully and then summarizes the "inequalities" in the system.[29] Suggestions are made for improving it. However, the Committee expressly reserves authority[30] to draw its own conclusions and make its own recommendations.

This article is an effort to discuss several questions raised by

---

24. N.M. Stat. Ann. §§ 29-1-8, 29-1-9(1953).

25. *Id.* § 29-1-9.

26. Nev. Comp. Laws §§ 3395.01, 3395.02 (Supp. 1931-41).

27. N.M. Stat. Ann. §§ 30-1-1, 57-3-3(1953).

28. McDonald v. Senn, 53 N.M. 198, 201, 204 P.2d 990, 991 (1949): "The law in this state regarding the property rights of husband and wife is statutory, but was modeled after the civil law of Spain and Mexico and those laws will be looked to for definitions and interpretations. . . ."

29. Report, c. XII, p. 137.

30. *Id.* Foreword, p. 3. The Senate Committee filed its own separate two page report in January, 1955. After reciting the authority for the study and the nature of the Committee's composition and work, the following *Findings and Recommendations* were stated:

> "The Community Property Law of New Mexico is a complicated, interrelated structure of law based on our present statutes and on court decisions. The committee finds that in its operation it is basically fair in its application to all who in their daily lives come within its operation. The committee doubts its ability to improve on a system derived from human experience dating back to early Spanish history and therefore recommends no change in the basic structure of our existing law.
>
> "The committee, however, finds that recent court decisions have caused uncertainties in two aspects of the law and therefore recommends legislation for the purpose of clarifying these two aspects. . . ."

Here the Committee expressed its concern over *In re* Trimble's Estate, 57 N.M. 51 (1953) and Chavez v. Chavez, 56 N.M. 393 (1952) and submitted proposed legislation, introduced in the 22d Legislature (1955) as Senate Bills 291 and 296, which declared that a joint tenancy may be proved by a preponderance of the evidence and requiring an instrument in writing to effect a transmutation or change of status of real property. These bills were passed but only that on proof of joint tenancy was signed into law.

This is the total result of two years of work, a long Report which cost a good deal of money and which had for its stated goal: "Recommendations toward equalizing the rights and obligations of women under the community property system. . ." and was prompted by proposed legislation which would have granted the wife testamentary power over her interest in the community property, a right which existed under Spanish law and exists in all of the community states except New Mexico and Nevada. See note 3 *supra*.

the Report. In addition, others will be asked. Proposed changes will be suggested.

It was agreed at a meeting of the Committee that a rough and ready distinction could be made between technical matters and the broader policy considerations suggested by the Resolution. The distinction is preserved in the Report[31] and is followed here although with complete awareness of the Committee's privilege to view the distinction as no more than an approximate, and at times overlapping, one.

Policy Questions

The "Legal" Community

Antenuptial agreements. Assuming that the community property method is not to be abolished as has been suggested,[32] an initial question is presented by a statute which reads:

> Section 57-3-1 *"Law applicable to property rights. . . .* The property rights of husband and wife are governed by this chapter unless there is a marriage settlement containing stipulations contrary thereto."[33]

On the face of it this statute permits a prospective husband and wife to employ methods other than the community for property ownership. Shall this be continued? Another statute[34] allowing husband and wife "to hold property as joint tenants, tenants in common, or as community property" refers to postnuptial agreements but supports the same policy of free choice of the form of ownership. The statute above referring to marriage settlements contemplates antenuptial property arrangements although the expression is often loosely applied to postnuptial agreements also. Postnuptial agreements are separately and expressly provided for in the statutes.[35]

In New Mexico should the parties before marriage be permitted to contract to hold property out of community? What effect should be given to such an agreement made in another state by persons who become domiciled in New Mexico? Shall such agreements apply only to property *in esse*, or also to after-acquired property?[36]

---

31. *Id.* c. XIII, p. 153.
32. *Ibid.*
33. N.M. Stat. Ann. § 57-3-1(1953).
34. *Id.* § 57-3-2.
35. *Id.* § 57-2-6 *et seq.*
36. See 1 de Funiak, Principles of Community Property §§ 135, 136 (1943).

No questions are intended to be raised here concerning optional or contract community systems which obtained for short times in Oklahoma and Oregon.[37]

Postnuptial agreements. Since the decision in *Chavez v. Chavez*[38] it is clear that postnuptial agreements are valid, even when they involve a transformation in character of separate or community property. That case overruled *McDonald v. Lambert*[39] which actually involved an antenuptial verbal agreement and was so understood by the district court, but which was decided in the Supreme Court as if it were a postnuptial agreement. The *McDonald* case temporarily voided the effect of statutes[40] which expressly provide for postnuptial agreements.

As a matter of policy should husband and wife be permitted to contract to hold property out of community?[41] Suppose they are business partners. How will the Uniform Partnership Act affect them?[42] At one point the Report concludes, "Thus, either a married man or woman may enter a partnership."[43] Does this include a husband and wife partnership? Before the Uniform Act was adopted either husband or wife could be the partner of a third person.[44] If husband and wife commercial partnerships or postnuptial agreements are permitted will they apply to after-acquired property and wages?

The repealed community property law of Oregon and Pennsylvania[45] provided for easy property transactions between husband and wife involving community property *in esse.* No provision was made for postnuptial agreements transforming community property into separate property.

Transmutations. The existence and free use of other forms of concurrent and separate ownership between husband and wife other than community property raise the question of how far transmutations from community to separate and vice versa

---

37. See Oregon Laws 1943, c. 440, p. 656. The Oregon system was patterned after Oklahoma's and was repealed in 1945. In 1947 another community property law was enacted which was subsequently repealed. See also Commissioner of Int. Rev. v. Harmon, 323 U.S. 44 (1944).

38. 56 N.M. 393, 244 P.2d 781 (1952).

39. 43 N.M. 27, 85 P.2d 78 (1938).

40. N.M. Stat. Ann. § 57-2-6(1953).

41. See Turley v. Turley, 44 N.M. 382, 103 P.2d 113 (1940) for dicta relevant to this question.

42. N.M. STAT. ANN. § 66-1-1(1953).

43. REPORT, c. VIII, p. 104.

44. See Adams v. Blumenshine, 27 N.M. 643, 204 Pac. 66, 20 A.L.R. 369 (1922).

45. Ore. Laws 1947, c. 525, § 9, p. 912; Pa. Acts 1947, No. 550, § 9, p. 1425.

should be permitted.[46] Gifts back and forth are not unusual. "Joint bank accounts,"[47] which are probably the most common method of transmuting the wages and salaries of husband or wife, or both, into a form of separate but undivided interests possessing the sought after incident of survivorship, are widely used in New Mexico. The question of the quantum of proof in the joint bank account situations necessary to show intent has not been raised as it has in the joint deed cases where the rule is that the evidence must be "clear, strong and convincing."[48] The explanation for this may be found among the following: (1) The holding in an earlier case[49] which did not involve community property or a transmutation but a deposit of the husband's separate property in a joint account with his wife. After the husband's death the court declared that the intent to create survivorship rights in a joint bank account is more easily found where the deposit is made in the name of the husband "or" wife. (2) The effect given to the depositor's agreement with the bank usually found on the application and signature card.[50] Moreover, a statute protects the bank against double payment.[51] (3) No situation has arisen since In re *Trimble's Estate*[52] that has been significant enough to carry to the Supreme Court.

Perhaps the only limitation on transmutations should be the rules against fraudulent transfers and other remedies open to creditors. It would seem that in family ownership matters

46. See Clark, *Transmutations in New Mexico Community Property Law*, 24 ROCKY MT. L. REV. 273 (1952).

47. This phrase is susceptible of different interpretations in different jurisdictions. See Kepner, *The Joint and Survivorship Bank Account—A Concept Without a Name*, 41 CALIF. L. REV. 596 (1954); Townsend, *Creation of Joint Rights Between Husband and Wife in Personal Property*, 52 MICH. L. REV. 779, 957 (1954). Some states call it a joint tenancy. New Mexico frankly recognizes it as something *sui generis*. Menger v. Otero County State Bank, 44 N.M. 82, 98 P.2d 834 (1940).

48. See Chavez v. Chavez, 56 N.M. 393, 244 P.2d 781 (1952).

49. Menger v. Otero County State Bank, 44 N.M. 82, 98 P.2d 834 (1940).

50. The following form is used by the largest New Mexico bank: "The undersigned joint depositors hereby agree each with the Albuquerque National Bank, all of Albuquerque, New Nexico, that all the sums heretofore or hereafter deposited by said joint depositors, or either of them, with said bank to their credit as such joint depositors shall be owned by them jointly with right of survivorship and be subject to the check or order or receipt of either of them or survivor of either of them, and payment thereof shall discharge said bank from liability to either or to their heirs, executors, administrators or assigns of either. This agreement shall not be changed or terminated except by written notice to said bank, and such notice shall not affect the right of the bank or said depositors hereunder with relation to deposits theretofore made."

51. N.M. STAT. ANN. § 48-10-3(1953).

52. 57 N.M. 51, 253 P.2d 805 (1953).

flexibility should not be discouraged. The Report discusses several aspects of transmutation.[53]

Community Property and Common Law Estates

In community property states should joint tenancies and tenancies in common be permitted between husband and wife? The present law[54] expressly provides for them. There are sound arguments pro and con.[55]

It appears that joint tenancy deeds are widely used in New Mexico's most populous county. This probability was discussed in a recent case[56] which has been strongly criticized. The case held that a deed to husband and wife in the form of joint tenancy did not transmute the property from community to separate property. The property was purchased with community funds. When the husband died the wife petitioned for letters of administration alleging that the property was community. Later it was discovered that the deed was in the form of joint tenancy. The wife then claimed all the property by right of survivorship as against a creditor, the hospital that had cared for the husband in his last illness. The only evidence of any intent to transmute community into separate property was the form of the deed. The court said: "Stripping aside the technicalities of evidentiary force, the root spirit of all of these decisions is *intent*, and rightly so. Ultimately, if the dual estates of the common and civil law can exist together compatibly, the amalgam must be the true intention of the parties. . . ." The court then decided that the general presumption of community property was not overcome because the intent to transmute was not "clear, strong and convincing" as shown by more than a mere preponderance of evidence. The community property statute does not expressly cover joint tenancies.

Special attention is given in the Report[57] to the *Trimble* case and the problems of joint tenancy. The Report contains a careful sampling from real estate records of nine counties "chosen on the basis of geographical location and diversity of economic interests." The Report's conclusion is that joint tenancy deeds are "fairly extensively used" in New Mexico.

---

53. REPORT, c. V, p. 27, c. VI, p. 57.
54. N.M. STAT. ANN. § 57-3-2(1953).
55. REPORT, c. III, p. 19, c. XII, p. 151.
56. *In re* Trimble's Estate, 57 N.M. 51, 253, P.2d 805 (1953).
57. REPORT, c. III, p. 19, c. XII, p. 151, c. XIII, p. 155.

The Report[58] sets out in full the suggestions made to the Committee for "correcting" the *Trimble* decision. There are a number and they vary from the desire to abolish joint tenancies between husband and wife to proposals for reducing the extraordinary burden of proof to show a joint tenancy. The Report's summary of these problems is particularly good.

In this same connection the question might be raised, why not allow tenancies by the entirety in New Mexico? The arguments against them given in *Hernandez v. Becker*[59] are not entirely convincing. At the present time many people taking property, particularly their homes, in joint tenancy do not realize that either party has the power to break up that tenancy. The argument that no one will purchase such an interest is irrelevant. When creditors are in pursuit the question is: May the creditor reach this particular interest on the ground that the debtor has a power over it which the creditor now would like to exercise (or have the bankruptcy trustee exercise)? The origin of tenancy by the entirety is obscure[60] but it seems to have been designed to meet this very problem. For all practical purposes a tenancy by the entirety is little more than a special kind of joint tenancy between husband and wife which neither has the right nor the power to break up. This seems to be the one notable example, along with the trust theory, of the common law developing an attitude toward the family as an economic unit of at least two persons.

The question has already been raised as to the existence of a commercial partnership between husband and wife.[61] Some community states declare that the business and marital partnerships are incompatible.[62]

Assume that a husband and wife, using all the community property they own, enter a business partnership. The New Mexico Uniform Act[63] declares:

> Section 66-1-25 "A partner's right in specific partnership property is not subject to dower, curtesy or allowances to widows, or next of kin, *and is not community property.*"

58. *Id.* c. XIII, p. 155.
59. 54 F.2d 542 (10th Cir. 1931). See also McDonald v. Senn, 53 N.M. 198, 204 P.2d 990, 10 A.L.R.2d 966 (1949).
60. See 3 HOLDSWORTH, HISTORY OF ENGLISH LAW 126 (1927).
61. See page 87 *supra*.
62. See 1 DE FUNIAK, PRINCIPLES OF COMMUNITY PROPERTY § 148 (1953).
63. N.M. STAT. ANN. § 66-1-1(1953).

(The italicized phrase was apparently copied from California.)[64]

Does this mean that a transmutation has taken place? Are the spouses now "tenants in partnership?" What kind of property is the income from the business, separate or community? The Report does not go into these questions.

Whether or not commercial partnerships are allowed between husband and wife, some thought should be given to the advisability of following partnership analogies in dealing with the marital community. The resemblances are superficial and the differences vital. There is a strong trend to regard the business partnership as an "entity" for certain purposes.[65] Arizona and Washington regard the community as an entity and have involved themselves in considerable practical difficulty not to mention specious legal reasoning.[66] It is clear that the courts do not generally regard the community an an entity in bankruptcy[67] although a commercial partnership and its individual members enjoy the benefits of that attitude.

This discussion raises the elementary question of whether the family as a basic unit of society is to be given certain considerations or priorities that individual members do not have but which are enjoyed by other social institutions or legal organizations. This is essentially the problem raised in tort cases and cases involving the rights of creditors.

Presumptions

Presumptions are an integral part of the New Mexico community property system. Their significance generally in community property law is explained by one writer[68] as follows:

> "In every one of the old community property states there is a presumption that all property acquired by either

---

64. See CAL. CORPORATIONS CODE § 15025(2)(e) (Deering, Supp. 1953); 1 DE FUNIAK, PRINCIPLES OF COMMUNITY PROPERTY § 80 (1943).

65. See Bankruptcy Act of 1898 as amended in 1938, 52 STAT. 845, 11 U.S.C. § 23 (1952); REPORT, c. VII, p. 101.

66. See, *e.g.*, Donn v. Kunz, 52 Ariz. 219, 79 P.2d 965 (1938); King v. Williams, 188 Wash. 350, 62 P.2d 710 (1936).

67. See Moore, *The Community Property System and the Economic Reconstruction of the Family Unit: Insolvency and Bankruptcy*, 11 WASH. L. REV. 61 (1936). In Washington the community entity may go through bankruptcy but a discharge apparently does not release the individual spouses entirely. See 1 DE FUNIAK, PRINCIPLES OF COMMUNITY PROPERTY § 180 (1943). What the law is in New Mexico is far from clear. See REPORT, c. VIII, p. 92.

68. Ganong, *Community Property and Presumptions*, 28 ORE. L. REV. 157, 167 (1949).

spouse during the marriage is community property. It is a fundamental part of a true community system. It existed under the Spanish law. . . . Such a presumption represents the social policy of a true community state. It is also supported by the probability that property acquired during marriage is more likely to be community than separate, and it provides a uniform rule in cases where satisfactory evidence is lacking, which are not infrequent. . . ."

The subject is an extremely technical one and will be given only general consideration here. The Report[69] devotes special attention to the nature of presumptions and also to the amount of evidence necessary to overcome or displace them.

The present New Mexico community property statute[70] creates the following presumptions:

1. That all property acquired after marriage is community.

2. That property acquired by a married woman alone or with a third person, by an instrument in writing, is separate property (in the latter case, the interest of a "tenant in common").

3. That property acquired by a married woman and her husband *described as such in the instrument* is community.

The statute does not expressly cover joint tenancies. It has been suggested[71] that in the following sentence the italicized phrase "the presumption is that the married woman takes the part conveyed to her, as tenant in common *unless a different intention is expressed in the instrument*" encompasses a joint tenancy deed.

A fourth presumption must also be considered: the presumption of a gift to the wife of one-half where property stands in the name of a man and woman who are husband and wife but who are not described as such in the instrument.[72] This presumption, although it may not have been decisive, appears in a case which is discussed elsewhere[73] and is further analyzed in the Report.[74] The case prompted the legislature to add the third presumption

---

69. REPORT, c. V, p. 27.
70. N.M. STAT. ANN, § 57-4-1(1953).
71. REPORT, c. V, p. 51.
72. August v. Tillian, 51 N.M. 74, 178 P.2d 590 (1947).
72. See Clark, *Presumptions in New Mexico Community Property Law: The California Influence*, 25 So. CALIF. L. REV. 148 (1952).
74. REPORT, c. V, p. 27, c. XIII, p. 157.

listed above in 1947.[75] It is believed that that amendment is no more than a clarification of the first general presumption in favor of community.[76]

All of these presumptions are rebuttable except with respect to bona fide encumbrancers or purchasers, in which cases the presumptions are conclusive. The statute does not, however, prescribe the degree of proof or nature of evidence which will overcome the presumptions. These questions have become particularly troublesome since the decision of In re *Trimble's Estate*[77] because (1) it required the quantum of proof to overcome the general presumption of community property to be extraordinary ("clear, strong and convincing" and more than a mere preponderance of the evidence) and (2) it leaves in doubt the degree of proof and the nature of the evidence necessary to overcome the other presumptions.[78]

Apart from the problems involved in distinguishing presumptions from inferences, and the difficulties in applying presumptions, it must be stated that the purpose of the general presumption is clear: (1) It states the social policy behind community-of-property thinking and (2) it has the practical effect of resolving doubts in favor of co-ownership between the spouses as against claims of separate ownership. The commingling cases are examples.[79]

It has already been stated that the community property statutes do not refer specifically to joint tenancies which are permitted in New Mexico but must be expressly created. If the problems augured in the *Trimble* case are to be met, special attention must be given to joint tenancies. It is believed that the New Mexico community property statutes should be redrafted with the following policy considerations uppermost in mind:

1. This is a community state which has established the principle of co-ownership of family property by husband and wife.

2. Attacks on titles and uncertainty connected with the *form* of ownership should be reduced.

---

75. N.M. Laws 1947, c. 191, p. 393.

76. See Clark, *Presumptions in New Mexico Community Property Law: The California Influence*, 25 So. Calif. L. Rev. 149 (1952).

77. 57 N.M. 51, 253 P.2d 805 (1953).

78. Report, c. XIII, p. 156.

79. See Stroope v. Potter, 48 N.M. 404, 151 P.2d 748 (1944).

3. The form of a deed should be controlling (*i.e.*, the form should be taken as evidence of the state of mind of the grantees that they intended the deed to be in a particular form) except in unusual circumstances such as fraud, duress, *etc.*

The discussion in the Report[80] concerning the effect of presumptions as rules of evidence or rules of property points out that the real problem in both cases is to determine the amount of evidence to overcome or displace a presumption. Any new legislation must not ignore that problem.

In addition to the suggestions for corrective legislation contained in the Report[81] another idea is advanced herein for the Committee's consideration. A simple statute could be drafted which would follow the theory contained in the Model Code of Evidence, Rule 703 on Legitimacy,[82] and would read something like this:

> Whenever it is established that any property was acquired during the marriage by husband and wife, the property shall have the status of community property and the party asserting that it is separate property has the burden of producing evidence and the burden of persuading the trier of fact beyond a reasonable doubt that the property is separate property.

This would comport with the rule established in *Chavez v. Chavez*[83] and In re *Trimble's Estate.*[84]

Another statute could be drafted which would refer specifically to joint tenancies and tenancies in common and make it necessary to prove beyond a reasonable doubt that property held in this form is *not* separate property. It is believed that this type of statute should be applicable to both husband and wife. The present statute establishing presumptions in favor of married women only should be repealed. Still another statute might be enacted for the benefit of abstractors and title examiners which would create the beyond a reasonable doubt test where the words "sole and separate estate"[85] appear in a deed either to a man or woman. The conclusive presumption for the

80. REPORT, c. V, p. 27.
81. *Id.* c. XIII, p. 153.
82. A.L.I., MODEL CODE OF EVIDENCE (1942).
83. 56 N.M. 393, 244 P.2d 781, 30 A.L.R. 2d 1236 (1952).
84. 57 N.M. 51, 253 P.2d 805 (1953).
85. The phrase "sole and separate" would seem to raise a rebuttal presumption under the present statute, N.M. STAT. ANN. § 57-4-1(1953) of separate property since an "intention is expressed in the instrument."

benefit of the same class of persons now protected by the statute should be retained.

The above suggestions are made with full recognition of their common law influence. For under the civil law the actual ownership was more important than the form of the title.[86] However, it would seem that the experience of the code countries and the history of titles in this country demonstrate the soundness of these proposals. Moreover, it is believed that the aggravated ills of *Chavez v. Chavez*[87] and In re *Trimble's Estate*[88] would be arrested if not cured.

Creditors' Rights and Liability to Third Persons

Great confusion prevails in this area, and not just in New Mexico.[89] No attempt will be made to resolve it in this summary. However, the main outlines of the difficulty can be pointed out.

A clear policy must be adopted with respect to:

1. Liability for the husband's antenuptial and postnuptial debts.

2. Liability for the wife's antenuptial torts.

3. Liability of the community property for torts, "community" and separate, of either spouse.

Answers to these problems are hinted at in some of the cases. They are not entirely clear in the statutes. One case[90] lays down the rule that the community property may be taken on execution of the wife's separate postnuptial tort. The case held that her half of the community was liable. Suppose her half were not enough to satisfy the judgment? Is the rule of *McDonald v. Senn*[91] applicable to the husband's torts also? What is a "community tort," if there is such a wrong?

The above is no more than a sketch of some of the substantive problems. If certain creditors' rights are recognized, then procedural methods must be improved for enforcing them by (1) establishing the order of liability of community and separate property and (2) clarifying the priorities among com-

---

86. See 1 DE FUNIAK, PRINCIPLES OF COMMUNITY PROPERTY § 60 (1943).
87. 56 N.M. 393, 244 P.2d 781, 30 A.L.R.2d 1236 (1952).
88. 57 N.M. 51, 253 P.2d 805 (1953).
89. See Daggett, *Policy Questions on Marital Property Law in Louisiana*, 14 LOUISIANA LAW REVIEW 528 (1954); 1 DE FUNIAK, PRINCIPLES OF COMMUNITY PROPERTY §§ 167-70, 178-80 (1943).
90. McDonald v. Senn, 53 N.M. 198, 204 P.2d 990, 10 A.L.R.2d 966 (1949).
91. *Ibid.*

munity creditors and individual antenuptial and postnuptial creditors of the spouses.

The Arizona statute[92] may be a guide in this matter. Any new legislation should not overlook bankruptcy problems and the vast penumbra in this area.[93]

Before remedies for the above problems are proposed there should be a re-examination of the conflict of interests between the family and those outside of it, for example, creditors. Therein lies the basis of any determination of policy. This means, of course, that exemption statutes, insolvency procedures and family support and expense statutes should be studied and re-appraised. Obviously community property principles would play only a part in such a project.

Income, Increases and Profits from Separate Property

A controversial issue is purposely raised by this question: Should the present New Mexico statutes be changed to make the income and profits of separate property community property? This is the law of Louisiana, Texas and Idaho.[94] This was the original Spanish law. Why was it changed and is it advantageous to the family unit?

The present statutes are stepchildren of the Married Women's Acts. These acts were followed, blindly many times, in the late nineteenth century. They were promoted by the commendable desire to allow married women in the common law states to own and control their own property. They were inspired by equity's realistic treatment of the woman of property. However, under the community property system a married woman always owned her separate property. The *corpus* of such property always remained separate. But the income and fruits belonged to the marital partnership which presumably made maximum use of the *corpus*. The basis for this practice and the changes that have developed have been explained as follows:

> "One of the principal aims of the Spanish law was protection of the family, and toward that end property was kept in a family as much as possible. Community of property was one of the methods for achieving this goal. The limitation on succession was another. The ownership of separate property by either or both spouses was an inextricable but

92. ARIZ. CODE ANN. § 63-305 (1939).
93. REPORT, c. VIII, p. 157.
94. 1 DE FUNIAK, PRINCIPLES OF COMMUNITY PROPERTY § 71 (1943).

entirely subordinate element in the Spanish system. Under modern community property statutes decided emphasis is placed on separate property. Thus in five community States the 'rents, issues and profits' of separate property remain separate instead of becoming 'acquets and gains' of the marriage.

"The Spanish law's recognition of separate property seems to have been mainly for the purpose of returning such property to the family line of the particular spouse, who, during his or her lifetime or marriage had the right to its use and enjoyment. There were express limitations on the testamentary right of a spouse to dispose of separate property beyond the spouse's immediate family.

"At least in this area of old Spanish law, the emphasis was on *use* rather than 'ownership'. Hence the recognition of usufructuary and other rights in the marital partnership, and the rule that the increase and income from separate property was community property."[95]

The Married Women's Acts were not designed to correct any injustices in a system of this nature. But they were not fully understood by the New Mexico settlers who brought this legislation with them. The confusion created by these acts is a matter of record:

"The personal and property rights of married women are in a sadly muddled condition. The confusion which existed under the Compiled Laws, of 1884, was worse confounded by the acts of 1887, and in order to harmonize the two or make either one intelligible, further legislation is necessary. This is one of the most important changes necessary in our laws to bring them in harmony with the legislation in other parts of the Union. . . ."[96]

The legislation making the income and profits of separate property separate property has probably engendered the greatest confusion and inequities to be found in the system.

"The right of husband or wife to own separate property was an integral part of Spanish community property law and is an even more important, and at times a distorted,

95. Clark, *Matrimonial Law in New Mexico and the Western United States*, MATRIMONIAL PROPERTY Vol. II, pp. 89-138, Comparative Law Series, University of Toronto (1955).

96. NEW MEXICO STATE BAR PROCEEDINGS 26 (1888).

feature of the community systems in the United States where the category of separate property has been greatly enlarged by statute. Under Spanish law separate property remained separate property. This is still the settled rule in all the community states. However, under Spanish law, and under the present law of Idaho and Texas, the *income and fruits* of separate property become community property. Today by statute in the other community States *such increases and profits* remain separate property. The proposition that 'the rents, issues and profits' of separate property are separate property is being re-examined these days for several reasons. First, the application of such a rule is very difficult, no matter how clearly it is stated in the statute, because of the general presumption in favour of community property and the problems involved in tracing funds. Second, such a rule theoretically requires that the average middle class family keep three sets of books of account, one for each spouse's separate income or profits and one for the community gains. Third, it has the effect of further enlargement of lien and equity theories which are already amorphous and unwieldy. The idea of preserving the separate identity of the *income and fruits* of separate property betrays the influence of English common law separation of property theories which Professor Kahn-Freund and others have shown to be inadequate in modern family life.

"In a few of the community States, as previously explained, the wife has also been given complete ownership of her wages and earnings which, of course, is a statutory contradiction of community property principles."[97]

It is suggested that further study be given to the community property statutes of the so-called "new community states," especially Pennsylvania, Oklahoma and Oregon, which took notice of this difficult problem.[98] Those states repealed their systems, but that is no criticism of this particular point.

The Report analyzes this general problem and offers suggestions for alleviating it.[99]

---

97. See note 95 *supra*.

98. See 1 DE FUNIAK, PRINCIPLES OF COMMUNITY PROPERTY § 71 (1943); Daggett, *Louisiana Legislation of 1944—Matters Pertaining to the Civil Code* 6 LOUISIANA LAW REVIEW 1 (1944).

99. REPORT, c. XIII, p. 159.

Conflict of Laws and Problems of Descent and Distribution

One area which the Report admittedly[100] does not attempt to cover is Conflicts. Yet the subject is relevant to any study of marital property law[101] and particularly community property.

New Mexico's population has greatly increased in the past decade.[102] The new residents, many of them presumably from non-community states, have brought property and funds with them. Many of these new residents will, in a short time, become indistinguishable from the older residents; they will raise families, retire and leave property to their heirs. Many others, however, live on or near military and atomic energy installations and within an area of federal jurisdiction which is not always clearly or realistically defined. These people "reside" in New Mexico for some purposes and yet for other purposes they are treated by the law as outsiders.[103] These circumstances create doubt and uncertainty in property, inheritance and other marital matters. The legislatures of the individual states and the Congress of the United States[104] cannot ignore this. It is believed that the New Mexico legislature should anticipate some of the problems.

Two recent New Mexico decisions[105] involving a 1951 amend-

---

100. *Id.* c. I, p. 12.

101. See MARSH, MARITAL PROPERTY IN CONFLICT OF LAWS (1952); 1 ARMSTRONG, CALIFORNIA FAMILY LAW 537 *et seq.*, §§ G, I (1953).

102. The New Mexico population in 1940 was 531,818. In 1950 it was 681,187, an increase of 28.1%. In the continental United States during the same period the increase was 14.5%. 1 1950 CENSUS OF POPULATION—NUMBER OF INHABITANTS.

103. See Arledge v. Mabry, 52 N.M. 303, 197 P.2d 884 (1948); Chaney v. Chaney, 53 N.M. 66, 201 P.2d 782 (1949), holding that persons living at Los Alamos had no right to vote or obtain a divorce because land acquired in New Mexico by the United States through condemnation was not "in New Mexico" within meaning of constitutional provisions dealing with rights of electors, and persons at Los Alamos are not "residents of the state" within meaning of the divorce statute. See subsequent legislation creating Los Alamos county and correcting these conditions: N.M. STAT. ANN. § 15-15-1(1953).

104. 68 STAT. 961 (1954) (Atomic Energy Act). "There is hereby retroceded to the State of New Mexico the exclusive jurisdiction heretofore acquired from the State of New Mexico by the United States of America over the following land of the United States Atomic Energy Commission in Bernalillo County and within the boundaries of the Sandia Base, Albuquerque, New Mexico. [There follows the legal description of the area.]

"This retrocession of jurisdiction shall take effect upon acceptance by the State of New Mexico. Approved August 30, 1954." *Id.* c. 19, § 3.

Governor E. L. Mechem accepted state jurisdiction on September 20, 1954.

Senator Anderson's amendment, however, does not cover other areas in New Mexico where questions of "exclusive jurisdiction" are equally relevant.

105. Crownover v. Crownover, 274 P.2d 127 (N.M. 1954); Wilson v. Wilson, 272 P.2d 319 (N.M. 1954).

ment to the New Mexico statute[106] on the residence requirement in divorce actions, which amendment reads:

> ". . . and provided further, persons serving in any Military branch of the United States Government who have been continuously stationed in any Military Base or installation in the State of New Mexico for such period of one (1) year, shall for the purposes hereof, be deemed residents in good faith of the State and County where such military base or installation is located."

exemplify one aspect of the general problem. The New Mexico Supreme Court has in effect through its interpretation of the provision decided that the New Mexico legislature has the power to define "residence" or physical presence, as being equal to "domicile" for the purpose of divorce. This seems to ignore the Full Faith and Credit Clause of the United States Constitution and the cases[107] discussing the traditional concept of domicile as the basis of jurisdiction in divorce. In any event, the cases call attention to Conflicts problems. The divorce problem is not a direct part of the Committee's community property study, but the property consequences of divorce certainly are.

The property rights of married persons employed at or residing on atomic energy installations, military posts and other quasi-federal reservations in New Mexico should be made clearer. As these people become older and accumulate more property rights, with the same or a new spouse, their problems will multiply. Many of the homes and other tangible property owned by these people were purchased with funds brought to this state, which funds were legally the property of one or the other individual spouse. So long as there is no divorce and neither spouse dies, practical arrangements concerning ownership are possible between the spouses. However, dissolution of the marriage by divorce or death demands that the law find an answer to problems of ownership and inheritance. If the "source theory" is followed logically in these situations it is apparent that much property now believed to be community property clearly is not.

This general problem requires attention in two areas. One is concerned with property owned by living persons who may

---

106. N.M. Laws 1951, c. 107, § 1, p. 166.

107. See Alton v. Alton, 207 F.2d 667 (3d Cir. 1953), *judgment vacated*, 74 Sup. Ct. 736 (1954); Williams v. North Carolina, 325 U.S. 226 (1945); see also Granville-Smith v. Granville-Smith, 214 F.2d 820 (3d Cir. 1954), *cert. granted*, 75 Sup. Ct. 60 (1954).

wish to sell, transmute, or encumber it, and the other concerns the estates of deceased persons.

Living persons.

It is suggested that a statute be considered which would set forth the community property policy of this jurisdiction in clear language. Arizona has the following statute:[108]

> "The marital rights of persons married out of this state, who may move to this state, shall in regard to property acquired in this state during the marriage be regulated by the laws of this state."

Notice that the Arizona statute does not employ the phrase "real and personal property." Nor does it refer to persons who "reside" in the state or are "domiciled" there. Any proposed New Mexico legislation should consider the implication of all of these terms. The distinction between residence and domicile must be recognized in view of the recent divorce cases. Another aspect of the general problem can be illustrated by referring specifically to the married persons employed by the Sandia Corporation or at Los Alamos and the service man attached to a military base in New Mexico who "resides" with his or her family in the state, who may vote and even get a divorce, but who may consciously possess a definite intention to return to Iowa or New Jersey, thus barring him or her from acquiring "domicile" in the traditional sense. Are the man's wages or salary community property? May his wife's wages be garnished by a community creditor? Is the family home which is held by a deed to husband and wife, who are so described in the instrument, community property? Is the family car held in the husband's name community property? The husband and wife have a right to know with some degree of certainty, the burdens and benefits of various forms of ownership of marital property. It is obvious from these elementary questions that the "source" or time of acquisition theory in these situations could lead to interminable and expensive litigation which would undermine the family.

Deceased persons.

Testamentary power. Most of the people now moving into the state probably have normal life expectancies. However, clarification is needed at once with respect to their property

108. Ariz. Code Ann. § 63-306 (1939).

rights. California has pioneered the problem.[109] Statutes have been passed providing for the descent of separate property in the same manner as community property if, at the time it was acquired, it would have been community property under California law.[110]

It has been suggested that California statutes be amended to include real property.[111] If new legislation is proposed in New Mexico serious consideration should be given to the provisions of the California Probate Code and the suggestions that have been made for improving them. It is believed that careful draftsmanship will recognize the general rule that the situs of land ordinarily governs its devolution and yet appropriate language can be used in order to follow community property principles.

This type of legislation would, of course, require further study of the very problem which prompted the New Mexico Report:[112] the granting of testamentary power to the wife over her share of the community estate. There has been no objective showing[113] that the community property states, and there are six, which permit the wife this power have had unusual or insuperable problems as a consequence. It would be absurd to conclude that New Mexico and Nevada, which do not grant the wife this power, have had a unique problem with wives predeceasing husbands. Statistics and mortality and longevity tables are all to the contrary.[114] It should be recalled, also, that the New Mexico statutes were patterned after California's[115] at a time when the married woman in that state had no more than an expectant interest in the community property.[116] Not to allow her to dispose by will of property she did not own or control was entirely logical and understandable. However, since 1927 the California wife has had a "present, existing and equal"[117] interest

---

109. See CAL. PROB. CODE § 201.5 (Deering, 1949); *In re* Way's Estate, 157 P.2d 46 (Cal. App. 1945); Estate of Thornton, 1 Cal.2d 1, 33 P.2d 1, 92 A.L.R. 1343 (1934).

110. CAL. PROB. CODE §§ 201.5, 202, 203 (Deering, 1949).

111. Notes, 35 CALIF. L. REV. 121 (1947), 19 SO. CALIF. L. REV. 39 (1945).

112. See note 3 *supra*.

113. See REPORT, c. XII, pp. 148, 151, for reasons against allowing wife testamentary power.

114. *Id.* c. II, p. 15.

115. See McDonald v. Lambert, 43 N.M. 27, 85 P.2d 78 (1938), *overruled in* Chavez v. Chavez, 56 N.M. 393, 244 P.2d 781 (1952). Until 1923 the California statute gave all the community property to the husband upon the wife's death.

116. See Van Maren v. Johnson, 15 Cal. 308 (1860).

117. CAL. CIV. Code § 161a (Deering, 1949).

in the community property and testamentary power over it has been granted to her.[118] In New Mexico the wife is in the position of owning a "vested" interest in the community property which will inure to the benefit of her separate judgment creditor,[119] but upon her death she is denied the power and the privilege of leaving the same property to the man who was largely responsible for accumulating it because "No other course would be logical unless the lawmakers desire to add to the sorrows of a bereaved husband the further burden of the enforced liquidating of his business affairs upon the death of the wife."[120]

The rationale of In re *Chavez's Estate* is not as solid as the tax savings it has engendered. At the present time the latter are the principal justification for reliance on the case. The decision is based on an attitude toward marriage and the family which has little sociological support today. It is a summary of tax theories which have been outmoded for two decades, and it is an example of statutory interpretation which sees a clean line between tax matters and other property ownership concepts. The prophetic phrases of the case have been greatly overvalued and they have little support in statistics or experience.

Intestate succession.

The New Mexico statute[121] which provides that in cases of intestacy of the husband, three-eighths of the community property shall go to the surviving children in equal shares is a vestige of the early civil law. It no longer serves the purpose originally intended which in an agricultural society was to keep land in the family line. Such a method of disposition is impractical and expensive in a money and personal property-owning society. The statute needs re-examination. Where the surviving children are minors the provision is particularly unworkable.[122] The California statutes are offered as examples of the type of statute needed in New Mexico.

Methods of Changing the Law

The Report[123] emphasizes the policy matter involved in choosing the method by which the community law may be im-

118. CAL. PROB. CODE § 201 (Deering, 1949). The wife's testamentary power has existed since 1923 and relates only to property acquired since that date. Boyd v. Oser, 23 Cal.2d 613, 145 P.2d 312 (1944).
119. McDonald v. Senn, 54 N.M. 198, 204 P.2d 990, 10 A.L.R.2d 966 (1949).
120. *In re* Chavez's Estate, 34 N.M. 258, 280 Pac. 241, 69 A.L.R. 769 (1929).
121. N.M. STAT. ANN. § 29-1-9(1953).
122. See REPORT, c. XII, p. 148.
123. *Id.* c. XIII, p. 153.

proved. If, as a result of the Committee's study and recommendations, changes in the present law are proposed the decision as to the method selected for accomplishing the changes should be the product of careful thought.

Codification has not proved to be a cure-all in many fields of law. Piecemeal legislation has not always brought about the desired changes without also, in many cases, creating complications larger than those it attempts to correct. The Married Women's Acts may be cited in support of this statement.

Some of the legislation needed will be primarily curative or clarificatory in nature. In this area the Report[124] wisely cautions against collision with constitutional principles which, if not thoroughly understood by legislative draftsmen, may result in legislation that will be given prospective effect only by the courts. The unfortunate and confused experience of California in the realm of legislative draftsmanship and judicial interpretation[125] should be a clear warning to the New Mexico Legislature.

TECHNICAL CHANGES

Several topics discussed in the preceding pages illustrate the interrelationship of policy and technical matters. The following summary may be viewed either as an extension of policy considerations, or as a distinct category of problems which can be largely eliminated by changes in the present law.

Contracts and Conveyances

In view of a recent decision[126] the statute[127] delegating certain powers of management and control to the husband is in need of clarification. *Henderson v. Treadwell*[128] involved a real estate contract for the sale of community property signed by a married man posing as single. The purchaser moved on the premises and made payments and improvements. Later, as a part of a divorce decree, the contract was set over to the wife of the seller. The case decided that the purchaser under the contract acquired rights that would be protected; that the purchaser had a right to a deed to the property. The court held that the mar-

124. *Id.* c. XIII, p. 158.

125. See Armstrong, *"Prospective" Application of Changes in Community Property Control—Rule of Property or Constitutional Necessity?*, 33 CALIF. L. REV. 476 (1945). See also Boyd v. Oser, 23 Cal.2d 613, 145 P.2d 312 (1944).

126. Henderson v. Treadwell, 58 N.M. 230, 269 P.2d 1108 (1954).

127. N.M. STAT. ANN. § 57-4-3(1953).

128. 58 N.M. 230, 269 P.2d 1108 (1954).

ried woman, who had made various promises to the purchasers that they would get a deed, was estopped by her conduct and could not rely on the fact that her husband alone had signed the contract.

The present statute does not expressly cover real estate contracts which are widely used in New Mexico. However, the husband has authority to make all ordinary contracts for the community. But an earlier case[129] held that a contract for the sale of community realty was unenforceable unless jointly executed by both spouses. Another case[130] held that a deed by a husband as sole grantor was absolutely void and did not convey even his interest in the community property. The theory of that case was relied on by the two dissenting justices in the real estate contract case.[131]

An amendment to the statute should clarify the rules applicable in these circumstances. Perhaps the rule of *Jenkins v. Huntsinger*[132] should be changed to make a deed by one spouse voidable merely and not absolutely void as is the present rule.

Presumptions and the Retroactive Effect of Changes

It is believed that the part of the decision in *August v. Tillian*[133] which was not abrogated by the amending of 1947[134] should be changed so that property now standing in the names of husband and wife who are not described as such in the instrument will be held to be community property, or separate property in which each has an equal although undivided interest. At the present time the rule is that one-half of such property is the separate property of the wife and the other half is community property, thus allowing the wife a three-fourths interest.

The unwelcome ramifications of In re *Trimble's Estate*[135] have already been discussed. Technical methods for handling presumptions of community property or joint tenancy in a clear manner can be devised.

It is believed that the decisions in the above cases are not "rules of property"[136] which if altered would disturb "vested

129. Adams v. Blumenshine, 27 N.M. 643, 204 P.2d 66, 20 A.L.R. 369 (1922).
130. Jenkins v. Huntsinger, 46 N.M. 168, 125 P.2d 327 (1942).
131. Henderson v. Treadwell, 58 N.M. 230, 269 P.2d 1108 (1954).
132. 46 N.M. 168, 125 P.2d 327 (1942).
133. 51 N.M. 74, 178 Pac. 590 (1947).
134. N.M. Laws 1947, c. 191, § 1, p. 393.
135. 57 N.M. 51, 253 P.2d 805 (1953). See pages 93–95 *supra*.
136. See Justice Seymour, concurring specially in Brown v. Gurley, 267 P.2d 134, 142 (N.M. 1954).

rights." Legislation can be drafted which will have retroactive effect[137] and thereby clear away much uncertainty concerning titles and the quantum of proof necessary to show a particular form of ownership, or the status of specific property as separate or community.

Agency Problems

The Report[138] recommends that general agency problems be kept out of problems of control and management. However, it might be possible to clarify the managerial powers of the husband by a minor statutory change. *Frkovich v. Petranovich*[139] indicates that there is no "head" of the community realty. This statement is to be doubted except where it is applicable to the power to convey or encumber community realty. Some one certainly has the power to make decisions concerning the *use* of community realty.

The powers of attorney between spouses, including those of minor spouses, need statutory integration and clarification. The Report contains suggestions on this matter.[140]

Rights and Priorities of Creditors

A statute is needed which will take care of both tort and contract creditor situations, clarify insolvency and bankruptcy remedies, and determine what kind of property, community or separate, and in what order, a creditor may seek satisfaction.[141]

"Instrument in Writing"

If the present statute on presumptions is altered or improved, some thought should be given to a definition of the phrase "instrument in writing" contained in the statute.[142] In some states the phrase has been limited in interpretation to include titles to real property only.[143]

Insurance

Provision should be made for situations, not at all rare, in which life insurance premiums have been paid out of commu-

137. See Clark, *Management and Control of Community Property in New Mexico*, 26 TULANE L. REV. 324 (1952).

138. REPORT, c. XII, p. 144.

139. 48 N.M. 382, 151 P.2d 337 (1944).

140. REPORT, c. VII, p. 75.

141. See page 95 *supra*.

142. N.M. STAT. ANN. § 57-4-1(1953); see REPORT, c. XIII, p. 17.

143. See Dorsey v. Barba, 226 P.2d 677 (Cal. App. 1951), 38 Cal.2d 350, 240 P.2d 604 (1952); Pacific Tel. & Tel. Co. v. Wellman, 98 Cal. App.2d 151, 219 P.2d 506 (1950).

nity funds for long periods of time although the policy, having been purchased before marriage, is separate property.[144] Either the proceeds of the policy should be prorated on the basis of the percentage of the premiums paid in from community or separate funds, or one-half of the premiums paid out of community funds, plus interest, should be returned to the spouse who does not share in the proceeds. The urgency of this problem can be gleaned from the Report's[145] discussion of *Wissner v. Wissner*[146] which has established a rule with respect to National Service Life Insurance which is contrary to community property principles but is not binding in commercial insurance cases. The practical necessity for a clear way to determine the respective spouses' interest in life insurance proceeds or policies is illustrated graphically in both death cases and divorce-property settlement cases.

Community Property Ownership v. Duty of Support

The Report[147] points out the confusion in the understanding of the two concepts and states that the distinction is fundamental. Clarification of the statutes on divorce, separation,[148] and property settlement procedures[149] would help dispel much of this confusion.

It is believed that a "family expense" statute[150] should be enacted. This type of statute deals with the obligations of marriage and is not concerned with whether property is separate or community. The Report[151] does not look favorably on this type of legislation. However, it is believed that such legislation would be entirely appropriate in community states where the wife actually owns part of the family resources and not merely her pin money. Such a statute should (a) cover more than "necessaries" which are all that most support statutes include, (b) make *both* spouses personally liable, but the wife only secondarily liable after the husband. It appears that most statutes intended this effect, but the courts in giving them a literal reading extended personal liability to the husband only.[152]

---

144. *In re* White's Estate, 43 N.M. 202, 89 P.2d 36 (1939).
145. REPORT, c. VI, p. 69.
146. 338 U.S. 655 (1950).
147. REPORT, c. XIII, p. 154.
148. N.M. STAT. ANN. § 22-7-1(1953).
149. *Id* §§ 57-2-6—57-2-13.
150. See 3 VERNIER, AMERICAN FAMILY LAWS § 160 (1935).
151. REPORT, c. XII, p. 145, c. II, p. 15.
152. See 3 VERNIER, AMERICAN FAMILY LAWS § 160 (1935).

An amendment to the California statute[153] makes the wife's wages liable for necessaries furnished the community. The amendment is evidence of the existing confusion over support and community property ownership principles. The New Mexico statute[154] exempting a wife's wages from liability for her husband's debts was copied from California. It is made apparent by the California amendment[155] that California failed to understand that the statute did not exempt the wife's wages from *community* debts, at least for necessaries. In New Mexico the wife's wages, being community property, are liable for community debts and are not merely liable for community debts arising out of the purchase of necessaries. As the Report[156] seems to indicate, it is the husband's separate debts for which the wife's wages cannot be taken. However, statutory clarification of the point would be helpful.

Descent and Distribution

Clarification is needed of the meaning of "decedent's estates" used in the statutes,[157] particularly for tax purposes and for the purpose of determining the source of payment for funeral expenses, gravestones, expenses of administration and, perhaps most importantly, executors' and attorneys' fees. When a married man predeceases his wife, and the Report[158] carefully marshals the evidence for this possibility, should the base for attorney's fees be the entire community estate or only half of it? In re *Stutzman's Estate*[159] foreshadows these problems. It is believed that the practice is by no means uniform in the state or even in the same law office.

Testamentary power. (1) It has not been demonstrated by the experience of the other community states that allowing the wife testamentary power over her interest in the community property has resulted in excessive hardship, difficult legal problems or a decline in economic enterprise.[160] Two of the least populous and least wealthy states, Nevada and New Mexico, do not grant the wife this power. It would not be reasonable to assume that only these two states possess a proper understand-

---

153. CAL. CIV. CODE § 168 (Deering, 1949).
154. N.M. STAT. ANN. § 57-3-6(1953).
155. CAL. STAT. & CODE AMEND. 1497 (1937).
156. REPORT, c. VIII, p. 89.
157. See *In re* Stutzman's Estate, 57 N.M. 710, 262 P.2d 990 (1953); N.M. STAT. ANN. §§ 29-1-9, 31-16-3(1953).
158. REPORT, c. II, p. 15.
159. 57 N.M. 710, 262 P.2d 990 (1953).
160. REPORT, c. XII, pp. 150-151, raises these questions.

ing of the problem. The justification for the denial in New Mexico is tax savings.[161] The possibilities expressed in In re *Chavez's Estate*[162] remain, but the probabilities, which are far more relevant, that wives will predecease husbands,[163] are not great. As a caveat to the *Chavez* case it should be emphasized that:

(a) the case was a tax decision

(b) The case was decided before the new era of taxation which is based on dominion and control theories and not on formal ownership or title

(c) the case contradicts the idea that the wife owns one-half of the community estate.

(2) Changes in the statutes. Before changes in testamentary provisions are made, if any are contemplated, consideration should be given to the statutes of Idaho and Louisiana,[164] which limit the extent to which a spouse may leave his or her share of the community property by will. For comparative purposes the Idaho statute is quoted:

Section 14-113, Idaho Code 1948 reads:

> "Devolution of Community Property—Upon the death of either husband or wife, one-half of all of the community property shall go to the survivor, subject to the community debts, and the other half shall be subject to the testamentary disposition of the deceased husband or wife, in favor only of the survivor, the children, the grandchildren or parents of either spouse, or one or more of such persons, subject also to the community debts; provided, that not more than one-half of the decedent's half of the community property may be left by will to a parent or parents, unless limited to an estate for life or less . . . . [other provisions unimportant]"

One criticism of the statute is made. There should be a provision for leaving a portion of the decedent's property, to be determined by the legislature, to charitable institutions or for

161. In New Mexico when the wife predeceases the husband, "the entire community, without administration, belongs to the surviving husband." N.M. STAT. ANN. § 29-1-8(1953). This statute has been interpreted to mean that no state succession tax is collectible when the wife dies, *In re* Chavez's Estate, 34 N.M. 258, 280 P.2d 241, 69 A.L.R. 769 (1929). The same rule was followed in a federal estate tax case, Hernandez v. Becker, 54 F.2d 542 (10th Cir. 1931).

162. 34 N.M. 258, 280 P.2d 241, 69 A.L.R. 769 (1929).

163. REPORT, c. II, p. 15.

164. Arts. 1493, 1494, LA. CIVIL CODE of 1870.

similar purposes. The tax savings aspects of donations and the public benefit therefrom should not be overlooked.

Intestate succession. The California and Idaho statutes do not provide that upon intestacy a portion of the decedent's interest should go to the children. New Mexico has such a provision which should be abolished.[165] Reasons for such a change are stated at page 103 *supra.*[166] It is also suggested that a summary probate procedure statute for small estates be enacted in New Mexico. The present statute[167] is so limited as to be worthless for the purposes discussed herein.

Jurisdiction in Probate

The lawyer handling a probate matter should know with more than reasonable certainty whether a particular question should be raised in the probate or the district court. A recent case[168] draws attention to the lawyer's uncertainty in New Mexico.

It seems clear that the probate court, which in New Mexico is a separate county court[169] usually presided over by a layman, has always exercised both judicial and administrative functions. But serious questions have been raised as to its jurisdiction to try titles to realty[170] or determine the status of specific property as separate or community.[171] Recent legislation[172] attempted to clarify the first matter. With respect to the second question legislative clarification is needed because of:

(1) The present constitutional problem of probate jurisdiction[173]

165. N.M. STAT. ANN. § 29-1-9(1953). The statute declares that in the absence of testamentary disposition by the husband of his one-half of the community estate, such property "goes one-fourth to the surviving wife and the remainder in equal shares to the children of the decedent and further as provided by law. . . ." One-fourth of the husband's one-half means the surviving wife then has a total of 5/8 of the entire community estate and the children receive 3/4 of 1/2 or 3/8. See Weinmann, *Surviving Spouse's Inheritance of the Decedent Spouse's Interest in the Community in an Intestate Succession: A Comparative Study of the Law of Mexico, Quebec and Louisiana*, 28 TULANE L. REV. 480 (1954).

166. See page 103 *et seq. supra.*

167. N.M. STAT. ANN. §§ 31-1-30—31-1-32(1953) (summary administration limited to personal property the cash value of which is not more than $1000).

168. *In re* Conley's Estate, 276 P.2d 906 (N.M. 1954).

169. N.M. STAT. ANN. § 16-4-1(1953).

170. See Dunham v. Stitzberg, 53 N.M. 81, 201 P.2d 1000 (1949).

171. See note 168 *supra.*

172. N.M. CONST. Art. 6, § 23 (1949 amendment), granting probate courts jurisdiction to determine heirship with respect to real property.

173. N.M. CONST. Art. 6, § 23; Dunham v. Stitzberg, 53 N.M. 81, 201 P.2d 1000 (1949).

(2) The possible right to jury trial in disputes over the nature or status of property as separate or community.

Taxes

Taxes are, of course, not merely a technical subject. They epitomize the inseparable connection between the determination of a purpose and the methods for attaining it. It is impossible therefore to summarize the New Mexico and federal tax structure in the family law area, or make suggestions to clarify or strengthen it. However, a few situations which exist by virtue of statute or case law and which may create future problems can be outlined. These and others are pointed out in the Report.[174]

(1) The different tax consequences, state and federal, of joint tenancy and community property ownership are significant[175] but are not clearly understood.

(2) The New Mexico succession tax[176] is not chargeable against the entire community estate when the husband dies first. Only half of the estate is includible in the gross estate.[177] However, if the husband is the surviving spouse, none of the community estate is subject to the succession tax.[178]

(3) Since 1948[179] the above rule has been applicable with respect to the federal estate tax when the wife survives. An earlier federal case, *Hernandez v. Becker*,[180] following the New Mexico succession tax rule decided that where the husband survives, none of the community estate is includible in the decedent wife's gross estate for federal estate tax purposes.

At the present time the above rules affect the valuation of community property for purposes of computing capital gains and losses. If the wife survives the husband a new basis for valuation is acquired at the husband's death. But since the entire community property "belongs to" the New Mexico hus-

---

174. REPORT, c. XI, p. 127.

175. See Marshall, *Joint Tenancy, Taxwise and Otherwise*, 40 CALIF. L. REV. 501 (1952).

176. N.M. STAT. ANN. § 31-16-1 *et seq.* (1953).

177. REPORT, c. XI, pp. 132-133.

178. *In re* Chavez's Estate, N.M. 258, 280 P.2d 241, 69 A.L.R. 769 (1929).

179. 26 FED. CODE ANN. §§ 800 *et seq.*, 811(e)(2) was replaced in 1948. This restored the community property law as it existed before 1942. See INT. REV. CODE § 2040 (joint interests), § 2506(c)(2)(B)(C) (community property rules) (1954).

180. 54 F.2d 542 (10th Cir. 1931).

band who survives his wife, he does not receive the benefit of the federal law[181] authorizing the new valuation.

(4) A New Mexico case[182] decided under the Federal Revenue Act of 1942 raised the question of the ultimate liability for payment of federal estate taxes. The case declared that this was a local law matter. The Report[183] to the Committee in the analysis of the case, states: "No New Mexico decision was found that determined the question of ultimate liability . . . as between distributive interests of the state." However, in applying apportionment in the *Gallagher* case,[184] the court commented:

> "We have not tallied the jurisdictions on each side, but although the earlier rule (ultimate liability borne by the residue) may still represent the majority opinion of jurisdictions passing on the question, we feel no compunction to adhere inelastically to a rule which in view of this Court is not productive of substantial justice. Certainly the vitality of our legal system derives in large part from the function of our courts in applying its *root* concepts, among them that of equal treatment, to ever new and diversified problems. . . ."

(5) Transfers of property between spouses and transmutations of separate into community property, and vice versa, with all their attendant complications, take place against the background of state and federal gift and estate taxes[185] where further technicalities are to be expected.

CONCLUSION

Society is confronted, more seriously than ever before, with the disintegration of the family. The Married Women's Acts and the "equal rights"[186] statutes for women do not seem to have discouraged the trend and they may have heightened it. Much of the difficulty in this area obviously lies outside the scope of a marital property study. However, the family, like other social institutions, has an economic as well as cultural framework. This was true under all earlier systems and remains true today. But the legal protections erected by the common law to sustain the family unit, although many of them are still with us, became

181. See note 179 *supra*; REPORT, c. XI, p. 136.
182. *In re* Gallagher's Will, 57 N.M. 112, 255 P.2d 317 (1953).
183. REPORT, c. XI, p. 132.
184. *In re* Gallagher's Will, 57 N.M. 112, 130, 255 P.2d 317, 328 (1953).
185. REPORT, c. XI, p. 127.
186. See WIS. STAT. § 6.015 (1935); 3 VERNIER, AMERICAN FAMILY LAWS § 150 (1935).

outmoded during the Industrial Revolution and the rise of political democracy. Beginning a century ago, the Married Women's Acts obtained legal recognition for these historical developments.

These acts were efforts to carry by law to middle class married women the property rights already established in equity for the wealthier classes. In large measure they accomplished their purpose, yet at the same time the economic interests of the spouses were *in law* pulled apart rather than together. This did not *in fact* always happen largely because of the functional and realistic attitudes of most married persons with respect to the family resources. This general outlook is now a major part of federal tax law.

An important problem for the law is to find ways to accommodate, with proper legal procedures and safeguards, the co-ownership practices of married persons. The persons most concerned are those who, either because of lack of funds, or the mistaken belief that his services are superfluous, never consult a lawyer, even about the matter of taking title to the family home. Improvements in family law are not urgently needed for those who can afford legal services. These persons may receive some tax or other benefits as a consequence of improvement or clarifications in the law, but in most cases they probably have legal counsel to advise them.

The utility and convenience of a marital property system should not be judged merely by the facility with which a division of property can be had upon divorce, or tax matters handled upon divorce or death, or even because there are certain tax advantages to be had as a result of alimony, support or separation decrees or agreements.[187] The system should be judged by the manner in which it fulfills the needs of the individual and the group, in this case the family and society.[188]

Many husbands and wives are employed;[189] the per capita income and with it the average family income is rising steadily in the United States. In the use and expenditure of this income

187. See Kragen, Stoke, Oliver, & Buckley, *The Marriage Undone: Taxwise*, 42 CALIF. L. REV. 408 (1954), for a California example of the type of study needed in all states.

188. See Tenbroek, *The Impact of Welfare Law upon Family Law*, 42 CALIF. L. REV. 458 (1954). This article appears in an issue devoted entirely to family law which contains several original and much-needed studies in the field.

189. REPORT, c. II, p. 15.

and property for the benefit of the family, concurrent ownership ideas are advantageous and adaptable. It is believed that community of property principles, despite all the accumulated difficulties delineated and alluded to here, furnish the "only significant analogy"[190] in which a solution to problems of joint ownership and control may be found.

The community states, therefore, as leaders in this field, must take steps to clarify their own systems. The New Mexico experience and the Committee Report may provide some helpful suggestions with which to begin.

---

190. See Townsend, *Creation of Joint Rights Between Husband and Wife in Personal Property*, 52 MICH. L. REV. 779, 784 (1954); Daggett, *Policy Questions in Marital Property Law in Louisiana*, 14 LOUISIANA LAW REVIEW 528 (1954).

Some Principles of Texas Community Property Law

*William O. Huie**

Basic Spanish Principles

The Texas community property system is derived from the Spanish law. The Spanish community property rules, which were the law of the land when Texas was under the sovereignty of Spain and Mexico, were retained by the Texas Republic when the English common law was adopted in 1840.[1] But the original Spanish rules have been greatly modified during the intervening century. Some of the changes have been intentional, reflecting a change in ideas as to the proper status of married women. Others have resulted from the infiltration of rules and principles of English common law and equity, sometimes because of lack of full information and understanding of the original civil law principles.

Under the Spanish law the spouses were equal partners[2] as to all financial enterprises during the continuance of the marriage, unless otherwise agreed in a marriage contract. Both spouses contributed to the partnership their time and efforts and the use of and revenue from their individual wealth. The individual capital of each spouse consisted of the property owned at marriage and the property acquired after marriage by inheritance or by gift to the individual.[3] At the dissolution of the partnership the separate capital of each spouse was restored before the division of the profits either by recognizing individual ownership of specific property on hand or by allowing reimbursement from the property on hand,[4] all of which was presumed to be community property.[5]

---

* Professor of Law, The University of Texas.

1. Tex. Laws 1840, p. 3, 2 LAWS OF TEXAS 177 (Gammel 1898).

2. See 1 DE FUNIAK, PRINCIPLES OF COMMUNITY PROPERTY 264 (1943).

3. 1 *id.* §§ 63, 69.

4. As to reimbursement, see the translations of Spanish commentaries in the second volume of de Funiak's work: Matienzo, 2 *id.* at 143, 213, 214, 246, 268, 269; Gutierrez, 2 *id.* at 186, 187; Azevedo, 2 *id.* at 170, 171; Llamas y Molina, 2 *id.* at 411.

5. 1 *id.* § 60.

Texas has retained many of the basic principles of the Spanish law. The idea of a marital partnership has been retained, and the Texas definitions of separate and community property closely resemble those of the Spanish law. Separate ownership of specific property was confined within narrow limits by the definitions of the 1840 statute,[6] but in the Constitution of 1845 the wife's separate property was defined as "all property, both real and personal . . . owned or claimed by her before marriage, and that acquired afterwards by gift, devise, or descent,"[7] and an 1848 statute contained a similar definition of the separate property of both husband and wife.[8] All other property acquired during the marriage by either the husband or the wife was community, the statute said. Later constitutions have contained the same definition of the wife's separate property,[9] and there has been no effective change of the statutory definitions.[10] In Texas today, as under the Spanish law, each spouse retains separate ownership of the property owned at marriage and of the property received by gift or inheritance during the marriage, but property acquired during the marriage by the personal efforts of either spouse is community, and the revenue from the separate property of both spouses goes into the community.

Tracing Separate Property Through Changes in Form

Under the Spanish law it was possible in certain exceptional cases to establish separate ownership of particular property by tracing separate property into its product. For example, land received in exchange for separate land was separate.[11] Also separate land could be sold and the proceeds reinvested in separately owned land.[12] But the tracing of separate property to establish separate ownership of the product was narrowly con-

6. Tex. Laws 1804, p. 3, 2 LAWS OF TEXAS 177 (Gammel 1898).

7. TEX CONST. Art. 7, § 19 (1845), 2 LAWS OF TEXAS 1923 (Gammel 1898).

8. Tex. Laws 1848, c. 79, p. 77, 3 LAWS OF TEXAS 77 (Gammel 1898).

9. TEX. CONST. ANN. Art. 16, § 15 (Vernon, Supp. 1954).

10. An attempt to change the definitions by putting the revenue from separate property into the separate estate was held invalid as to the revenue from the wife's separate property in Arnold v. Leonard, 114 Tex. 535, 273 S.W. 799 (1925), and in 1929 the legislature restored the older definitions of the separate estates of both spouses, Tex. Laws 1929, c. 32, p. 66, 26 LAWS OF TEXAS 66 (Gammel 1929). For the present statutory definitions, see TEX. REV. CIV. STAT. ANN. Arts 4613, 4614, 4619 (Vernon, 1951).

11. It is clear that tracing to establish separate ownership was permitted upon an exchange of land. Judging from the broad language of the writers, the same principle may have been applied to other kinds of property acquired by exchange as distinguished from purchase. See the translations from Matienzo, 2 DE FUNIAK, PRINCIPLES OF COMMUNITY PROPERTY 142 (1943), and Gutierrez, 2 *id.* at 186.

12. See the translations from Matienzo, 2 *id.* at 143, Azevedo, 2 *id.* at 174, 175, and Gutierrez, 2 *id.* at 186.

fined. The general rule was that property bought during the marriage with separate funds was community property,[13] the spouse whose funds were used receiving reimbursement from community assets at the dissolution of the marital partnership.[14]

In Texas the ownership tracing principle has been greatly extended. The leading case was *Love v. Robertson*,[15] decided in 1851. The opinion in that case shows that the departure from Spanish law resulted from a failure to understand fully the Spanish rules. The husband had used his separate money to buy two slaves, Peter and Finn. He paid cash for Peter. For Finn he paid in cash with separate funds $330 of a total purchase price of $800; the balance was paid later out of community funds. After the husband's death a controversy arose over whether the slaves were separate property or community property. It appears from the authorities now available that the Spanish law would have awarded ownership of the slaves to the community, and the husband's heir would have received reimbursement from the community for the separate funds used in making the purchase, but apparently no adequate exposition of the Spanish law was available. Language of a prior case indicated that under the Spanish law property bought by either spouse after marriage was community property even though it was paid for with separate funds, but there had been no recognition in the authorities brought to the court's attention of the Spanish rule that the separate capital so invested in community property was to be restored at the dissolution of the community. The possibility of reimbursement as an alternative to ownership was not suggested by counsel nor considered by the court.[16] In the absence of

13. See Savenant v. Le Breton, 1 La. 520, 522 (1830). According to Matienzo, the money brought by the spouses to the marriage became community property forthwith; hence anything bought with it became community property. See the translation in 2 DE FUNIAK, PRINCIPLES OF COMMUNITY PROPERTY 143 (1943). See also the translation of Gutierrez, 2 *id.* at 186, 187. There was not complete harmony among the Spanish writers, and although the rule stated above seems to have been accepted by most of them, Professor de Funiak has concluded that there was only a rebuttable presumption that property bought with separate funds was bought for the community. See 1 *id.* § 77.

14. See the translations from Matienzo and Gutierrez, *supra* note 13.

15. 7 Tex. 6 (1851).

16. Although the Texas court was looking to Louisiana cases for guidance, the Louisiana cases directly in point were not brought to the court's attention. In Brown v. Cobb, 10 La. 172 (1836), it had been held that a slave bought by the husband with his separate funds was community property because the conveyance to the husband contained no language to indicate that he intended for the slave to be his separate property. In Young v. Young, 5 La Ann. 611 (1850), it had become established that in such a case the husband would be allowed reimbursement from the community for the amount of his separate funds used in making the purchase.

compensation to the husband for his separate funds, awarding the slaves to the community would have been a very unjust result. To avoid what it deemed an obvious injustice to the husband, the court concluded that property bought with separate funds should be separate, and that payment of part of the purchase price with separate funds should give a fractional separate interest. Peter was separate; Finn was owned by a mixed title, 330/800ths separate and 470/800ths community.

From the time of that decision it has been established in Texas that the principle of tracing separate property through changes in form to establish separate ownership of the product is one of general applicability.[17] It is not confined to exceptional situations, as was true under the Spanish law, but is applied to usual transactions, such as a purchase of property with separate funds. It is applied even though only a fraction of the total consideration is paid with separate funds.[18]

Intention as Sometimes Controlling under Application of Trust Principles

The opinion in *Love v. Robertson*[19] cited no trust cases and did not use trust terminology, but the ownership tracing principle the court was applying in that case is the same principle which enables the beneficiary of a trust to trace the trust property through changes in form to establish separate ownership of new acquisitions by the trustee. Within a few years the Texas courts were using trust language and were looking to trust cases as controlling precedents.

In *Smith v. Strahan*,[20] decided in 1856, the husband had used his separate property to buy land in his wife's name. Looking to the law of trusts as developed in common law jurisdictions, the court held that an intent to make a gift of the property to the wife would be presumed in the absence of evidence to the contrary, but that the presumption could be rebutted by parol evidence that a gift was not intended. Rebutting the presumption of gift would raise a purchase-money resulting trust in favor of the husband, equitable ownership vesting in him as separate property, unless a loan to the wife was intended.

In the converse case, where the wife's funds are used to

17. Rose v. Houston, 11 Tex. 324, 62 Am. Dec. 478 (1854); Speer, Law of Marital Rights in Texas § 426 (3d ed. 1929).

18. Gleich v. Bongio, 128 Tex. 606, 99 S.W.2d 881 (1937).

19. 7 Tex. 6 (1851).

20. 16 Tex. 314, 67 Am. Dec. 622 (1856).

buy land in the husband's name, there is a presumption of a resulting trust in favor of the wife as her separate property,[21] a presumption which can be rebutted by oral evidence that a gift or loan[22] to the husband was intended. Evidence of a gift would place ownership in the husband as his separate property. If the wife's funds are loaned to the husband, the money thereby becomes community property in the absence of further evidence,[23] and property bought with the money would likewise be presumed to be community property.

The likelihood that a gift to the wife is intended would seem as great in a case where the husband uses community funds to buy property in the wife's name as in a case where he uses his separate funds to make such a purchase. But in the former case a gift to the wife is not presumed in the absence of further evidence. Where community funds are used to make the purchase in the wife's name it was first thought that the community property law fixed ownership in the community and that an intent to make a gift to the wife could not be given effect.[24] That notion was soon rejected and an intent to make a gift to the wife was given effect although proved merely by parol evidence,[25] but the civil law tradition, under which property standing in the name of either spouse is presumed to be community, was strong enough to prevent a presumption of gift from the mere fact that the husband takes title in the wife's name when he buys property with community funds.

When title to property bought with separate funds is taken in the name of both spouses, the equitable ownership will again depend, in the final analysis, upon the intention of the parties at the time of acquisition. There are several possibilities as to

21. There is substantial conflict in other jurisdictions whether a gift to the husband or a resulting trust to the wife should be presumed, most courts presuming a trust to the wife. 2A BOGERT, TRUSTS AND TRUSTEES § 460 (1953); Note, 113 A.L.R. 339 (1938). In Texas it has been assumed without discussion that there is a presumption of a trust to the wife. Matador Land & Cattle Co. v. Cooper, 87 S.W. 235 (Tex. Civ. App. 1905). In accord are cases where proof that a wife's funds were used to buy property, title being taken in the husband's name, was held sufficient to establish separate ownership in the wife. Evans v. Welborn, 74 Tex. 530, 12 S.W. 230, 15 Am. St. Rep. 858 (1889); Blum v. Rogers, 71 Tex. 668, 9 S.W. 595 (1888); Yoe v. Montgomery, 68 Tex. 338, 4 S.W. 622 (1887); Ross v. Kornrumpf, 64 Tex. 390 (1885).

22. Levy v. Williams, 50 S.W. 528 (Tex. Civ. App. 1899), *writ of error refused.*

23. Money borrowed by the husband during the marriage is presumed to be community property. Foster v. Hackworth, 164 S.W.2d 796 (Tex. Civ. App. 1942). The problem of determining the separate or community character of property acquired on credit is discussed page 125 *infra.*

24. See Smith v. Strahan, 16 Tex. 314, 323, 67 Am. Dec. 622, 626 (1856).

25. Higgins v. Johnson's Heirs, 20 Tex. 389, 70 Am. Dec. 394 (1857).

intent. One is that the spouse whose funds were used is to have separate equitable ownership of the entire title. A second possibility is that each of the spouses is to own an undivided half interest as separate property. A third possibility is that community ownership is intended. The fact that title is taken in the name of both spouses would seem to furnish a strong indication that the property is intended to belong to both spouses, either as community property or as co-owners by separate titles. However, the Texas cases involving the problem have extended the presumption of a resulting trust to the situation where title is taken in the name of both spouses. According to those cases, the presumption of community is rebutted merely by evidence that the property was paid for with separate funds; that evidence alone will be sufficient to establish separate equitable ownership of the entire title in the spouse whose funds were used in the absence of further evidence to rebut the presumption of a resulting trust.[26] No real consideration of whether the presumption of a resulting trust will effectuate the probable intention of the parties is indicated by the opinions in those cases, and perhaps a full consideration of the question would result in a conclusion that the presumption of community should be given controlling effect in the absence of evidence that separate equitable ownership was intended.

Where the evidence establishes that title was taken in the name of both spouses with the intent that the property should be community property, the Texas cases have given effect to the intent, holding that the property is community property although bought with separate funds.[27] In such a case the spouse whose separate funds were used would ordinarily be entitled to reimbursement from community assets at the dissolution of the

26. See Foster v. Christensen, 67 S.W.2d 246, 249 (Tex. Com. App. 1934), and Sparks v. Humble Oil & Refining Co., 129 S.W.2d 468, 470 (Tex. Civ. App. 1939), *error ref.* (separate funds of wife); Jones v. Jones, 181 S.W.2d 988, 991 (Tex Civ. App. 1944), *writ of error refused for want of merit*; and Cummins v. Cummins, 224 S.W. 903, 904 (Tex. Civ. App. 1920) (separate funds of husband).

27. Jones v. Jones, 181 S.W.2d 988, 991 (Tex. Civ. App. 1944); Cummins v. Cummins, 224 S.W. 903, 904 (Tex. Civ. App. 1920). But see Sparks v. Humble Oil & Refining Co., 129 S.W.2d 468, 470 (Tex. Civ. App. 1939), *error ref.*, where the court expresses a contra view, relying on the opinion in Gleich v. Bongio, 128 Tex. 606, 88 S.W.2d 881 (1937). The statements in those opinions are derived from a misapplication of the well-established Texas view that the separate or community character of property depends on the application of the law to the facts, not on the mere intention of the parties. That principle, which is discussed pages 121–25 *infra*, does not prevent the intention of the spouses from being a controlling operative fact in certain cases.

marital partnership.[28] The general rule that property bought with separate funds becomes separate is therefore not a fixed rule of uniform application; it is a rule of presumed intent, justifiable only in those circumstances where a presumption of a resulting trust will effectuate the probable intention of the parties.

Full recognition that the rule under which property bought with separate funds becomes separate is based on a presumption that separate ownership is intended will result in significant restrictions on the application of the rule, for there are a number of situations where an inference of an intention to invest separate funds for community benefit would be more reasonable than an inference of an intention to invest for the benefit of the separate estate. For example, where separate funds are invested in a stock of merchandise, it would be virtually impossible to preserve the corpus of the separate estate in the form of specific identifiable assets into which the original separate funds could be traced; mingling of principal and income is almost inevitable. It would be reasonable to assume that a spouse who makes such an investment of separate funds would prefer to preserve his or her separate capital in the form of a claim for reimbursement from community assets, thereby avoiding the difficulties involved in trying to trace separate funds through changes in form.

The results of the Texas cases furnish support for a conclusion that reimbursement from community assets is the only remedy that will actually be available to a spouse who invests separate funds in a mercantile enterprise. The courts have never expressly stated that the ownership tracing principle is not appropriate in that kind of case, but the claims to ownership of specific property have usually been denied because of the mingling of separate and community funds,[29] while under similar facts claims to reimbursement of separate funds or property absorbed in the operation of a business have been successfully maintained.[30] The analysis that will go far to explain and reconcile the results of the cases is simply that the ownership tracing

28. Dakan v. Dakan, 125 Tex. 305, 83 S.W.2d 620 (1935).

29. Hardee v. Vincent, 136 Tex. 99, 147 S.W.2d 1072 (1941); Gibson v. Gibson, 202 S.W.2d 288 (Tex Civ. App. 1947); Walker-Smith Co. v. Coker, 176 S.W.2d 1002 (Tex Civ. App. 1943), *error ref. w.o.m.*

30. Schmidt v. Huppmann, 73 Tex. 112, 11 S.W. 175 (1889); Tittle v. Tittle, 221 S.W.2d 576 (Tex. Civ. App. 1948). A reimbursement theory also seems to be the proper explanation for the holdings in Hartman v. Hartman, 253 S.W.2d 480 (Tex. Civ. App. 1952), and Farrow v. Farrow, 238 S.W.2d 255 (Tex. Civ. App. 1951).

principle is not applicable to separate money spent in the operation of a business for community benefit; in those cases, instead of presuming that individual ownership of property bought with separate funds is intended, it is proper to presume an intention to invest the separate funds for community benefit, the individual spouse to receive reimbursement later from community assets.

That approach may also furnish an explanation for the recent holding of the Texas Supreme Court in *Norris v. Vaughan.*[31] One of the important holdings in that case was that interests in oil and gas leases acquired by the husband during the marriage were community property although the interests were paid for and developed with the husband's separate funds. Since the basis for the court's conclusion is not entirely clear, the circumstances of the case will be stated in some detail.

The leasehold interests in controversy were acquired during the marriage by partnerships of which the husband was a member at the time of the marriage. Some of the interests, referred to in the opinion as the McDowell and Tayor wells, were acquired under "farmout" agreements negotiated by the husband, under which one of the partnerships drilled certain wells in return for assignments of leasehold interests. Two other leases, referred to in the opinion as the Hill and Cantrell leases, were acquired direct from the lessors. The latter leases were not negotiated by the husband; they were procured by other members of a partnership in which the husband owned a one-fourth interest. Only nominal amounts were recited as the cash consideration for the Hill and Cantrell leases; one recited five dollars and the other ten. The drilling of the leases was done by the partnerships with partnership funds. From an audit of the partnership books it was concluded that no community funds had been used in the drilling of the wells; apparently all of the net income earned subsequent to the marriage had been withdrawn from both partnerships, and the court treated the case as if the drilling had been done with the husband's separate funds. Presumably the court also took the same view as to the partnership funds used in paying the nominal cash bonuses and delay rentals of the Hill and Cantrell leases, although the opinion contains no express statement to that effect.

If the leasehold interests were acquired for the partnerships, not for the partners individually, there might be some difficulty

31. 260 S.W.2d 676 (Tex. 1953).

in reconciling the court's analysis with the usual concept of the nature of a partner's interest in partnership property, but assuming the correctness of the court's basic approach, the holding can be stated in a simple form that eliminates the partnership aspect of the case. Viewing the case as one where a husband has acquired leasehold interests during the marriage and has used his separate funds to pay for and develop the leases, the Supreme Court refused to determine the ownership of the interests by looking to the character of the funds so used. Reversing the court of civil appeals on that point, the Supreme Court held that the leasehold interests were community property and that the separate estate should be reimbursed from community assets the amount of the separate funds spent. The court reasoned that the leases should be regarded as a product of the husband's personal efforts, referring to the talent and labor involved in the making of the deals by which the leases were acquired. The Hill and Cantrell leases, which were acquired through the efforts of the husband's partners, were also held to be community property. As to them it was reasoned that the efforts of the husband's partners should be regarded as the husband's own efforts for the purpose of deciding the question before the court.

The reasoning in the opinion does not furnish an entirely satisfactory explanation for the court's decision. The effort, skill, and judgment involved in making investments of separate funds have not in the past been regarded as a sufficient basis for awarding ownership to the community of property acquired with separate funds.[32] Why in this case did the court feel it was necessary to regard the leases as a product of the husband's efforts instead of looking to the character of the consideration given in exchange for them?

Perhaps the court's decision can be justified on the ground that the ownership tracing principle was not an appropriate one for the solution of the problem before the court. When the husband uses $20,000 of his separate money to buy a tract of land, it can properly be said that the money has been exchanged for the land, and a presumption of a resulting trust in favor of the husband's separate estate arises, under the established Texas rule. But the leasing of property for mineral development does not involve a comparable exchange of value equivalents. The bonus paid for the lease may be very large or very small; in

32. Cabell v. Menczer, 35 S.W. 206 (Tex. Civ. App. 1896); Evans v. Purinton, 34 S.W. 350 (Tex. Siv. App. 1896), *error ref.*

many cases it would be only a nominal part of the total return the lessor would expect from the lease. Strange results could be obtained if the separate or community character of a mineral lease were allowed to depend on the separate or community character of the funds used to pay the bonus. The husband could use five dollars of his separate funds to acquire a lease in unproven territory, risk many thousands of dollars of community funds in drilling a test well, and then claim the lease for his separate estate after its value had been established by production. Nor would it be desirable to let the separate or community character of the lease depend upon whether separate or community funds are used to pay the delay rentals, the payment of which merely entitles the lessee to defer the commencement of drilling operations. The desire on the part of the lessor to obtain development of the minerals is normaly the principal inducing cause for his execution of a mineral lease, and it would not be entirely unrealistic to say that the lessee receives the leasehold interest in exchange for a total consideration consisting of the bonus, the delay rentals, and whatever time and money the development and operation of the leased premises may involve. But the leasehold must be given a separate or community character at the time it is acquired; at that time the amount that may be spent in the future on delay rentals and on drilling and operating expenses cannot be known.

The simplest solution of the problem would be to regard mineral leases acquired by either spouse during the continuance of the marriage as community property, allowing reimbursement at the dissolution of the community to the spouse whose separate funds have gone into the acquisition and development of the leases. That is the solution that was actually found by the Supreme Court in *Norris v. Vaughan,* and although the court's explanation of its decision causes uncertainty as to the circumstances under which the case will be controlling, it should be regarded as an important precedent establishing that there are some situations where the ownership tracing principle is not appropriate and will not be used, and that cases where separate funds are used to acquire and develop mineral leases fall within that category.

If a conclusion of community ownership of certain types of property acquired with separate funds is based on a presumption of intent to acquire the property for the community, a different conclusion could be expected in cases where an intent to acquire for the separate estate is clearly manifested by reliable evidence at the time the property is acquired. But from the opinion in *Norris v. Vaughan,* which relies upon the theory that the effort involved in finding and negotiating the leases gave them a community character, it seems possible that intention will not be controlling in cases where oil and gas leases are acquired with separate funds. It may be that in those cases the Texas court is returning to an approach essentially like that of the Spanish law and will simply say that the property is community because acquired during the marriage otherwise than by gift, devise, or descent, even though acquired with separate funds.

Property Acquired on Credit

The character of property as separate or community is fixed at the time it is acquired, whether it is bought with cash or on credit. When property is bought for cash it can be regarded as standing in the place of and taking its character from the money for which it is exchanged. But when property is bought on credit it is received in exchange not for money or other property but for a mere promise to pay. Since the character of the property must be fixed at the time it is acquired, the character of the funds that are later used to pay the purchase-money debt cannot control. If property is community at the time it is acquired, the later use of separate funds to pay the purchase-money debt will not give the property a separate character.[33] A right of reimbursement can be established by tracing separate funds into the payment of the purchase-money debt,[34] with subrogation in some cases to the rights of the creditor,[35] but not ownership of the property.

The controlling rule in most credit acquisition cases is the presumption that property acquired on credit during the marriage is community;[36] usually there will be no evidence to rebut the presumption. If property is acquired partly for cash and partly on credit, the presumption of community is applied to the credit portion of the purchase price even though the down payment is made in whole or in part with separate funds. If the husband buys land for a total purchase price of $20,000, using his separate funds to make a down payment of $5,000 at the

33. Goddard v. Reagan, 28 S.W. 352 (Tex. Civ. App. 1894).
34. Allen v. Allen, 101 Tex. 362, 107 S.W. 528 (1908).
35. Van v. Webb, 147 Tex. 299, 215 S.W.2d 151 (1948).
36. Foster v. Hackworth, 164 S.W.2d 796 (Tex. Civ. App. 1942); Speer, Law of Marital Rights in Texas § 369 (3d ed. 1929).

time of the deed and giving his notes for the balance, in the absence of further evidence the husband will own an undivided one-fourth interest in the land as his separate property and the community will own an undivided three-fourths interest.[37] To the extent of the credit portion of the purchase price, the undivided three-fourths, the courts say that the property is bought on community credit.

What evidence will be sufficient to rebut the presumption of community in cases involving credit acquisitions? On that question there is an area of uncertainty in the Texas law, and some confusion. The courts speak of separate and community credit, and sometimes seem to have in mind a characterization of an obligation as separate or community on the basis of the character of the property that the creditor can reach to satisfy the obligation. But such a concept will not explain the holdings of the cases. For example, when a married woman buys land on credit, the seller is usually unable to hold her liable for the purchase price and therefore cannot force payment out of her separate estate,[38] but the fact does not prevent a court from holding that the land belongs to the wife as her separate property if there is an agreement at the time of acquisition that the purchase-money debt is to be discharged with the wife's separate funds. Furthermore, it is possible for the property to become the wife's separate property even though the seller does hold a legally enforceable claim for the purchase price against the husband and the community. There have been several cases holding that land conveyed to the wife was entirely her separate property although the purchase-money note was signed by both the husband and the wife and the vendor could have held the husband and the community liable but could not have reached the wife's separate estate; in those cases the controlling fact was that the husband and the wife had agreed at the time the property was acquired that the purchase-money debt was to be paid out of the wife's separate estate.[39]

But some uncertainty in the law was introduced by language in *Gleich v. Bongio*.[40] In that case the court said:

---

37. Gleich v. Bongio, 128 Tex. 606, 99 S.W.2d 881 (1937).

38. Houston Loan & Investment Co. v. Abernathy, 131 Tex. 601, 117 S.W.2d 1089 (1938).

39. McClintic v. Midland Grocery & Dry Goods Co., 106 Tex. 32, 154 S.W. 1157 (1913); Schuster v. Bauman Jewelry Co., 79 Tex. 179, 15 S.W. 259, 23 Am. St. Rep. 327 (1890); Foster v. Christensen, 67 S.W.2d 246 (Tex. Com. App. 1934) (conveyance to husband to wife).

40. 128 Tex. 606, 612, 99 S.W.2d 881, 884 (1937).

"The mere intention of the husband and wife cannot convert property purchased with an obligation binding upon the community into the separate estate of either spouse. To accomplish that purpose the vendor must have agreed with the vendee to look only to his or her separate estate for the satisfaction of the deferred payments."

Although that language seems to have been intended by the court as a statement of existing law as derived from prior cases, actually it contained two new requirements for rebutting the presumption of community in cases where property is acquired on credit: (1) the vendor must participate in an agreement that the purchase-money debt is to be paid from the separate estate, and (2) the agreement must be that the vendor will look only to the separate estate for satisfaction. Both of the new propositions are inconsistent with prior decisions. In several cases holding that separate ownership in the wife had been established it affirmatively appeared that the husband had signed the purchase-money notes, with nothing to rebut the inference that in the event of default the creditor could reach community assets through a judgment against him.[41] And in one of the prior Supreme Court cases the vendor was not a party to the agreement that the purchase-money obligation would be paid with the wife's separate funds; the court's conclusion that the land was separate was based explicitly upon an agreement between the husband and the wife, with no mention of any participation by the vendor.[42]

The actual holding in *Gleich v. Bongio*[43] was not inconsistent with those prior decisions; only the language was. The case was one where the husband used his entire separate estate to make a down payment on the purchase price of land bought largely on credit. It was a clear case for the application of the presumption of community as to the credit portion of the purchase price. There was no agreement between the husband and the wife as to how the balance of the purchase price would be paid and no other evidence to justify a claim that the presumption of community as to the credit portion had been rebutted.

It is very doubtful, therefore, that the language quoted above will be followed. A few later civil appeals opinions have

41. Note 39 *supra*.
42. McClintic v. Midland Grocery & Dry Goods Co., 106 Tex. 32, 154 S.W.
43. 128 Tex. 606, 99 S.W.2d 881 (1937).
1157 (1913).

purported to follow it,[44] but the decisions can be justified on other grounds, and there has been at least one inconsistent holding by a court of civil appeals.[45]

It seems probable, therefore, that Texas will continue to permit the husband to lend community credit to the wife in order that she may buy property for her separate estate. An agreement between the husband and the wife at the time of the deed that the purchase-money debt will be paid out of the wife's separate estate will probably continue to be sufficient to rebut the presumption of community even though the vendor relies on the husband's promise to pay. Also, despite the language quoted above, Texas courts will doubtless continue to hold that the husband can make gifts to the wife by buying property for her on credit, including community credit.[46]

A somewhat different problem is presented in the situation where the husband attempts to rebut the presumption of community and establish separate ownership in himself of property bought on credit. From the language in *Gleich v. Bongio*[47] it appears that it would be sufficient to prove an agreement between the husband and the vendor at the time of the acquisition that the vendor will look only to the husband's separate estate for satisfaction of the obligation. But if the property is bought on the husband's general credit without any agreement of that kind, the community being reachable by the vendor to satisfy the obligation, would an agreement between the husband and the wife at the time of the acquisition that the purchase-money debt will be paid out of the husband's separate estate be effective to establish separate ownership? It could be argued that the husband can lend community credit to the wife to enable her to acquire property for her separate estate because the husband is the manager of the community[48] and that, since the wife does not have general managerial power over the community, she does not have power to bind herself by a consent to the husband's use of community credit in the acquisition of property for his separate estate.

44. Gorman v. Gorman, 180 S.W.2d 470 (Tex. Civ. App. 1944), *error dism.*; Price v. Service Bureau, 165 S.W.2d 794 (Tex. Civ. App. 1942), *error ref. w.o.m.*

45. Edsall v. Edsall, 240 S.W.2d 424 (Tex. Civ. App. 1951). The holding in Rath v. Rath, 218 S.W.2d 217 (Tex. Civ. App. 1949), also seems difficult to reconcile with the language in *Gleich v. Bongio.*

46. Goldberg v. Zellner, 235 S.W. 870 (Tex. Com. App. 1921).

47. 128 Tex. 606, 99 S.W.2d 881 (1937).

48. The management of the community during the continuance of the marriage is discussed page 139 *infra.*

At the opposite extreme it is arguable that even without the wife's consent the husband should be able to use his general credit to acquire property for his separate estate. A recent decision by a court of civil appeals permits him to do so if he has the intention at the time of the credit acquisition to discharge the obligation with his separate funds. In *Edsall v. Edsall*[49] the husband desired to sell a tract of his separate land and use the proceeds to buy a different tract, but he consummated the purchase of the new tract before the sale of the old tract, using his general credit to obtain the money to pay for the new tract. He borrowed the money from a bank, giving his promissory note, and used the money to pay for the new tract. One week later he sold the old tract and used the proceeds to discharge the note. In subsequent litigation over the separate or community character of the new tract the trier of fact found that at the time the husband obtained the loan he had the intention to sell his separate land and pay the note with the proceeds of the sale. In view of that finding, a conclusion that the borrowed money and the land bought with it belonged to the husband's separate estate was upheld.

In another civil appeals case involving a similar situation the husband secured the wife's consent to the use of community cash in the acquisition of a new tract of land for the husband's separate estate, it being agreed at the time of the purchase contract that other land belonging to the husband's separate estate would be sold and the proceeds used to pay the balance of the purchase price and to reimburse the community for community funds used in making the down payment. It was the view of the court that under the circumstances there was no impediment to effectuating the agreement of the spouses that the new acquisition should be the husband's separate property.[50]

If the husband owns an ample separate estate at the time of the credit acquisition there would be little risk of injustice to the wife in allowing the husband to use his general credit to acquire property for his separate estate provided his intention to buy for his separate estate and pay the purchase-money debt with his separate funds could be established by reliable evidence contemporaneous with the purchase. If the husband's subjective intent were allowed to control in the absence of evidence of that kind, he might be tempted to claim the best investments for his

49. 240 S.W.2d (Tex. Civ. App. 1951).
50. Rath v. Rath, 218 S.W.2d 217 (Tex. Civ. App. 1949).

separate estate and leave the others for the community. In the *Edsall* case[51] the husband's intent to borrow the money for his separate estate and repay the loan with separate funds seems not to have been manifested by any recital in the note or any other reliable evidence exactly contemporaneous with the loan, but since only a week elapsed between the borrowing of the money and the repayment of the loan with separate funds, the court's decision involved no great risk of injustice to the wife.

Agreements Between the Spouses

In Texas the general rule is that the spouses cannot change the separate or community character of property by mere agreement. That contractual disability has two aspects. They are unable to contract to change in advance the character of property to be acquired in the future; that is, they cannot by contract substitute new rules for the rules of law by which the separate or community character of property is determined.[52] And after property has been acquired they cannot change the ownership from separate to community or vice versa merely by declaring their intention in a formal transfer.[53] Property takes its character as separate or community by reason of the law operating on the facts, and if the spouses wish to change the character of property, they can do so only by providing the proper facts on which the law can operate.

That the spouses would be unable to modify the rules determining the character of property by a postnuptial contract was made clear by the language of the 1840 statute which retained the Spanish community property system upon the adoption of the English common law.[54] The same statute also indicated that prospective spouses would as a general rule be free to alter their marital property rights by a written contract entered into prior to the marriage. The statute was derived from the Louisiana Civil Code,[55] under which the general validity of antenuptial marriage contracts is well established,[56] and if the question had

---

51. Edsall v. Edsall, 240 S.W.2d 424 (Tex. Civ. App. 1951).

52. Brokaw v. Collett, 1 S.W.2d 1090 (Tex. Com. App. 1928); Cox v. Miller, 54 Tex. 16 (1880).

53. Tittle v. Tittle, 148 Tex. 102, 220 S.W.2d 637 (1949); King v. Bruce, 145 Tex. 647, 201 S.W.2d 803 (1947); Kellett v. Trice, 95 Tex. 160, 66 S.W. 51 (1902); Bruce v. Permian Royalty Co., 186 S.W.2d 686 (Tex. Civ. App. 1945), *error ref. w.o.m.*

54. Tex. Laws 1840, p. 3, 2 LAWS OF TEXAS 177 (Gammel 1898); TEX. REV. CIV. STAT. Arts. 4610-4612 (1925).

55. Arts. 2305-2310, LA. CIVIL CODE OF 1825; Arts. 2325-2330, LA. CIVIL CODE of 1870.

56. DAGGETT, THE COMMUNITY PROPERTY SYSTEM OF LOUISIANA 114 (2d ed. 1945).

been litigated at an earlier time probably the Texas courts would have been generaous in upholding the validity of such contracts. But not until the case of *Gorman v. Gause*[57] in 1933 was in contended that the contractual disability of the spouses extended to antenuptial as well as postnuptial contracts. By that time the court seems to have lost touch with the civil law tradition under which marriage contracts were encouraged and freely upheld. Landmark decisions in the early twentieth century had given sanctity to the statutory definitions of separate and community property and to the constitutional definition of the wife's separate property.[58] In *Gorman v Gause* an antenuptial contract stipulating against the community regime and providing for separate ownership of all property acquired during the marriage was held invalid as an attempt to modify in advance the character of property to be acquired. The statute only permits such contracts as are not contrary to some rule of law, it was reasoned, and "[c]ertainly the Constitution and statutes defining the status of property acquired during the marriage constitutes a 'rule of law.' "[59] Furthermore, the opinion of the commission of appeals added, if the legislature does not have the power to add to the wife's separate estate, surely the parties themselves cannot do so by antenuptial agreement.[60]

There was dictum in *Gorman v. Gause* that some antenuptial contracts affecting marital property rights could be sustained as not contravening any law of the state. For instance, it could be agreed that the husband would convey to the wife one-half of property he might acquire during the marriage by gift, devise or descent, or that a certain portion of the community estate, when acquired, would be conveyed by him to the wife and made her separate property. In such a case the property would take the character given it by law, the court reasoned, and then would be subject to being disposed of as the parties had obligated themselves to do in the antenuptial contract.[61] But as will be seen from the discussion to follow, there is reason to doubt that the types of contracts mentioned in the court's dictum could be sustained. The difficulty lies in the requirement that the character of property be determined by the law operating on the facts, not by here agreement of the parties.

57. 56 S.W.2d 855 (Tex. Com. App. 1933).

58. Arnold v. Leonard, 114 Tex. 535, 273 S.W. 799 (1925); Kellett v. Trice, 95 Tex. 160, 66 S.W. 51 (1902).

59. Gorman v. Gause, 56 S.W.2d 855, 858 (Tex. Com. App. 1933).

60. *Ibid.*

61. *Ibid.*

As an original proposition, it would seem that the legal definitions by which the separate or community character of property is to be determined were intended to fix the rights of the spouses in acquisitions from third persons and were not intended to apply to transactions between the spouses affecting the ownership of property already acquired. However, the opposite view taken in the leading case of *Kellett v. Trice*[62] is the established Texas law. The legal definitions, as modified by the ownership tracing principle, are given controlling effect in transactions between the spouses. If the husband and wife want to convert their separate property into community property or vice versa, they must do it in such a way that the transaction can be fitted into the legal definitions. The wife's separate property cannot be converted into community property by gift, it was held in *Kellett v. Trice,* because the law says that property acquired by gift is separate. But the wife's separate property can be changed by a gift into the husband's separate property[63] because the law says that property the husband receives by gift is separate; the transaction fits into the legal definition and the law operating on the fact accomplishes the desired result. The husband can convert community property into the wife's separate property by a gift to her,[64] and it seems that the wife can convert community property into the husband's separate property by a gift to him.[65]

In Texas there is no general disability on the part of the spouses to bargain with each other, and they can change the character of property if the transaction can be fitted into the legal definitions or rules for determining the separate or community character of property. For example, the wife can lend her separate money to the husband[66] and thereby change the money into community property. The manner by which the husband acquires the money is such that under the established rules of law it becomes community property; it comes to the husband during the marriage, not by gift, devise, or descent, and not in exchange for separate property. Likewise, if the wife sells separate property to the husband, receiving payment in community funds, the property would be changed into community

62. 95 Tex. 160, 66 S.W. 51 (1902).
63. Riley v. Wilson, 86 Tex. 240, 24 S.W. 394 (1893).
64. Story v. Marshall, 24 Tex. 305 (1859).
65. Stratton v. Robinson, 67 S.W. 539 (Tex. Civ. App. 1902), *error ref.*; King v. Bruce, 145 Tex. 647, 657, 201 S.W.2d 803, 809 (1937).
66. Ryan v. Ryan, 61 Tex. 473 (1884); Cadwell v. Dabney, 208 S.W.2d 127 (Tex. Civ. App. 1948), *writ of error refused, no reversible error.*

property and the money would become the wife's separate money.[67] The rule that a new acquisition takes the character of what is given in exchange for it can be applied in a situation of that kind. It should follow that by either an antenuptial or a postnuptial contract Texas spouses can turn over their separate assets to the community at an agreed valuation under an agreement that restitution of a fixed amount will be made from community assets at the dissolution of the community. The practical operation of the community property system could be greatly simplified if contracts of that kind would become a matter of common custom.

The result of applying the legal definitions to transactions between the spouses has been to defeat the intention of the spouses in certain situations without any inquiry into whether or not there was any policy justification for doing so. The desires of the spouses have been frustrated by the application of the legal definitions in two types of situations: (1) gifts to the community, and (2) partitions of community property.

Gifts to the Community

Because of the legal definitions an attempted gift by one of the spouses to the community will not be effective to vest ownership in the community.[68] Will the attempted gift have any effect? If a third person attempted to make a gift to the community, presumably each of the spouses would acquire an undivided half interest as separate property.[69] Similarly, it could have been held that an attempted gift to the community by the husband or wife would at least be effective as a gift to the other spouse of an undivided half interest as separate property, but in the cases where the deeds disclosed the intent to vest title by gift in the community it was held that the attempted transactions were entirely ineffective.[70] Where the deeds did not disclose an intent to make a gift to the community, however, a different result was reached. In *Belkin v. Ray*[71] a conveyance of the wife's separate property to a trustee and a reconveyance to both the husband and the wife were held effective to vest an undivided half interest in each of the spouses, and oral evidence of an

---

67. See Kellett v. Trice, 95 Tex. 160, 171, 66 S.W. 51, 54 (1902).

68. Tittle v. Tittle, 148 Tex. 102, 220 S.W.2d 637 (1949); Kellett v. Trice, 95 Tex. 160, 66 S.W. 51 (1902).

69. *Cf.* Bradley v. Love, 60 Tex. 472 (1883).

70. See note 68 *supra.* For an excellent review of the cases, see Note, 28 TEXAS L. REV. 275 (1949).

71. 142 Tex. 71, 176 S.W.2d 162 (1943).

intent to vest title in the community was held inadmissible for the purpose of invalidating the conveyances.

Partitions of Community Property

The application of the legal definitions to transactions between the spouses also resulted in a conclusion that the husband and wife, while living together, could not convert community property into separate property by a voluntary partition.[72] However, the decisions striking down attempted partitions came at a time when there was thought to be a need for effective transactions of that kind.[73] The statutes and the constitutional definition of the wife's separate property were therefore amended expressly to allow voluntary partitions of community property at any time the spouses desire it.[74] It is expressly provided that the rights of existing creditors cannot be prejudiced by such a partition. A writing is required, and whenever the partition involves a valuation problem it is not effective until it has been approved by the district court, a requirement imposed for the protection of the wife.

The change in the law allows only voluntary partitions. It does not affect the Texas rule that neither spouse can compel a partition of community property during the continuance of the marriage.[75]

Agreements on Permanent Separation

Permanent separation of the spouses without a divorce does not dissolve the community. The usual rules for determining the separate or community character of property continue to apply to property acquired after a separation in the absence of an agreement to the contrary.[76] And neither spouse can compel a dissolution of the community except by obtaining a dissolution of the marriage.[77]

---

72. King v. Bruce, 145 Tex. 647, 201 S.W.2d 803 (1947); Bruce v. Permian Royalty Co., 186 S.W.2d 686 (Tex. Civ. App. 1945), *error ref. w.o.m.*

73. Under the Revenue Act of 1942 there was discrimination against the residents of community property states in the application of the federal estate tax. It was thought that permitting a partition of community property would furnish a possible remedy. See Comment, 23 TEXAS L. REV. 483 (1946).

74. The Constitution was amended in 1948. See TEX. CONST. ANN. Art. 16, § 15 (Vernon, Supp. 1954). The statutory provisions were enacted in 1949. Tex. Laws 1949, c. 242, p. 450; TEX. REV. CIV. STAT. ANN. Art. 4624a (Vernon, 1951).

75. Martin v. Barnes, 17 S.W.2d 789 (Tex. Com. App. 1929).

76. Carter v. Barnes, 25 S.W.2d 606 (Tex. Com. App. 1930).

77. Martin v. Martin, 17 S.W.2d 789 (Tex. Com. App. 1929).

But the community property rules were not designed for the situation where the spouses have permanently separated and are not very appropriate in that context. There is likely to be a need at that time for an adjustment of the property rights of the spouses, and they ought to have contractual power to meet the need with a property settlement dissolving the community. Realizing the needs of the situation, the Texas courts have extended to spouses who have permanently separated or who are in the process of separating contractual powers denied to married couples who are living together. Property settlements on permanent separation are upheld if they are fair and equitable, even though they involve changing community property into separate property by a transaction that does not fit into the legal definitions.[78] One civil appeals case held invalid the part of a property settlement providing that future acquisitions would be owned by separate property, invoking the usual rule that the spouses cannot by agreement change in advance the character of property to be acquired in the future.[79] But the contrary view seems to be the prevailing view. According to the more authoritative cases a property settlement on permanent separation need not be confined to the property on hand at the time; the spouses can also validly stipulate against the continuance of the community and provide for individual ownership of property to be acquired in the future.[80]

The Statute of Frauds

An oral agreement between the spouses as to the separate or community character of land is sometimes ineffective because some statute require a writing. An oral gift of community land by the husband to wife would be ineffective because of the statute requiring conveyances of land to be in writing.[81] An oral agreement between the husband and the wife for the sale of community land to the wife as her separate property would be unenforceable because of the provision of the Statute of Frauds relating to contracts for the sale of interests in land.[82] Under the

---

78. Rains v. Wheeler, 76 Tex. 390, 13 S.W. 324 (1890); Speckels v. Kneip, 170 S.W.2d 255 (Tex. Civ. App. 1942), *error ref.*; Corrigan v. Goss, 160 S.W. 652 (Tex. Civ. App. 1913), *error ref.*

79. George v. Reynolds, 53 S.W.2d 490 (Tex. Civ. App. 1932), *error dism.*

80. Speckels v. Kneip, 170 S.W.2d 255 (Tex. Civ. App. 1942), *error ref.*; Corrigan v. Goss, 160 S.W. 652 (Tex. Civ. App. 1913), *error ref.* And see Coborn v. Collins, 244 S.W.2d 526 (Tex. Civ. App. 1951).

81. Tex. Rev. Civ. Stat. Art. 1288 (1925).

82. Tex. Rev. Civ. Stat. Art. 3995 (1925).

provisions of the Texas Trust Act enacted in 1943 an express trust of land is invalid unless there is a writing.[83]

Resulting and constructive trusts are not invalidated by the Texas Trust Act even though they are not evidenced by any instrument in writing.[84] A theory of resulting or constructive trust is often available to establish equitable ownership in one of the marital estates through the tracing of funds into the purchase although the legal title is vested in another of the estates Thus, if the wife's separate funds are used with her permission to buy land in the husband's name, the purchase price being paid in cash at the time of the deed, in the absence of further evidence the equitable ownership of the land would be in the wife as her separate property under a presumption of a purchase-money resulting trust.[85]

If the wife turns her separate funds over to the husband to be used by him in buying property in her name for her separate estate, and the husband, violating her instructions, uses the money to buy property in his own name, the wife would have a choice of remedies. She could claim separate equitable ownership of the property as the beneficiary of a constructive trust,[86] or she could claim a right to restitution of her money with an equitable lien on the property as security.[87]

But as a general rule a resulting or constructive trust must be based upon the facts at the time the land is acquired. If land is bought on credit during the marriage without any agreement at the time of the deed as to how the price is to be paid, the presumption of community is controlling and the land takes that character. The subsequent use of separate funds to pay the purchase-money debt would not change the ownership of the land;[88] it would merely give a right of reimbursement from the community in favor of the spouse whose funds were used. Furthermore, an oral agreement between the spouses at the time the debt was paid could not be effective to change the land into separate property because of the Statute of Frauds.[89] The

---

83. Tex. Laws 1943, c. 148, § 7, p. 232; Tex. Rev. Civ. Stat. Ann. Art. 7425b-2 (Vernon, 1951).

84. See Texas Trust Act, § 2; Tex. Rev. Civ. Stat. Ann. Art. 7425b-2 (Vernon, 1951).

85. See the authorities cited in note 21 *supra*.

86. Sparks v. Taylor, 99 Tex. 311, 90 S.W. 485, L.R.A.(n.s.) 381 (1906).

87. 3 Scott, Trusts 2432, § 508 (1939).

88. Goddard v. Reagan, 28 S.W. 352 (Tex. Civ. App. 1894).

89. Allen v. Allen, 101 Tex. 362, 107 S.W. 528 (1908).

transaction would be classified as an attempted sale or conveyance of land from the community to the separate estate.

Where the deed by which the property is acquired reserves an express vendor's lien, however, there is a problem as to the effect of the concept that the vendor retains legal title until the lien has been discharged. In *Johnson v. Smith,*[90] decided prior to the Texas Trust Act, the Supreme Court held that an oral trust of land was enforceable when it had been declared by the vendee subsequent to the deed but contemporaneously with the discharge of an express vendor's lien, relying on the concept that the legal title does not pass to the vendee until the express vendor's lien is discharged. Using the same concept, in a case where the husband used the wife's separate funds to discharge a vendor's lien under an oral agreement between the spouses that the wife would have a separate equitable interest in the property, a court of civil appeals allowed the wife to establish *pro tanto* equitable ownership on a theory of an enforceable express trust.[91] The Trust Act would now prevent the enforcement of an oral express trust of land even if declared contemporaneously with a transfer of legal title, but it is possible that in a case similar to *Johnson v. Smith* arising out of facts occurring subsequent to the Trust Act the courts might now find that a constructive trust to prevent unjust enrichment could be justified by invoking the same title concept used in that case. But the reasoning in *Johnson v. Smith* has never been entirely consistent with the refusal to allow a purchase-money resulting trust in cases where funds of one person have been used to discharge a vendor's lien on land belonging to another;[92] and in order to avoid further disturbance from an anomalous holding, *Johson v. Smith* should be relegated to the limbo of obsolete precedents by refusing to extend it beyond the context of express oral trusts.

The Parol Evidence Rule

Where property is conveyed during the marriage to either the husband or the wife or both, it is presumed to be community property in the absence of any recitals in the deed indicating separate ownership.[93] Frequently, however, the deed to one of the spouses will contain recitals affecting ownership. The extent

90. 115 Tex. 193, 280 S.W. 158 (1926).

91. Walkup v. Stone, 73 S.W.2d 912 (Tex. Civ. App. 1934), *error dism.*

92. Smith v. Buss, 135 Tex. 566, 144 S.W.2d 529 (1940); Oury v. Saunders, 77 Tex. 278, 13 S.W. 1030 (1890); Lusk v. Palmer, 87 S.W.2d 790 (Tex. Civ. App. 1935).

93. SPEER, LAW OF MARTIAL RIGHTS IN TEXAS § 352 (3d ed. 1929).

of the effect depends upon what the recitals are and how they come to be inserted in the deed. In some cases the recitals would operate to rebut the presumption of community and raise a presumption of separate ownership.[94] In some cases the ownership of the property depends entirely on the recitals because of the applicability of the parol evidence rule.

The parol evidence rule has long been applied to a conveyance by one spouse to the other. When a deed from the husband recited that the property was conveyed to the wife "for her separate use and benefit," it was held that the recital was contractual and the parol evidence rule prevented enforcement of an oral agreement by the wife to hold title in trust for the community.[95] According to the language of the opinions, a recital in a deed from the husband that the property is conveyed to the wife as her separate property would be given the same effect.

Where the husband buys property with community funds, taking title in the wife's name through a deed which recites that the conveyance is to the wife as her separate property, there has been some difference of opinion as to the applicability of the parol evidence rule. According to the earlier authorities the parol evidence rule would not be applicable to exclude evidence of an agreement with the wife that the property would belong to the community.[96] The rule would not apply, it has been said, because the husband was not a party to the deed.[97] A different view was taken, however, in *Lindsay v. Clayman,*[98] a recent decision by the Texas Supreme Court. Where the husband was a party to the transaction, although not a party to the deed,[99] the parol evidence rule was applied to prevent proof of an oral agreement that the wife was to hold legal title in trust for the community, where the recitals of the deed inserted at the husband's direction stated that the property was conveyed to the wife as her separate property.

---

94. McCutchen v. Purinton, 84 Tex. 603, 19 S.W. 710 (1892).

95. McKivett v. McKivett, 123 Tex. 298, 70 S.W.2d 694 (1934); Kahn v. Kahn, 94 Tex. 114, 58 S.W. 825 (1900).

96. McCoy v. Texon Royalty Co., 124 S.W.2d 877 (Tex. Civ. App. 1939), *error dism., judgm. cor.*; see McCutchen v. Purinton, 84 Tex. 603, 604, 19 S.W. 710, 711 (1892).

97. See Pointer v. Pointer, 197 S.W.2d 504, 505 (Tex. Civ. App. 1946).

98. 151 Tex. 593, 254 S.W.2d 777 (1952).

99. The husband was a party to a written contract to buy the property, which also contained a recital that the property was to be the wife's separate property, but the court did not seem to regard that fact as decisive. The court relied upon and quoted with approval from Loeb v. Wilhite, 224 S.W.2d 343 (Tex. Civ. App. 1949), *error ref. n.r.e.*, where a similar holding was one of several grounds of decision, and the element of the husband's being a party to the contract to buy was not present in the *Loeb* case.

The holding in that case seems sound as applied to cases where both spouses are active parties to the transaction, the separate or community character of the property depends upon the intention of the spouses, and the recitals in the deed can properly be regarded as a written integration of an agreement between them as to the character of the property. But those elements are not present in all cases. Of course a spouse should not be bound by a recital of which he did not know and to which he did not consent. And even if there is knowledge and failure to object, it might be improper to regard the writing as an integration of an agreement between the spouses. For example, if the husband, using community funds under his management to buy property, has the draftsman insert in the deed a recital that the property is conveyed to the husband as his separate property, evidence that the wife knew of the recital and made no objection would probably not be sufficient to bind the wife by an application of the parol evidence rule. It could be said that she was not a party to the transaction, or that the writing could not properly be regarded as an integration of an agreement between her and her husband that the property was to be the husband's separate property.

Even where both spouses are parties to the transaction, the parol evidence rule would not prevent extrinsic evidence to show that a deed contained incorrect factual recitals. It could be shown, for example, that a deed was actually a deed of gift although it recited that a valuable consideration was being paid for the property.[100] Or a recital that separate funds had been used in buying property could be contradicted by evidence that community funds were used.[101]

Control and Management During the Marriage

Under the Texas law prior to 1913 there was unified management of all three of the marital estates. The husband had the management of his own separate property, the wife's separate property,[102] and the community property.[103] It was necessary for the wife to join in conveyances of her separate land and of the homestead,[104] and her assent was necessary to dispositions

---

100. Bradley v. Love, 60 Tex. 472 (1883).
101. See McCutchen v. Purinton, 84 Tex. 603, 604, 19 S.W. 710, 711 (1892).
102. Tex. Rev. Civ. Stat. Art. 4621 (1911).
103. *Id.* Art. 4622.
104. It is still necessary, as a general rule, that both husband and wife join in a conveyance of the wife's separate land or of the homestead. Tex. Rev. Civ. Stat. Ann. Arts. 4614, 4617, 4618 (Vernon, 1951).

of her separate personalty,[105] but the general rule was that the husband had sole management and control of all of the property.

Since he was the manager of the community, the law gave to the husband full authority to bind the community estate by incurring debts. The debts incurred by him during the marriage were normally classified as community debts,[106] although the creditor could levy upon the husband's separate property as well as upon community property.[107] The corpus of the wife's separate estate could not be reached to satisfy debts incurred by the husband,[108] although the community revenue from her property could be reached.

The giving of sole managerial power to the husband was properly accompanied by a lack of contractual power in the wife. If the husband's control of the community estate was to be effective, he had to have control over the incurring of obligations as well as over the cash expenditures. Until early in the twentieth century the wife had no power to bind herself or the husband by ordinary contracts; the only debts for which the wife could be held liable were those for the reasonable value of necessaries furnished to her for herself and her children and reasonable expenses incurred for the benefit of her separate property.[109]

The development of modern ideas as to the proper status of married women made necessary some change in the Texas law as to management of the marital estates. One change was made in 1911; a statute enacted that year provided a method by which a married woman could have her disabilities of coverture removed and be declared a *feme sole* for mercantile and trading purposes, thereby acquiring full contractual power.[110] The joinder of the husband in a petition to the district court was required, and it was necessary for the court to determine whether or not the removal of the disability would be to the wife's best interest. The statute made clear that upon issuance of the order removing the disability the wife was to have full contractual power and that her separate estate was to be liable for debts incurred by her, but did not make plain the extent to which the

---

105. See Bledsoe v. Fitts, 105 S.W. 1142, 1145 (Tex. Civ. App. 1907), *error ref.*

106. Speer, Law of Martial Rights in Texas § 382 (3d ed. 1929).

107. See Moody v. Smoot, 78 Tex. 119, 123, 14 S.W. 285, 286 (1890).

108. Le Gierse & Co. v. Moore, 59 Tex. 470 (1883).

109. Tex. Rev. Civ. Stat. Arts. 4624, 4625 (1911); Harris v. Williams, 44 Tex. 124 (1875).

110. Tex. Laws 1911, c. 52, p. 92, 15 Laws of Texas 92 (Gammel 1911).

order would be effective to give her other managerial powers over her separate estate or the community revenue produced by her property and efforts. The provisions of the 1911 statute were carried into the 1925 revision and are still in effect,[111] but the judicial decisions involving the statute have not been illuminating.[112]

A radical change in the allocation of managerial power between the spouses came in 1913. With a statute enacted that year Texas embarked on an experiment in divided management of community property.[113] One way of giving the wife an equal share in management would have been to put the community estate under the joint control of the spouses, allowing each of them an equal voice as in the case of ordinary partnerships. Instead of that Texas chose to divide the management, giving each spouse exclusive control over a part of the community estate. The division was evidently intended to be along the same natural lines that ownership is divided in the modified common law states. In addition to her separate property the wife was to manage the revenue from her property and her own earnings; the husband was to continue as manager of his separate property, the revenue from it, and his earnings.

In order to make effective the wife's exclusive control it was necessary to free the types of community under her management from liability for debts incurred by the husband. The creditors of the husband were to look only to his separate property and the part of the community estate under his management; the creditors of the wife were to look only to her separate property and the part of the community under her management.

The 1913 scheme seems basically sound. In determining the managerial authority of the spouses and the rights of third persons dealing with them, the law was to be as simple as is the determination of ownership in the non-community states. For those purposes there was to be no need to distinguish between income and principal or between income produced by property and income produced by personal efforts. It was to be comparatively easy to determine which spouse had authority to act, and

---

111. The statute, as amended in 1937, now appears as TEX. REV. CIV. STAT. ANN. Art. 4626 (Vernon, 1951).

112. It has even been held that the 1911 statute was intended to impose restrictions on powers the legislature did not grant to married women until 1913, apparently due to a failure to notice that the original statute antedated by two years the grant of powers contained in the 1913 statute. Hirshfeld & Co. v. Evans, 127 Tex. 254, 93 S.W.2d 148 (1936).

113. Tex. Laws 1913, c. 32, p. 61; 16 LAWS OF TEXAS 61 (Gammel 1914).

the authority was to be where the spouses and people dealing with them would normally expect it to be. The individuality of each spouse was fully recognized by the award of managerial power. At the same time the advantages of a community property system were retained by keeping unchanged the laws affecting beneficial ownership. Being equal owners of community property, the spouses would continue to have an equal interest in the financial success of the marriage and to be bound together by the knowledge that they were working together toward a common goal. They were still to be equal partners, but instead of one partnership there were to be two, one managed by the husband and one managed by the wife.

But the 1913 plan as outlined above was never quite put into effect. An important part of the plan was a grant of full contractual power to the wife, a power she would obviously need in order to be an effective manager of her separate property and the part of the community put under her control. However, the governor objected to the giving of contractual power to married women, and the bill as finally passed did not contain any express grant of contractual power.[114] That defect in the law has been partially cured by judicial decision. Considerable contractual power in married women has been derived by implication from the express grant of power to manage and control property,[115] but the decisions have not been uniformly liberal[116] and Texas married women are still handicapped as managers by serious restrictions on their contractual powers and by large areas of uncertainty and confusion in the law as to the extent of their powers.

There was also some lack of clarity in defining the part of the community estate committed to the wife's management. The types of community property that were to be liable for the wife's debts were described as "the personal earnings of the wife, and the income, rents and revenues from her separate property."[117] But in describing the types of community that were to be under the wife's exclusive control and exempt from the

---

114. A summary of the legislative history of the 1913 act appears in Red River National Bank v. Ferguson, 109 Tex. 287, 293, 206 S.W. 923, 926 (1918).

115. Levin v. Jeffers, 122 Tex. 83, 52 S.W.2d 81 (1932); Cauble v. Beaver-Electra Refining Co., 115 Tex. 1, 274 S.W. 120 (1925); Gohlman, Lester & Co. v. Whittle, 114 Tex. 548, 273 S.W. 808 (1925); Whitney Hardware Co. v. McMahan, 111 Tex. 242, 231 S.W. 694 (1921).

116. Grant Lumber Co. v. Jones, 139 Tex. 647, 164 S.W.2d 1019, (1942): Hirshfeld & Co. v. Evans, 127 Tex. 254, 93 S.W.2d 148 (1936).

117. Tex. Laws 1913, c. 32, p. 61, 16 Laws of Texas 61 (Gammel 1914).

husband's debts, the statute listed the wife's personal earnings and only certain varieties of income from her separate property; not all varieties of income from her separate property were included. The list included rent from the wife's separate real estate, interest on her bonds and notes, and dividends on her stock,[118] but said nothing as to interest from her separate savings account, revenue from the leasing of her separate chattels, income from her separate business, or the receipts from a sale of crops grown on her separate land. The fact that all of the revenue from the wife's separate realty or personalty was made subject to her debts strongly indicates that the listing of specific items was intended to be illustrative, not exclusive, but that question has not yet ben entirely settled.

For a time, there were cases holding that the listing was exclusive. In *First National Bank of Lewisville v. Davis*[119] it was held that the husband had power to mortgage cotton grown on the wife's separate land to secure a community debt incurred by him because the cotton could not be classified as "rent from the wife's real estate." In several cases the husband's creditors were allowed to reach the revenue from the wife's separate business,[120] apparently without any consideration being given to the possibility that revenue of that kind may have been put under the wife's exclusive contrlo and exempted from the husband's debts by the provisions of the 1913 statute. In a civil appeals case it was reasoned that revenue from the wife's separate copywright could be reached by the husband's creditors because it was not included in the list of exempted items.[121]

But the recent decision in *Bearden v. Knight*[122] furnishes strong support for the opposite view. In that scholarly opinion the Supreme Court looked back to the general plan of the 1913 statute and concluded that *First National Bank of Lewisville v. Davis*[123] should be overruled. The exact holding was that all of the revenue from the wife's separate land, whether technically classifiable as rent or not, is under the wife's exclusive management and free from liability for the husband's debts. The opinion was confined to revenue from land, for that was the problem

118. *Ibid.*

119. 5 S.W. 2d 753 (Tex. Com. App. 1928), overruled by Bearden v. Knight, 149 Tex. 108, 228 S.W.2d 837 (1950).

120. Hardee v. Vincent, 136 Tex. 99, 147 S.W.2d 1072 (1941); Walker-Smith Co. v. Coker, 176 S.W.2d 1002 (Tex. Civ. App. 1943), *error ref. w.o.m.*

121. Simmons v. Sikes, 56 S.W.2d 193 (Tex. Civ. App. 1932), *error dism.*

122. 149 Tex. 108, 228 S.W.2d 837 (1950).

123. 5 S.W.2d 753 (Tex. Com. App. 1928).

before the court, but there is reasoning in the opinion that would be equally applicable to revenue from personalty. Hence there is still doubt as to revenue from personalty of types not specifically listed, but it seems entirely possible that the Supreme Court will now find that the statutory listing is not exclusive but illustrative, and that the present statutes exempt from the husband's debts and commit to the wife's exclusive management all varieties of income from her separate property, real and personal.

An omission in the 1925 revision of the Texas statutes has further complicated the problem of determining the extent of the wife's managerial powers over community property. The act of 1913 expressly gave to the wife exclusive power to manage her personal earnings and the listed varieties of income from her separate property, in addition to exempting those items from the debts of the husband. In the 1925 revision the express provision giving the wife power to manage those items was omitted, although the provision exempting them from the husband's debts was retained[124] along with the provision subjecting the wife's personal earnings and the revenue from her separate property to liability for debts incurred by the wife.[125] In the text usually relied on by courts and lawyers in Texas it is concluded that the 1913 plan by which the wife was given management of part of the community estate was abandoned with the 1925 revision,[126] but there is ample internal evidence in the statutes to show that the legislature did not so intend. The exemption of the listed items from the husband's debts was continued,[127] although the only purpose of the exemption was to make effective the wife's control. The provision subjecting the wife's earnings and the revenue from her separate property to liability for her debts, which also was continued in the 1925 revision,[128] can be justified only on the ground that the wife was intended to have control over that part of the community estate. The omission in the 1925 revision can be explained in part by the attempted change in the definitions of separate property that occurred in 1917 and 1921,[129] the new definitions being carried into the 1925 revision[130] before the decision in *Arnold v. Leonard*[131] established the un-

124. Tex. Rev. Civ. Stat. Art. 4616 (1925).
125. *Id.* Art. 4623.
126. Speer, Law of Marital Rights in Texas § 347 (3d ed. 1929).
127. Tex. Rev. Civ. Stat. Art. 4616 (1925).
128. *Id.* Art. 4623.
129. Tex. Laws 1917, c. 194, p. 436, 17 Laws of Texas 436 (Gammel 1917); Tex. Laws, c. 130, p. 251, 20 Laws of Texas 251 (Gammel 1920).
130. Tex. Rev. Civ. Stat. Arts. 4613, 4614 (1925).
131. 114 Tex. 535, 273 S.W. 799 (1925).

constitutionality of the attempted change. At the time the 1925 revision was prepared, it must have been thought that it would be unnecessary to give the wife express power to manager the rent from her real estate, the interest from her bonds and notes, and the dividends from her stock, because she was being given express power to manage her separate estate, and all of those items were made part of her separate estate by the ned definitions which put all of the revenue from her separate property into the separate estate.[132] The omission of the express provision giving the wife poper to manage her personal earnings cannot be explained in that way, but in view of the other provisions from the 1913 act that survived the revision it seems plain that the omission of that provision was inadvertent. However, in the case of *Porrorff v. J. D. Adams Co.*[133] the court of civil appeals relied upon the omission in the 1925 revision for the proposition that the wife no longer has power to manage her personal earnings. The recent decision in *Bearden v. Knight*[134] establishes that no significance is to be given the omission of the express provision giving the wife power to manage the rent from her real estate, and in view of the court's scholarly review in that opinion of the entire statutory history of the control and exemption provisions, it is possible that *Pottorff v. J. D. Adams Co.* will be overruled and the wife's managerial authority over her earnings restored to her without the necessity for an amendment of the statutes.

There is another serious problem as to whether property under the wife's management will remain under her management after a change in form. If the wife accumulates the rent from her separate estate and uses it to buy additional land, does the wife have the management of the new community land, or does it come under the husband's management? The only answer consistent with the division of management contemplated by the 1913 plan is that the new acquisition comes under the wife's management. If there is to be an estate under the wife's exclusive management, she must be able to invest and reinvest the funds of that estate without interference from the husband or his creditors. But under the present Texas authorities the answer to the question is far from clear.

The uncertainty is caused by the holding in *Strickland v.*

---

132. Tex. Rev. Civ. Stat. Art. 4614 (1925).
133. 70 S.W.2d 745 (Tex. Civ. App. 1934), *error ref.*
134. 149 Tex. 108, 228 S.W.2d 837 (1950).

Wester.[135] In that case the Texas Supreme Court held that when the wife invests her earnings in land, the exemption from the husband's debts comes to an end and the husband's creditors can reach the land. The opinion offered no explanation for that conclusion; it was merely stated that the question had received careful consideration. Did the court give consideration to the fact that the exemption from the husband's debts was an integral part of a plan for dividing the management of the community estate between the spouses, a plan under which the wife was to have exclusive control of her personal earnings? Or was the court thinking of the exemption of the wife's earnings as something comparable to the exemption of such items as current wages and the tools of a trade? Did the court mean to imply that when the wife is given the exclusive power to manage community funds derived from certain sources, her power ends as soon as the funds are invested in other property, or did the court assume that the omission in the 1925 revision had terminated the wife's power to manage her personal earnings? The opinion leaves those questions unanswered.

In the prior case of *Hawkins v. Britton State Bank*[136] it had been held that the wife had exclusive management of hay-harvesting equipment bought with rent from her separate farm; the husband had no power to convey the equipment to his creditors in payment of debts owed by him. The fact that the rent from the wife's separate land was under her exclusive management was deemed sufficient to justify the conclusion that the equipment bought with the rent was also under the wife's exclusive management, free from the debts and control of the husband. The *Hawkins* case was not questioned in the *Strickland* case and is still a respected precedent.[137]

The *Hawkins* and *Strickland* cases are not in direct conflict. They could be reconciled by distinguishing between the wife's personal earnings and revenue from separate property, confining the *Strickland* case to situations where the wife's personal earnings are traced into other property. They could also be reconciled by confining the *Hawkins* case within narrow limits. If the wife is to manage her separate farm effectively, she must have control not only of the receipts from the operation of the farm but also of the farm equipment bought for use on the farm.

135. 131 Tx. 23, 112 S.W.2d 1047 (1938).

136. 122 Tex. 69, 52 S.W.2d 243 (1932).

137. In Bearden v. Knight, 149 Tex. 108, 228 S.W.2d 837 (1950), the *Hawkins* case was relied on as a controlling precedent.

The *Hawkins* case could be justified on the ground that giving the wife exclusive management of the hay-harvesting equipment was necessary in order to make effective the grant to her of exclusive authority to manage her separate farm. But neither way of reconciling the two cases will give full effect to the purposes of the 1913 statute. The holding in the *Strickland* case is inconsistent with the purposes of the 1913 plan and should be overruled.

Succession on Death

On the death of a spouse intestate, the decedent's half of the community property is inherited by the decedent's children or their descendants.[138] A provision that the surviving spouse is entitled to the other half appears in the statute of descent, but the survivor does not receive his half by inheritance; it is settled that each spouse owns half of the community property during the marriage and that on the death of one spouse the other simply continues to own a half interest.[139] If there are no children or descendants surviving the decedent, the decedent's half of the community is inherited by the surviving spouse.[140]

When there are children or descendants, the surviving spouse inherits one-third of the intestate's separate personalty and a life estate in one-third of the separate land.[141] If there are no children or descendants, the surviving spouse inherits all of the separate personalty and either one-half or all of the separate land, depending on whether or not the decedent leaves a surviving parent, brother, or sister.[142]

Except for certain allowances[143] and the homestead rights of a surviving spouse and minor children,[144] under Texas law each spouse has complete testamentary power over his or her half of community property and over all of his or her separate property.[145]

Division on Divorce

In Texas the court has a great amount of discretion in dividing the property of the spouses on divorce. At that time the

138. Tex. Rev. Civ. Stat. Art. 2578 (1925).
139. Jones v. State, 5 S.W.2d 973 (Tex. Com. App. 1928).
140. Tex. Rev. Civ. Stat. Art. 2578 (1925).
141. *Id.* Art. 2571.
142. *Ibid.*
143. As to the allowance for a year's support to the widow and minor children, see Tex. Rev. Civ. Stat. Ann. Arts. 3476-3484 (Vernon, 1952). As to the allowances in lieu of homestead and other exempt property, see *id.* Arts. 3485-3495.
144. Tex. Const. Art. 16, § 52 (1876).
145. Speer, Law of Marital Rights in Texas § 315 (3d ed. 1929).

court may do more than merely determine questions of ownership and act on claims for reimbursement. According to the statute, the court can make such division of the property of the spouses as it deems just and right, subject to the limitation that title to real estate must not be divested.[146] Subject to that limitation the court can take the property of one spouse and award it to the other if circumstances make it just to do so. The division of the community property need not be equal if the circumstances will justify awarding more than half of the community to one of the spouses.[147] The power of the court extends to the separate property of both spouses, as well as to the community property.[148]

The prohibition against divesting title to real estate is an important limitation on the divorce court's power, but the statute has been so construed as to allow the court significant power over land. The awarding to one spouse of as much as a life estate in the separate land of the other is not regarded as divesting title to real estate.[149] Furthermore, the court can impose a trust on the land of one spouse, awarding to the other a right to receive the income for life.[150]

The prohibition against divesting title to land applies to community land as well as to separate land.[151] But a partition is not a divesting of title within the meaning of the statute even though a sale is necessary to effect the partition.[152] According to some cases the divorce court may partition the community by awarding all of the community land to one spouse if the other is compensated for his or her interest with money or other assets,[153] but there is conflict, other cases holding that such a decree divests title to land in violation of the statute.[154]

It has been said that the trial court's discretion in dividing

---

146. TEX. REV. CIV. STAT. Art. 4638 (1925).

147. Trimble v. Trimble, 15 Tex. 19 (1855).

148. Hedtke v. Hedtke, 112 Tex. 404, 248 S.W. 21 (1923).

149. *Ibid.*

150. Keton v. Clark, 67 S.W.2d 437 (Tex. App. 1933), *error ref.*; see *Ex parte* Scott, 133 Tex. 1, 14, 123 S.W.2d 306, 313 (1939).

151. Reasonover v. Reasonover, 59 S.W.2d 887 (Tex. Civ. App. 1933).

152. Scannell v. Scannell, 117 S.W.2d 538 (Tex. Civ. App. 1938), upheld a sale of land to one of the spouses as a permissible method of effecting a partition.

153. Simons v. Simons, 23 Tex. 344 (1859); Walker v. Walker, 231 S.W.2d 905 (Tex. Civ. App. 1950); Daniel v. Daniel, 30 S.W.2d 801 (Tex. Civ. App. 1930).

154. Hartman v. Hartman, 253 S.W.2d 480 (Tex. Civ. App. 1952); Lewis v. Lewis, 179 S.W.2d 594 (Tex. Civ. App. 1944); O'Neil v. O'Neil, 77 S.W.2d 554 (Tex. Civ. App. 1934), *error dism.*

property on divorce will not be reversed on appeal in the absence of an abuse of discretion.[155] But the trial court must not act arbitrarily, and must give consideration to the property rights of both spouses. If there are no circumstances to justify a different disposition the court should award the property according to ownership, dividing the community equally between the spouses.[156]

Various factors can justify an unequal division. The financial needs of the members of the family are of the greatest importance. Permanent alimony is not allowed in Texas, but if there is enough property on hand at the time of the divorce the court can provide an effective substitute.[157] The court would usually be concerned with providing for the future support of the wife, but if the husband is the one who needs it the divorce court can provide for his support out of the wife's property.[158] If there are dependent children, their need for support can be taken into consideration in dividing the property,[159] but the court is not confined to the property on hand in making provision for the support of children under eighteen.[160] Other factors than need for support can be taken into consideration. The courts have never attempted to formulate a complete list. It is proper for the divorce court to consider the benefits that the innocent spouse would have received from a continuance of the marriage, the Supreme Court has said;[161] at least to that extent it is proper to consider who was at fault in the failure of the marriage. In one case the fact that the wife had acquired her wealth by gift from the husband was deemed significant.[162]

---

155. Hedtke v. Hedtke, 112 Tex. 404, 248 S.W. 21 (1923); Keton v. Clark, 67 S.W.2d 437 (Tex. Civ. App. 1933), *error ref.*

156. Reasonover v. Reasonover, 59 S.W.2d 887 (Tex. Civ. App. 1933).

157. Hedtke v. Hedtke, 112 Tex. 404, 248 S.W. 21 (1923); Keton v. Clark, 67 S.W.2d 437 (Tex. Civ. App. 1933), *error ref.*

158. Fitts v. Fitts, 14 Tex. 443 (1855).

159. Rice v. Rice, 21 Tex. 58 (1858).

160. See TEX. REV. CIV. STAT. ANN. Art. 4639a (Vernon, Supp. 1954).

161. Hedtke v. Hedkte, 112 Tex. 404, 409, 248 S.W. 21, 22 (1923).

162. Fitts v. Fitts, 14 Tex. 443 (1855).

The Community Property Law In Washington*

Harry M. Cross†

I. Introduction

Statutory Pattern

Washington's present community property laws have, in basic pattern, remained unchanged since the enactment in territorial days of the Code of 1881.[1] The statutes, in two separate sections,[2] provide that each spouse owns, separately, all property owned at the time of marriage, any property thereafter acquired gratuitously, and the rents, issues and profits of separate property. Property acquired after marriage otherwise than as provided in the two separate property sections is community property.[3]

The husband has management of all community property and inter vivos power to dispose of the community personal property[4] but cannot directly convey or encumber community

---

* Statutory citations, for the most part, are to the *Revised Code of Washington* (1953 format) for convenience, even though there are changes in the code from the phraseology of the session laws. Most of the statutes material to community property problems are included in Chapter 26.16 of that code.

In the interests of brevity the writer has usually confined case citations to the recent or to older illustrative cases rather than tracing the development of any paricular principle through the cases. It is believed that this will fairly demonstrate the current position of the Washington Supreme Court, and as one of the members of that court explained in suggesting citations in briefs only to the most recent case, it can be assumed that the reader has access to the digests and citators. Citations are further limited to Washington cases for two reasons: (1) this discussion is designed to present a summary picture of Washington's community property law, only; and (2) in many instances the Washington Supreme Court has limited its reported consideration to Washington cases, an approach frequently inevitable currently because a present problem may be the result of earlier developments peculiar to the Washington cases.

† Professor of Law, University of Washington.

1. The statutory pattern and its development are briefly summarized in Hill, *Early Washington Marital Property Statutes,* 14 Wash. L. Rev. 118 (1939).

2. Wash. Rev. Code 26.16.010, 26.15.020 (1953).

3. *Id.* at 26.16.030.

4. *Ibid.*

real property without the wife's joinder in the appropriate instrument.[5] Each spouse may devise or bequeath his or her half of the community property,[6] and may deal in all respects with his or her separate property as if unmarried.[7]

Man or Woman Unmarried

If property is acquired while a man and woman are living together, it can be community property only if the acquirer and the other are husband and wife.[8] The interests of the two if unmarried are necessarily separate property, but the resolution of the problems of ownershp between the two can be affected by the meretricious or innocent character of the relationship.[9] In the absence of evidence to the contrary the parties in a meretricious relationship will be presumed to have intended ownership to be where title is and no trust will be raised for the other.[10] The presumption is not conclusive.[11] If, however, it is the belief of one or both that they are validly married, the court will exercise an equity power to protect the innocent party or parties in determining the ownership,[12] but there is no application of a putative wife doctrine. When both persons participate in the acquistion (in a business or earning sense, not merely in a community property, husband and wife sense), the existence of any meretricious relationship is disregarded and their rights are resolved under ordinary partnership or joint venture principles.[13]

Time of Marriage

In most situations, of course, the two persons are husband and wife and inherently there is a preliminary problem of proof that they were married at the time of acquisition of the assets involved in the controversy.[14] It is not necessary, however, that there be direct testimony of the time of marriage.[15]

---

5. *Id.* at 26.16.040.
6. *Id.* at 11.04.060.
7. *Id.* at 26.16.010, 26.16.020.
8. Poole v. Schrichte, 39 Wash.2d 558, 236 P.2d 1044 (1951).
9. *Ibid.*
10. Walberg v. Mattson, 38 Wash.2d 808, 232 P.2d 827 (1951); Creasman v. Boyle, 31 Wash.2d 345, 196 P.2d 835 (1948).
11. *Ibid.*
12. Poole v. Schrichte, 39 Wash.2d 558, 236 P.2d 1044 (1951).
13. Poole v. Schrichte, 39 Wash.2d 558, 236 P.2d 1044 (1951); Hynes v. Hynes, 28 Wash.2d 660, 184 P.2d 68 (1947).
14. Chase v. Carney, 199 Wash. 99, 90 P.2d 286 (1939).
15. Proff v. Maley, 14 Wash.2d 287, 128 P.2d 330 (1942).

II. Management and Voluntary Disposition

For problems of management or voluntary disposition of community real and personal property, the court has evolved uniform rules. The husband is the statutory agent to manage all community property and to dispose of community personal property. Despite the language as to personal property that the husband has "a like power of disposition as he has of his separate personal property, except that he shall not devise by will more than one-half thereof"[16] the rule is settled that he must act for the community interests in a business sense.[17] Consequently the husband cannot make effective gifts of the community personal property without the consent of the wife.[18] The husband is not required to be a good manager; so long as he exercises his discretion in the community interest as he sees it, the wife is without power to frustrate his acts.[19] While the husband's management power is the same over all community property, he cannot dispose of community real property unless the wife participates in the transaction.[20] Basically the wife has neither a managing or disposing power over community property of any kind,[21] but the court has recognized an "emergency power" in the wife[22] and has recognized that the husband may either directly or through estoppel or ratification make her the agent to conduct community affairs or transactions.[23]

Two problems then arise as to any particular transaction: (1) whether the subject matter is real or personal property, and (2) whether the transaction is within the community "business" agency of the actor.[24]

Real or Personal Property

Determination of whether the interest is real or personal property is made in accordance with historical concepts, and

16. Wash. Rev. Code 26.16.030 (1953).
17. Sun Life Assurance Co. v. Outler, 172 Wash. 540, 20 P.2d 1110 (1933).
18. Marston v. Rue, 92 Wash. 129, 159 Pac. 111 (1916).
19. Hanley v. Most, 9 Wash.2d 429, 115 P.2d 933 (1941); Bellingham Motors Corp. v. Lindberg, 126 Wash. 684, 219 Pac. 19 (1923).
20. The statutory method of participation is joinder in the appropriate instrument, Wash. Rev. Code 26.16.040 (1953), but the case law recognizes her "participation" through estoppel or ratification.
21. Feise v. Mueller, 41 Wash.2d 409, 249 P.2d 376 (1952); McAlpine v. Kohler & Chase, 96 Wash. 146, 164 Pac. 755 (1917).
22. Marston v. Rue, 92 Wash. 129, 159 Pac. 111 (1916).
23. Lucci v. Lucci, 2 Wash.2d 624, 99 P.2d 393 (1940); Short v. Dolling, 178 Wash. 467, 35 P.2d 82 (1934).
24. Much of the discussion of this problem appears in Part V *infra*.

the court has held that the statute[25] requires the wife's joinder in execution of term leases,[26] grants of easements and profits,[27] mortgages of land,[28] as well as conveyances of or contracts to convey the fee estate.[29] On the other hand the leasehold interest is characterized as personal property and can be assigned or surrendered by the husband acting alone.[30] The statute is construed, however, to be for the protection of the wife, and the third person cannot disaffirm merely because the wife has not joined.[31] He must instead first request execution of the instrument by the wife.[32] The husband, as manager, apparently can put a person in possession of community land as periodic tenant.[33] If the wife has not joined in the conveyance or encumbrance the transaction can be nullified against the wishes of the transferee[34] unless the wife has ratified the husband's acts or has estopped herself to deny their effectiveness.[35]

The classification of the purchaser's interest under a real estate contract is not clear. Reasoning from the notorious statement in *Ashford v. Reese*[36] that the purchaser in an executory forfeitable contract has no interest, legal or equitable, in the land, it can be concluded that whatever the relationship might be the purchaser's interest at least is not real property, and hence

---

25. WASH. REV. CODE 26.16.040 (1953).

26. Bowman v. Hardgrove, 200 Wash. 78, 93 P.2d 303 (1939); Kaufman v. Perkins, 114 Wash. 40, 194 Pac. 802 (1921).

27. Northwestern Lumber Co. v. Bloom, 135 Wash. 195, 237 Pac. 295 (1925).

28. Campbell v. Sandy, 190 Wash. 528, 69 P.2d 808 (1937).

29. Colpe v. Lindblom, 57 Wash. 106, 106 Pac. 634 (1910). But the husband's managing power may extend to modification of the provisions of a previously executed contract to sell. See *In re* Horse Heaven Irrigation District, 19 Wash.2d 89, 95, 141 P.2d 400, 402 (1943).

In Geoghegen v. Dever, 30 Wash.2d 877, 194 P.2d 397 (1948), the court announced the rather startling proposition that a real estate broker employed by the husband could not secure a judgment for his commission against community property because the wife had not joined in the commission contract. To hold otherwise, the court felt, would permit the husband alone to encumber the real estate contrary to the provisions of the statute. McGlauflin v. Merriam, 7 Wash. 111, 34 Pac. 561 (1893) was followed despite an earlier statement in Philips & Co. v. Bergman, 130 Wash. 346, 227 Pac. 321 (1924) that the *McGlauflin* case apparently had been overruled *sub silentio.*

30. Gabrielson v. Swinburne, 184 Wash. 242, 51 P.2d 368 (1935); Tibbals v. Iffland, 10 Wash. 451, 39 Pac. 102 (1895).

31. Stabbert v. Atlas Imperial Diesel Engine Co., 39 Wash.2d 789, 238 P.2d 1212 (1951).

32. Colcord v. Leddy, 4 Wash. 791, 31 Pac. 320 (1892).

33. *Cf.* Ryan v. Lambert, 49 Wash. 649, 96 Pac. 232 (1908).

34. Benedict v. Hendrickson, 19 Wash.2d 452, 143 P.2d 326 (1943).

35. Campbell v. Webber, 29 Wash.2d 516, 188 P.2d 130 (1947); *In re* Horse Heaven Irrigation District, 19 Wash.2d 89, 141 P.2d 400 (1943).

36. 132 Wash. 649, 233 Pac. 29 (1925).

the husband can deal with it without the wife's joinder.[37] The court has, however, constantly retreated from this sweeping statement, and common practice is to require the wife's joinder in any assignment of the purchaser's interest, whether the assignee is a third person or the vendor. The husband may, as manager, default in payment of installments, thereby putting the vendor in a position to declare a forfeiture of the purchaser's interest.[38] In such a situation the husband's act in releasing the purchaser's interest is valid, even though the wife does not join, under the reasoning that the "release" is not a conveyance within the spirit of the statute but rather only a recognition of the fact that the previous interest has been lost. That the substance rather than the form is important is suggested in two additional situations in which the court has construed transactions as not being conveyances within the meaning of the statute: (1) an assignment for the benefit of creditors;[39] and (2) a declaration of abondonment of oyster lands.[40]

No mention is made above of a statute enacted in 1891[41] purporting to empower the record title holder to convey to an actual bona fide purchaser without joinder of the spouse unless an inventory asserting a community claim has been filed by the other spouse. Qualification as an "actual bona fide purchaser" is so difficult to achieve under the cases[42] that commonly the statute is ignored, and title examiners as a practical matter operate on the assumption, as an initial proposition, that any owner of a real property interest is married and that the interest is community property.

Neither spouse has testamentary power over more than his or her half of the community property. The statute expressly so

---

37. In the recent case of Jarrett v. Arnerich, 44 Wash.2d 55, 265 P.2d 282 (1954), the husband in concert with the vendor purported to surrender to the vendor in disregard of wife's wishes and rights. The court affirmed a judgment for plaintiff wife which in effect found there had been no surrender and said the wife, "as a member of the community, was entitled to notice of forfeiture." The basis of the decision appears to be that the husband exceeded his authority as statutory agent, with the knowledge of the vendor, and his act therefore was ineffective. The quoted statement is not necessary to the decision. It is not clear that it is a correct statement that the wife must participate before there is effective dealing with the community interest as purchaser under a forfeitable contract.

38. Converse v. LaBarge, 92 Wash. 282, 158 Pac. 958 (1916). But compare the comment in the preceding note.

39. Thygesen v. Neufelder, 9 Wash. 455, 37 Pac. 672 (1894).

40. Halvorsen v. Pacific County, 22 Wash.2d 532, 156 P.2d 907, 158 A.L.R. 555 (1945).

41. WASH. REV. CODE 26.16.095, 26.16.100, 26.16.110 (1953).

42. Campbell v. Sandy, 190 Wash. 528, 69 P.2d 808 (1937); Dane v. Daniel, 23 Wash. 379, 63 Pac. 268 (1900).

limits the husband's power over community personal property,[43] and the descent statute[44] makes it clear that the limitation extends to all community property.

A statutory provision,[45] unique to Washington, establishes a form of dispositive instrument commonly called a community property agreement. By this statute the husband and wife can enter into an agreement in deed form upon the status and disposition of the whole or any part of the community property, which agreement takes effect upon the death of either. A common form of this agreement provides for survivorship whereby all community property is vested in the survivor, and in it also laymen, who prepare many of them, embody both the present and prospective change of character of assets mentioned in Part IV, *infra.* To distinguish the common three-pronged contract from the agreement authorized by statute, the latter is here termed the "statutory community property agreement." The effect of such an agreement is to eliminate the testamentary power of each spouse as to his or her half of community property covered by the agreement.[46] The statutory community property agreement has no other inter vivos effect.[47] The statute does not limit the parties to survivorship dispositions, nor in any other fashion (except for preserving the rights of creditors), and despite the lack of a definitive decision, this writer believes any conceivable disposition not otherwise proscribed[48] could be made, even cutting off the survivor entirely or vesting only a life interest in the survivor with remainders over, *etc.* There is some support for this belief in In re *Dunn's Estate,*[49] though the instrument therein met the requirements both of a statutory community property agreement and of a joint will, and the survivor by joint will reasoning could in effect be limited to a life interest (though perhaps not technically a life estate as to his half) in all community property, both his and his deceased wife's halves.

---

43. WASH. REV. CODE 26.16.030 (1953).

44. *Id.* at 11.04.050.

45. *Id.* at 26.16.120. See Buckley, *The Community Property Agreement Statute,* 25 WASH. L. REV. 165 (1950).

46. *In re* Brown's Estate, 29 Wash.2d 20, 185 P.2d 125 (1947).

47. Hesseltine v. First Methodist Church, 23 Wash.2d 315, 161 P.2d 157 (1945).

48. *E.g.,* by the rule against perpetuities.

49. 31 Wash.2d 512, 197 P.2d 606 (1948). This view is not shared by the author of the Washington State Bar Association's pamphlet, "Have You Made a Will?" which states, "If the parties wish to provide for part of estate to go to children, it cannot be accomplished by such an agreement."

Life Insurance Policies

Cases involving management and voluntary disposition of life insurance policy rights need brief mention.[50] The power of the insured in inter vivos transactions conforms to the usual rules applicable to personal property. The husband insured can surrender the policy for cash payment and pledge it as security.[51] As pointed out in Part III, *infra*, to the extent that the policy is purchased with community funds, the policy and its proceeds are community property. With this as the starting point the court has developed a partially complete set of rules governing designation of the beneficiary of the policy. In the initial case, *Occidental Life Ins. Co. v. Powers*,[52] the court struck down entirely the husband's change of the beneficiary from his wife to his mother and secretary, reasoning that the designation of the beneficiary was an attempt to make a gift without consent of the wife, and therefore ineffective. This extreme position was distinguished in In re *Towey's Estate*,[53] in which the court upheld the payment of proceeds to the husband's executor who had been substituted for the wife as beneficiary. The husband's will was exclusively in favor of persons other than his wife, but the court said the wife's community interest was not affected by this change since half of the community assets administered by the executor would belong to the wife as her share. In other cases an original beneficiary designation of a third person (*i.e.*, someone other than the wife of the insured) has been frustrated at the suit of the wife on the authority of the *Powers* case, and in these situations apparently the proceeds become assets of the community estate, subject to administration.[54] Under this result the widow would at least secure half of the proceeds but not necessarily more. There is no case directly answering the problem of ownership of the proceeds where the change is from the wife to a third person as beneficiary: is the changes of beneficiary nugatory entirely so that the wife is to be treated as owner as if

50. Discussions of the Washington cases can be found in Recent Cases, 28 WASH. L. REV. 236 (1953), 26 WASH. L. REV. 223 (1951), 20 WASH. L. REV. 167 (1945); Papers Presented at Legal Institute, *Life Insurance as Community Property*, 16 WASH. L. REV. 187 (1941); Comment, 13 WASH. L. REV. 321 (1938).

51. Page v. Prudential Life Ins. Co., 12 Wash.2d 101, 120 P.2d 527 (1942); Seattle Ass'n of Credit Men v. Bank of California, 177 Wash. 130, 30 P.2d 972 (1934).

52. 192 Wash. 475, 74 P.2d 27, 114 A.L.R. 531 (1937).

53. 22 Wash.2d 212, 155 P.2d 273 (1945).

54. *E.g.*, National Bank of Commerce v. Lutheran Brotherhood, 40 Wash.2d 790, 246 P.2d 843 (1952); California-Western States Life Ins. Co. v. Jarman, 29 Wash.2d 98, 185 P.2d 494 (1947).

there had been no attempt to change, or is the change effective at least to the extent of eliminating the wife as beneficiary, so that in effect there is no designated beneficiary and the proceeds are therefore community assets in the estate of the deceased insured? The latter appears to be the sounder view despite the apparent singleness of the act of designating a different beneficiary. This position finds some support in the effectiveness of a change to the insured's executor in In re *Towey's Estate*,[55] and also in the approach in *Wilson v. Wilson*,[56] in which the court, dealing with a policy owned in shares part separate and part community determined the designation of the beneficiary in the policy, that is, the contract, should control to the extent possible without infringing on the community property policy of protection of the wife.

While certain results on the basis of these cases can be predicted with some assurance, the whole area is open to question by the 4-to-4 split of the court in *Aetna Life Ins. Co. v. Brock*[57] (with one judge not participating) on the advisability of continuing to follow the *Powers* case. If the *Powers* case principle is in the future rejected, then apparently the husband will be able to dispose of half of this asset by direct designation of a third person as beneficiary of his half of the community interest in the proceeds.

Joint Ownership

The court has not yet answered questions of ownership involving United States savings bonds purchased with community funds in which a stranger is named beneficiary or co-owner.[58] A somewhat similar problem inheres in the several joint "bank account" statutes[59] which provide that certain contracts with the financial institution can create survivorship rights. The only case[60] involving use of community funds did not reach the survivorship problem because the account was closed prior to the

55. 22 Wash.2d 212, 155 P.2d 273 (1945).

56. 35 Wash.2d 364, 212 P.2d 1022 (1949). The wife was named beneficiary as to ¾ of proceeds but the community interest was ⅘. She took ¾ as beneficiary; the other named beneficiary took ⅕ (separate interest) as beneficiary.

57. 41 Wash.2d 369, 249 P.2d 383 (1952).

58. WASH. REV. CODE 11.04.230 (1953) purports to make the survivor the sole and absolute owner.

59. It is recognized that these statutes are not limited to *bank* accounts, but for simplicity the term is used to include the several principal statutes: banks, *id.* at 30.20.015; mutual savings banks, *id.* at 32.12.030; savings and loan associations, *id.* at 33.20.030; credit unions, *id.* at 31.12.140.

60. Munson v. Haye, 29 Wash.2d 733, 189 P.2d 464 (1948).

death of the wife, who with community funds withdrawn had opened a new account with a stranger. The court held that the identification of the source of the account as community funds necessarily meant that the account was a community asset, in the absence of a clear showing of an intention to change the character of ownership into a joint tenancy. It being a community asset the wife had no power to give it away without the husband's consent.[61]

III. Character of Ownership as Separate or Community Property

"Time of Acquisition" Test

The basic statute provides that any property acquired during marriage and not within one of the statutory definitions of separate property is community property. The location of the record title in husband or wife or both is not controlling.[62] The first step in identifying the original character of any asset, then, involves determination of the marital status of the acquirer at the time of the acquisition. If the acquirer was unmarried his or her ownership then was necessarily separate. (The present character of the ownership may not be the same as its original character, but this is reserved for later discussion.)[63] The converse, however, cannot be so blandly asserted, that is, one cannot say that a particular asset acquired during marriage even if not a gift is necessarily community property, because the separate property definition encompasses rents, issues and profits of separate property; and the particular asset first acquired during marriage may, for instance, have been purchased with funds on hand at the time of the marriage—which funds necessarily are

61. Whether any arrangement short of the "separate property agreement" discussed in Part IV, *infra*, could supply the necessary intention to change the community character of the funds put into a joint account is not clear. The *Munson* case, *ibid.*, may, however, eliminate any problem in reaching a result in favor of the surviving spouse against the stranger designated a joint depositor by the decedent spouse.

62. Wash. Rev. Code 26.16.030 (1953). "Under our somewhat perplexing statutes relating to the acquisition of property, title to real property taken in the name of one of the spouses may be the separate property of the spouse taking the title, the separate property of the other spouse, or the community property of both of the spouses, owing to the source from which the fund is derived which is used in paying the purchase price of the property. If the fund is derived from the separate property of one of the spouses, the property purchased is the separate property of that spouse; if it is derived from the community property of both the spouses, it is the community property of both of them." Merritt v. Newkirk, 155 Wash. 517, 520, 285 Pac. 442, 444 (1930).

63. See Part IV, *infra*.

separate property assets which remain separate property so long as they can be traced in their mutations to the particular asset now at hand. The usual statement is that the character, as separate or community property, of any asset is to be determined as of the time of its acquisition,[64] but this must be understood to refer only to original assets whose source of acquisition cannot be traced (except perhaps to earnings of a spouse). So understood, the "time of acquisition" test will furnish the answer as to the character of the asset which was acquired by a single, total consideration paid by the acquirer, but when it is not clear that the total acquisition occurred at one time, the test has posed problems for the court. These latter situations include: (1) conveyance on partial payment with a balance still due under a purchase-money mortgage either to the vendor or a third person; (2) conveyance on partial payment and assumption of an existing mortgage for the balance; (3) conveyance on purchase of the vendor's interest subject to (without assuming) an existing mortgage; (4) conveyance on full payment to vendor, part of the funds having been secured by a mortgage on another asset (*i.e.*, not a purchase-money mortgage); (5) purchase on an installment contract with balance due vendor in the future, conveyance to await payment of all installments.

In the cases involving mortgages a reasonably certain pattern has been established which involves the "source doctrine" in determining (1) the ownership of the funds used in initial part payment, and (2) the character of the credit pledged *i.e.*, the nature of the obligation underlying the mortgage, which is presumed to be community obligation.[65]

The ownership of the funds used to make the partial payment will determine the ownership of that share of the asset, and the character of the credit pledged to pay the balance will determine the ownership of the remaining share,[66] without regard to the ownership of the funds ultimately used to discharge the debt for the balance.[67] Thus if separate credit is primarily pledged in the borrowing for the balance, the remainder will be separately owned even though community funds are used to pay the balance.[68] If community credit is pledged, the remainder is

64. *In re* Witte's Estate, 21 Wash.2d 112, 124, 150 P.2d 595, 601 (1944).
65. Bryant v. Stetson & Post Mill Co., 13 Wash. 692, 43 Pac. 931 (1896).
66. These rules were applied in *In re* Dougherty's Estate, 27 Wash.2d 11, 176 P.2d 335 (1947).
67. *In re* Finn's Estate, 106 Wash. 137, 179 Pac. 103 (1919).
68. *Ibid.*

owned as community property—and this even though the security is by purchase-money mortgage on the property[69] (and apparently even though the property is income-producing and in fact produces the income to discharge the obligation). The problems most commonly arise when the wife is the moving party and makes the initial payment from her separate funds. If the husband is the moving party, the presumption that an obligation he incurs is a community obligation[70] will not, as a practical matter, ordinarily be overcome even though he has separate credit and assets, if the transaction does not specifically show that only his separate credit is pledged. If a mortgage balance is assumed, the reasoning is the same as if there is a purchase-money mortgage.

If the wife makes the initial payment from her separate funds and acquires the balance by borrowing on the security of a mortgage on other separately owned land, there is authority that this is a pledge of separate credit even though the husband also signs the note.[71] That the debt is ultimately discharged by community funds is immaterial. The reasoning in the above situations apparently is that the time of acquisition is the time when there is created a binding obligation as to the balance of the price.

When the title is taken to the property upon the initial payment subject to an outstanding encumbrance, but no promise is made to pay that encumbrance, the share represented by the balance apparently is acquired when that encumbrance is discharged and not before, hence the funds used to pay the encumbrance will control the ownership of that share. Thus when the wife separately made the initial payment and community funds thereafter were used to discharge the non-assumed encumbrance, the initial share was the wife's separate property and the remainder was community property.[72]

In the above cases the remainder of the total acquisition cost was due as a lump sum, but there is nothing to indicate a different result when the remainder is due in installments.

On the other hand, when the title is not secured as the immediate result of the transaction, but rather only upon completetion of installment payments, as in the typical land-purchase

69. Walker v. Fowler, 155 Wash. 631, 285 Pac. 649 (1930).
70. Bryant v. Stetson & Post Mill Co., 13 Wash. 692, 43 Pac. 931 (1896).
71. *In re* Finn's Estate, 106 Wash. 137, 179 Pac. 103 (1919).
72. *Ibid.*

contract, the result in terms of ownership remains confused. The court purports to apply the time of acquisition test, but has vacillated in its identification of the time of acquisition. The matter appeared to have been put at rest by the statement in In re *Binge's Estate*,[73] that the ultimate acquisition is but the fruit of the original obligation and that the time of acquisition was the time at which the obligation became binding. This proposition is consistent with the solution in the mortgage acquisition cases, and no regard (in terms of ownership) need be had to funds used in ultimate discharge of the installments.[74] However, in In re *Dougherty's Estate*,[75] without indicating why, the court determined the ownership of personal property to be part separate and part community on the basis of the ownership of the funds used to discharge the installments. There has been no recent indication that the ownership relation of the spouses to property is affected in the slightest by the real or personal property character of the asset.

The result in the *Dougherty* case, though confusing, is not surprising in light of the court's treatment of proceeds of life insurance policies upon the death of the insured. In this latter type of case a clear pattern of pro rata ownership, part separate and part community, has been evolved,[76] despite the apparent inconsistency with earlier results and the statement in the *Binge* case concerning land contracts. In the installment purchase cases, and even the mortgage cases, to assert unequivocally that there is a single time of acquisition challenges credulity, but at least the time of the original obligation and its character can be identified.[77] There is a distinction which can be drawn between these two types of acquisitions and the life insurance proceeds: the installment purchase contract and the mortgage transactions do involve a fixed obligation that the obligee can

---

73. 5 Wash.2d 446, 105 P.2d 689 (1940).

74. Previously, in *In re* Kuhn's Estate, 132 Wash. 678, 233 Pac. 293 (1925), the court held the surviving widower was owner, separately, when he completed payments on the contract, and that the heirs of the wife only had a right to be reimbursed for one-half of the amount paid with community funds prior to the wife's death.

75. 27 Wash.2d 11, 176 P.2d 335 (1947).

76. Wilson v. Wilson, 35 Wash.2d 364, 212 P.2d 1022 (1949); Small v. Bartyzel, 27 Wash.2d 176, 177 P.2d 391 (1947).

77. Establishing that the credit is other than community credit may pose difficulties. The husband's signature alone will raise a presumption of community obligation, the wife's joinder adds nothing to this presumption. The use made of funds acquired does not appear controlling, *but cf.* Auernheimer v. Gardner, 177 Wash. 158, 31 P.2d 515 (1934); *In re* Finn's Estate, 106 Wash. 137, 179 Pac. 103 (1919) (as to the Drew tract); *In re* Binge's Estate, 5 Wash.2d 446, 498, 105 P.2d 689, 711 (1940).

require to be performed (even though alternative remedies may be available), whereas in the typical life insurance contract the insurer cannot compel the insured to keep the policy alive so that there will be proceeds about which to argue. If, therfore, there were one clear rule for the mortgage and contract cases, and a different rule for ownership of life insurance proceeds it would be understandable and defensible—the difficulty in this rationalization, however, is that there is not the slightest suggestion in the cases that this is the explanation for the difference in result; nor is there any other explanation.

Under the present state of case law, while the result in the mortgage and life insurance proceeds cases is predictable, respectable argument can be advanced in the stallment contract cases that the ownership of the asset is determined (1) at the time of and by the character of the original obligation (the mortgage rue); or (2) on a pro rata basis according to ownership of funds used to pay installments (the life insurance rule); or *perhaps* (3) only at the time of fulfillment of the contract and acquisition of title, which apparently will be controlled by marital status at that time.

Tracing and Commingling

In the area of commingled funds, or assets purchased therewith, the court has perhaps most clearly demonstrated the favor with which community property is viewed. The rule was well stated by Judge Steinert as follows:

> "Where separate funds have been so commingled with community funds that it is no longer possible to distinguish or apportion them, all of the commingled fund, or the property acquired thereby, is community property."[78]

Counterbalancing the commingling doctrine and the presumption that any property acquired by purchase during marriage is community property is the statutory provision that the rents, issue and profits of separate property are separate property. The particular problem frequently becomes one of tracing, under the rule that "[s]eparate property continues to be separate property through all of its changes and transitions so long as it can be *clearly* traced and identified, and its rents, issues, and profits likewise are and continue to be separate property."[79] (Italics supplied.)

78. *In re* Witte's Estate, 21 Wash.2d 112, 125, 150 P.2d 595, 601 (1944).
79. *Ibid.*

The statutory provision that rents, issues, and profits of separate property are also separate property not only simplifies the problem of ownerhip of assets secured by exchange or sale of a separately owned asset, but also underlies problems of tracing the change in form of separate property, of applying presumptions of community character of spouses' property, and of commingling separate and community funds. Despite this statutory rule, the beginning point for analysis of the character of any asset held in the name of a spouse is the presumption of community ownership. It is clear under the cases that the burden rests on the person asserting the separate ownership to establish that claim by clear and satisfactory evidence.[80]

Similarly, to establish the separate ownership of an asset now in hand as the present form of a previously held asset admittedly separate property, requires that the changes in form be clearly traced and identified.[81] The mere possibility that separate property has been changed to the present asset is not enough. In *Berol v. Berol*,[82] for example, the husband had, fourteen months after marriage, bought a single premium life insurance policy in which he designated his mother as beneficiary. This designation is an unauthorized "gift" if the premium was paid with community funds without the wife's consent and therefore ineffective.[83] The court held the requirement of clear and satisfactory evidence of the separate character of the funds was not met by the husband's bald statement that he paid the premuim from his separate funds even though he also showed separate funds were available. In concluding that the value of the policy should be treated as community property in making the divorce division, the court stated the separate funds so used should be traced with some degree of particularity.[84]

While mere continuous holding of a particular asset during marriage will not change its character from separate to community, nor will mere altering its form by exchanges, if the tracing burden is met, the income-producing asset inherently creates additional difficulties which are aggravated by the commingling doctrine. Although the court by the decision in In re *Brown's Estate*,[85] was by local lawyer gossip said to have con-

80. *Ibid.*
81. *Ibid.*
82. 37 Wash.2d 380, 223 P.2d 1055 (1950).
83. See discussion in Part II *supra*.
84. See also duPont de Nemours & Co. v. Garrison, 13 Wash.2d 170, 124 P.2d 939 (1942).
85. 124 Wash. 273, 214 Pac. 10 (1923).

cluded that a husband (with a separate estate) did not have to work for the community but could work exclusively for himself, it has long since recognized that the talent or capacity of each spouse is itself a community asset which when exercised produced community property.[86] Under this view it is theoretically impossible for a husband to work exclusively for himself in a separate property sense, and even though his entire toil and talent is engaged in managing or operating his separately owned property or enterprise there is at least a partial community property interest in any return.[87]

If the acquisitions by the husband come in part from his own work and in part from the earnings of his invested separate property, whether there is pro rata ownership of the acquisitions or only total community ownership depends upon the applicability of the commingling doctrine. If the husband's business enterprise is in corporate form his ownership will be represented by shares of stock. Ordinarily increase in the value of the stock (reflecting increase in the corporate value) will be rents, issues and profits of the separate property,[88] and no serious problem arises if the husband as operator of the corporate business is paid a reasonable salary for his toil and talent.[89] Establishment of this circumstance depends upon the testimony presented on the reasonableness of the salary and the corporate records revealing the payment of the salary.[90] The reasonable salary is held to be the measure of community property acquisition. In such a situation there is contemporaneous segragation of earnings and increment between the community and separate assets, hence no commingling problem arises. When the separately owned enterprise is not conducted in corporate form there is a practical probability of commingling of earnings from the investment and the husband's ability (separate and community, respectively),[91] and if the rule is abolute that commingling makes everything community property there is not much that can be done. Physical commingling of separate and community funds should present

86. *In re* Witte's Estate, 21 Wash.2d 112, 150 P.2d 595 (1944).

87. Of course the community income from the husband's endeavor may be entirely consumed by regular expenditures so that there is no community interest in a present accumulation. See State *ex rel.* Van Moss v. Sailors, 180 Wash. 269, 39 P.2d 397 (1934); Toivonen v. Toivenon, 196 Wash. 636, 84 P.2d 128 (1938).

88. *In re* Hebert's Estate, 169 Wash. 402, 14 P.2d 6 (1932).

89. *Ibid.* See also Hamlin v. Merlino, 44 Wash.2d 851, 272 P.2d 125 (1954).

90. *Ibid.*

91. Consider the situations in *In re* Witte's Estate, 21 Wash.2d 112, 150 P.2d 595 (1944); Salisbury v. Meeker, 152 Wash. 146, 277 Pac. 376 (1929).

no problem other than a "fungible goods" confusion problem,[92] at least in situations where records contemporaneously kept clearly indicate the respective acquisitions to be credited to separate property and community endeavor. If contemporaneous records are not available, the problem would appear to be one of "tracing" to the sources of the present accumulation.

At this point a policy problem arises: Should a commingled fund be conclusively presumed to be community property in the absence of a clear showing of an affirmative intent of the spouses to the contrary, which intent can be demonstrated only by establishing contemporaneous segregation? This appears to be the proposition advanced in a dictum recently,[93] and the result may be satisfactory in controversies between the spouses or a spouse and gratuitous successors of the other (heirs, devisees, donees), though at least one other recent case[94] does not conform. As suggested elsewhere[95] in many situations such a result would accord with the unexpressed intent of the spouses to throw all assets into the common pot for the benefit of the marriage. But a conclusive presumption in the absence of contemporaneous segregation could pose serious problems for third parties to whom a spouse was separately obligated, to say nothing of the problems under tax liabilities.[96] The commingling doctrine is, in this writer's opinion, simply a form of the presumption of the community character of an asset on hand during the marriage, and the common conclusion that the commingled funds are community property results merely from the failure to carry the burden to establish by clear and satisfactory evidence the asserted separate character, in whole or part, of the funds or asset acquired thereby. "Tracing" in the framework is merely the process of carrying that burden of proof; and while the

92. The applicable rules are discussed in BROWN, A TREATISE ON THE LAW OF PERSONAL PROPERTY §§ 30-36 (1936).

93. Hamlin v. Merlino, 44 Wash.2d 851, 858, 272 P.2d 125, 129 (1954).

94. Holm v. Holm, 27 Wash.2d 456, 178 P.2d 725 (1947). In a divorce the trial court concluded all community property should be divided equally and that the whole of the business property was community property by commingling. The Supreme Court modified the decree to preserve for the husband as his separate property the amount invested in the business at the time of marriage. Even though clearly there was commingling of the investment with later earnings, proof of the original amount was permitted. On the other hand no attempt was made by the court to apportion the later increment, but this may be of no particular significance since the court can award any property of the spouses as circumstances require.

95. Kizer, *Community Interest in Commingled Income, Derived from Personal Service and Separate Capital—Another View*, 23 WASH. L. REV. 8 (1948).

96. LeSourd, *Community Property Status of Income from Business Involving Personal Services and Separate Capital*, 22 WASH. L. REV. 19 (1947).

absence of a contemporaneous segregation may make the burden beyond carrying, it should not conclusively preclude the attempt. But it is conceded that the cases do not now answer the question of the significance of the absence of contemporaneous segregation.

Separate Property and "Community Relationship"

In addition to property owned by one spouse at marriage together with the rents, issues and profits thereof, the general statutes[97] provide that separate property also includes that acquired by gift, devise or inheritance. There is no doubt that the facts of a particular acquisitive transaction rather than the form of the transaction will govern the character of the ownership[98]—the court's position is clear that the statute speaks of donative acquisition.[99] Another statute [100] provides that the earnings of the wife and minor children living with her while living separate from her husband shall be her separate property. Beyond this point the statutes are silent, but the cases develop an additional requirement that there be a community relationship, not merely a marriage relationship, between the spouses in order that an asset be characterized as community property.

In addition to the statutory position of the wife as separate owner of her earnings while living apart from the husband, the court in *Wampler v. Beinert* some years ago held that the husband lost his power as manager of the community property when he deserted his wife.[101] Subsequently in the case of *Togliatti v. Robertson*[102] the court concluded that the husband's acquisition long after he and his wife had permanently separated was his separate property. It is not, from the *Togliatti* case, entirely clear whether the basis for the court's conclusion was a "separate property agreement" inferred from the long separation (discussed in Part IV, *infra*) or the lack of a community relationship between the spouses. In the most recent case, In re *Armstrong's Estate*,[103] separation followed entry of an interlocutory decree

97. WASH. REV. CODE, 26.16.010, 26.16.020 (1953).

98. Andrews v. Andrews, 116 Wash. 513, 199 Pac. 981 (1921); Mechem, *Progress of the Law in Washington: Community Property*, 8 WASH. L. REV. 1, 4-7 (1933).

99. Even though the asset is acquired by gift it can be community property, apparently, if the gift is to both of them with that intent (rather than as tenants in common). See Schilling v. Schilling, 42 Wash.2d 105, 107, 253 P.2d 952, 953 (1953). The power to control the character of property owned, discussed in Part IV, *supra*, also suggests this possibility.

100. WASH. REV. CODE 26.16.140 (1953).

101. 125 Wash. 494, 216 Pac. 855 (1923).

102. 29 Wash.2d 844, 190 P.2d 575 (1948).

103. 33 Wash.2d 118, 204 P.2d 500 (1949).

of divorce and shortly thereafter the particular asset was acquired by the husband. The court concluded the asset was his separately on the basis of the *Togliatti* case, stating that the wife had made no contribution to the acquisition. This suggests, at least, that the *Togliatti* reasoning of the lack of a community relationship is controlling. There is some further support for this conclusion in the *Wampler* case wherein the husband was supplanted from his community agent's position by his desertion of the wife, and in *Yates v. Dohring*,[104] involving the family expense statute,[105] where the court concluded the wife had not incurred a "family" expense when she had permanently separated from the husband and had refused to perform her ordinary marital duties. From this might be drawn the conclusion that only the "innocent" spouse can subsequently acquire separate property and that the "guilty" spouse's acquisitions would be community property, but in fact in the *Yates* and the *Togliatti* cases the separation was mutually desired and probably there was no "guilty" spouse. It is this writer's belief, therefore, that whenever there can be shown a permanent separation of the spouses, the subsequent acquisitions of either will be separate property even though there is no dissolution of the marriage. Proving that there has been a permanent separation may be troublesome, and can most easily be done by an action for divorce or separate maintenance, but even in the absence of such litigation there would appear to be no reason to deny possible adequacy of other proof. This would permit a separate acquisition by the "innocent" spouse who might be either, or both, if the separation was by mutual consent, and still permit the court to characterize the husband's subsequent acquisition as community property if he deserted the wife.[106]

IV. Transactions and Agreements Between Spouses

Separate and Community Property Agreements

The statute[107] authorizes conveyance of the grantor's community interest by either spouse to the other,[108] with the result

104. 24 Wash.2d 877, 168 P.2d 404 (1946).

105. Wash. Rev. Code 26.20.010 (1953).

106. *Id.* at 26.16.140, for the wife living separate from her husband, apparently mould make the deserting wife's subsequent acquisition separate regardless of her "guilt."

107. *Id.* at 26.16.050.

108. Payment with community funds will result in community ownership even though the title is taken in the wife's name, only, at the direction of the husband. An oral gift of real estate is ineffective. *In re* Parker's Estate, 115 Wash. 57, 196 Pac. 632 (1921). However, the court has held under

that the subject matter of the conveyance becomes the separate property of the grantee.[109] And of course the power of either spouse as to separate property is as complete as if he or she were unmarried,[110] so that conveyance by one to the other would be treated similarly to conveyances between strangers. The effect of the first mentioned statute is to empower spouses to change community property into separate property, and the court in *Volz c. Zang*[111] stated that if such a change was permissible, the reverse was also permissible (which is a non sequitur). In addition to this explanation the court in the *Volz* case reasoned that the favor with which community property is viewed and the fact that there is no express prohibition against the result, permitted the conclusion that separate property could be changed into community property by a document in deed form which clearly expressed the intention of the spouses to do so.[112] But even beyond this point the court has given effect to agreements between the spouses that any property acquired after the effective date of the agreement should be community property, and this, if the intention is established, without regard to the manner of acquisition of the particular asset.[113]

The rather general freedom accorded the spouses in dealings between themselves has resulted in recognition of what can be called "separate property agreements" by which not only presently held property becomes the separate property of the respective spouses,[114] but also any subsequently acquired property

---

somewhat comparable facts that the conveyance by the grantor, at the husband's direction, to the wife "as her sole and separate property" will make the property hers separately. Goodfellow v. LeMay, 15 Wash. 684, 47 Pac. 25 (1896).

109. WASH. REV. CODE 26.16.210 (1953) in transactions between the spouse put the burden of proof on the person asserting the good faith of the transaction.

110. *Id.* at 26.16.010, 26.16.020. See Scott v. Currie, 7 Wash.2d 301, 109 P.2d 526 (1941), in which the court applied a presumption of gift to the conveyance of land by the grantor to the wife at the direction of the husband who paid therefor with his separate funds.

111. 113 Wash. 378, 194 Pac. 409 (1920).

112. The mere conveyance by one spouse of a half interest in the grantor's separate property does not give the grantee a half interest as a community share, but rather makes the grantor and grantee tenants in common. Powers v. Munson, 74 Wash. 234, 133 Pac. 453 (1913).

113. These agreements are frequently called community property agreements but are *not* the statutory community property agreements referred to in Part II *supra*.

114. Burch v. Rice, 37 Wash.2d 185, 222 P.2d 847 (1950); *In re* Garrity's Estate, 22 Wash.2d 391, 156 P.2d 217 (1945); *In re* Martin's Estate, 127 Wash. 44, 219 Pac. 838 (1923). Aside from statute of frauds problem as to real property, oral agreements may be sufficient. Aetna Life Ins. Co. v. Brock, 41 Wash.2d 369, 249 P.2d 383 (1952). *Cf.* Leroux v. Knoll, 28 Wash.2d 964, 184 P.2d 564 (1947).

is separate property of one or the other, thereby preventing any acquisition of assets as community property. This appears to be the proposition although an early case[115] suggested that the agreement amounted to a continuing offer to make a gift whereby community property upon its acquisition immediately was changed into separate property. As discussed in Part V, *infra*, the effect as to third parties can differ substantially under one interpretation of the effect of the separate property agreement rather than the other.

The court, as pointed out in Part III, *supra*, has developed a recognition of a marriage relationship distinct from both a family relationship and a community relationship. In this framework it can be said that the court has also recognized that there might be both a family and a marriage relationship without there being a community relationship. While it is true that many separate property agreements are a part of separation agreements made in connection with divorce or separation of the spouses, there are also those between spouses intending to continue normal marriage and family relationships. The court, in the divorce and other cases, upholds the finality of separate property agreements as between the spouses,[116] if that is their intention, while at the same time reaffirming the power of the court in divorce and separate maintenance actions to adjust the property relationships of the parties without being bound by the character of particular assets before the court. In other words, although a factor to be considered is the character of the asset as separate or community property, the court in such actions may not only unequally divide the community property between the two but also award separate property of one to the other.[117] Written separate property agreements between spouses are not uncommon when they are separated or contemplate separation or divorce, but it is probable that oral agreements in other situations will be given effect if proved. Here the burden of clear and satisfactory evidence is required and may not be met.[118]

Improvements

Besides these purposeful arrangements between the spouses, there is an additional area of transactions between them involv-

115. Yake v. Pugh, 13 Wash. 78, 42 Pac. 528, 52 Am. St. Rep. 17 (1895).

116. See cases cited note 114 *supra*.

117. Patrick v. Patrick, 43 Wash.2d 139, 260 P.2d 878 (1953), or almost any divorce case involving property division.

118. Aetna Life Ins. Co. v. Brock, 41 Wash.2d 369, 249 P.2d 383 (1952); State v. Miller, 32 Wash.2d 149, 201 P.2d 136 (1948); Piles v. Bovee, 168 Wash. 538, 12 P.2d 914 (1932).

ing improvement of land held in one character by the use of funds held in another character. Theoretically the asset improved can be held as separate property of the wife or of the husband or as community property, and the improvement made with funds held in either of the other two characters. This factual situation presents the problem of creation of an equitable lien in favor of the improver for reimbursement. The rule is clear that such investment does not create an ownership in the asset in favor of the improver,[119] and further, it does not necessarily follow that there will be a lien for reimbursement.[120] A common problem of this sort turns around an assertion of community lien for improvement of the husband's separate property. In some situations the basic fact of improvement with community funds cannot be established,[121] for the court has concluded that if there are separate funds as well as community funds adequate to pay for the improvements, it will be presumed that the "proper" fund is the source of the improvement; hence separate funds made the improvement and the community has no lien.[122] Of course if there is no showing of the existence of separate funds, the basic pattern for the lien is established. As a practical matter it may well be more difficult to establish a lien in favor of the husband or the community interests when the improvement is made at the husband's direction on the wife's separate property, because of an assumption (or perhaps ill-defined presumption) that the husband intends to make a gift of the improvement.[123] It is not impossible to show the absence of such an intention, however.[124]

---

119. Leroux v. Knoll, 28 Wash.2d 964, 184 P.2d 564 (1947); Legg v. Legg, 34 Wash. 132, 75 Pac. 130 (1904).

120. *In re* Hart's Estate, 149 Wash. 600, 271 Pac. 886 (1928). It may be that the improver, or advancer of funds, has received full value for the advance, hence has no right to reimbursement. See Merkel v. Merkel, 39 Wash.2d 102, 234 P.2d 857 (1951), where in divorce award the court considered mortgage interest, tax and upkeep payments as no more than reasonable rental for use of land.

121. Pekola v. Strand, 25 Wash.2d 98, 168 P.2d 407 (1946). In Legg v. Legg, 34 Wash. 132, 75 Pac. 130 (1904), the lien was allowed for "labor" as well as "money" improvements. The *Pekola* case indicates the amount of contribution must be shown, but there is doubt of the corectness of the statement therein that he tlien is allowed only for funds advanced.

122. *In re* Woodburn's Estate, 190 Wash. 141, 66 P.2d 1138 (1937).

123. *In re* Hickman's Estate, 41 Wash.2d 519, 250 P.2d 524 (1952).

124. *Ibid.* In a 5 to 4 decision the court held the equitable lien of the community could be reached by the trustee in bankruptcy as an asset of the bankrupt community's estate. Conley v. Moe, 7 Wash.2d 355, 110 P.2d 172, 133 A.L.R. 1089 (1941). If the spouses could show gift or relinquishment of any potential lien and meet the burden of proving good faith required by WASH. REV. CODE 26.16.210 (1953), the result in this case might be avoided,

V. Involuntary Disposition

While many of the problems of this part could be discussed under the management of the community's affairs, controversy does not ordinarily arise unless there is disagreement on the extend of enforceability of the claim; thus these problems commonly are ones of involuntary disposition of community property. The genesis of many of the problems was the court's interpretation that the statute insulates community property from all obligations separate in character, whether ante- or post-nuptial.[125] Originally it was the position of the court that a distinction should be drawn between the availability of real property, on one hand, and personal property on the other, but the rule has now long been settled to the contrary.[126] In addition to the unavailability of the whole of the community property, the court has held that a separate obligation cannot be enforced even against the debtor's half interest in community property,[127] but only against his or her separate property (if any). These propositions compel classification of obligations as separate or community.

Non-tort Obligations

In the ordinary course of affairs, any non-tortious act by a husband will presumptively be done as statutory manager and will create a community obligation.[128] If his act is done in managing a community asset or conducting a community business, community liability will follow as well as a separate liability against him. Extraordinary acts will create community liability if the husband's purpose was to benefit the community.[129] The actual accrual of benefit is unnecessary,[130] the lack of good

---

but otherwise a creditor may be in a stronger position to assert the lien than the improver.

On the other hand the court has given effect to the separate equitable lien over the claim of a community creditor to proceeds from the sale of a contract purchaser's interest. Farrow v. Ostrom, 16 Wash.2d 547, 133 P.2d 974 (1943).

125. Wash. Rev. Code 26.16.200 (1953) protects separate property from separate debt of other spouse; post-nuptial separate debt: Katz v. Judd, 108 Wash. 557, 185 Pac. 613 (1919).

126. Schramm v. Steele, 97 Wash. 309, 166 Pac. 634 (1917).

127. Stockland v. Bartlett, 4 Wash. 730, 31 Pac. 24 (1892).

128. Fisher v. Hagstrom, 35 Wash.2d 632, 214 P.2d 654 (1950); Fies v. Storey, 37 Wash.2d 105, 221 P.2d 1031 (1950); Whitehead v. Satran, 37 Wash.2d 724, 225 P.2d 888 (1950).

129. Beyers v. Moore, 145 Wash. Dec. 62, 272 P.2d 626 (1954).

130. *Ibid.*

judgment is immaterial,[131] and the dissent of the wife is irrelevant.[132]

Suretyship obligations executed by the husband furnish the common problem. Unless there was the intent to benefit the community, directly or indirectly, the argument will be that there has been an attempt to make a gift of the community credit[133] which is no more effective, without the wife's consent, than is a similar donative transfer of title to community property.[134] It was once held that the wife would be presumed to consent to the pledge of community credit to assist a child of the husband and wife,[135] but this case was directly overruled on the basis that the husband's agency was for conduct of the business of the community,[136] with the result that benefit to the community property or furtherance of a community purpose must be intended before liability will extend beyond separate responsibility of the husband. This rule is not as restrictive as might appear at first blush because (1) the burden of proof is on the one asserting the separate character of the transaction,[137] and (2) the intended benefit may be indirect as well as direct. The community purpose has been found, for example, in going surety for a corporation in which there are community funds invested,[138] in reviving an obligation by payment on a note barred by time,[139] in participating in financing the development of a golf club[140]—in other words, apparently community liability will exist if a community asset is somehow (no matter if only remotely) connected with the particular transaction, or if personal activity of a spouse is furthered.

In many transactions funds or other assets are immediately acquired by entering into the obligation. It is not entirely clear whether the use made of the funds is significant in determining the character of the obligation. In support of the conclusion of community liability the court has recently pointed out that the

131. Hanley v. Most, 9 Wash.2d 429, 115 P.2d 933 (1941); Bellingham Motors Corp. v. Lindberg, 126 Wash. 684, 219 Pac. 19 (1923).
132. Note 131 *supra*.
133. Zarbell v. Mantas, 32 Wash.2d 920, 204 P.2d 203 (1949).
134. See discussion in Part II *supra*.
135. Stevens v. Naches State Bank, 136 Wash. 137, 238 Pac. 918 (1925).
136. Sun Life Assurance Co. v. Outler, 172 Wash. 540, 20 P.2d 1110 (1933).
137. Beyers v. Moore, 145 Wash. Dec. 62, 272 P.2d 626 (1954).
138. Horton v. Donohoe-Kelly Banking Co., 15 Wash. 399, 46 Pac. 409 (1896).
139. Catlin v. Mills, 140 Wash. 1, 247 Pac. 1013 (1926).
140. Olympia Building & Loan Ass'n v. McCroskey, 172 Wash. 148, 19 P.2d 671 (1933).

funds were used for community purposes,[141] which may be merely indicated that the burden of proving a separate obligation has not been carried, but in a case[142] in which the wife's separate property was mortgaged to secure the advance, the court clearly held that the use of the funds for non-community purposes, prusuant to the pre-existing intention of the spouses, was irrelevant—the funds when first received, said the court, were acquired by the husband's pledge of community credit and were available for any community purpose.

The unavailability of community property to separate creditors poses a practical problem to those extending credit to unmarried persons. The truth apparently is that this insulation is not asserted by most recently married persons, but credit managers are confronted with what is loosely called "marital bankruptcy" in a wide variety of situations. The supplier of goods may be able to reach the goods which retain their separate property character, but the supplier of services does not even have this small consolation—how (or why) would the dentist, for example, recapture the product of his labors?

Conflicting policies of the community property system and divorce-alimony rules have collided head-on under this principle. The court has only partly met the problem of continuing protection to the divorced wife and children—obviously a separate obligation of the husband since it arises prior to his later marriage. In one case[143] the court held real property owned as community property of the husband and his second wife cannot be reached to satisfy the divorce decree awards, even though it had previously held that garnishment of the husband's salary was permissible.[144] This may be a limited throw-back to an abandoned distinction[145] between the real and personal property rights and powers of the husband, but perhaps the dissenting judge had a better idea when he suggested that the second wife just took an "encumbered" husband.

Whether the husband or wife is the moving party there will probably always be separate liability, but no presumption of community liability arises from the wife's obligations. In two types of situations community liability may result from the

---

141. Fies v. Storey, 37 Wash.2d 105, 221 P.2d 1031 (1950). See also *In re* Binge's Estate, 5 Wash.2d 446, 485, 105 P.2d 689, 706 (1940).

142. Auernheimer v. Gardner, 177 Wash. 158, 31 P.2d 515 (1934).

143. Stafford v. Stafford, 10 Wash.2d 649, 117 P.2d 753 (1941).

144. Fisch v. Marler, 1 Wash.2d 698, 97 P.2d 147 (1939).

145. Schramm v. Steele, 97 Wash. 309, 166 Pac. 634 (1917).

wife's obligations: (1) transactions falling within the "family expense" statute[146] which create three-way liability (separate-husband, separate-wife, and community), and (2) transactions by the wife for a community purpose which the husband either has authorized or ratified, or the community character of which he has estopped himself to deny.[147] To avoid community liability after he acquires sufficient knowledge of the transaction, the husband must act promptly, but this prerequisite provides substantial protection against community liability from many acts of the wife.[148]

Clearly the husband may formally appoint the wife agent to conduct community affairs,[149] but in addition the wife's agency may be established by a course of conduct so that her acts may create community liability. A peculiar offshoot, of undefined scope, appeared in *Lucci v. Lucci*[150] in which the wife's agency was found and a separate liability was imposed on the husband as well as the community liability. The wife's conduct of a grocery clearly benefitted the two of them in a community property sense and comparable liability for a loan used in ordinary community transactions follows, but there would appear to be nothing in the borrowing which benefited the husband in a separate property sense. The usual approach of the court in resolving problems of liability can be epitomized in referring to the husband-wife community as an "entity."[151] Conceivably the unexpressed reasoning of the court is that all community contractual transactions necessarily and unavoidably involve the husband's action as managing "principal" with the result that "entity" reasoning is inappropriate. There is nothing, however, to delineate the significance of the case.

---

146. WASH. REV. CODE 26.20.010 (1953).

147. Conner v. Zanuszoski, 36 Wash.2d 458, 218 P.2d 879 (1950); Williams v. Beebe, 79 Wash. 133, 139 Pac. 867 (1914). See also Feise v. Mueller, 41 Wash.2d 409, 249 P.2d 376 (1952).

148. Jones, Rosquist, Killen Co. v. Nelson, 98 Wash. 539, 167 Pac. 1130 (1917).

149. WASH. REV. CODE 26.16.060 (1953).

150. Lucci v. Lucci, 2 Wash.2d 624, 99 P.2d 393 (1940).

151. Though of course the court does not uniformly reach results on the basis that this "entity" is the principal in the agency law sense. See Mechem, *Progress of the Law in Washington: Community Property*, 7 WASH. L. REV. 367-70 (1933). The clearest rejection of the "entity" reasoning was made in Bortle v. Osborne, 155 Wash. 585, 285 Pac. 425, 67 A.L.R. 1152 (1930), in which the court held a tort cause of action did not survive against the community after the death of the tortfeasor spouse. This particular result has been changed by a 1953 statute, WASH. REV. CODE 4.20.045 (1953), discussed in Richards, *Washington Legislation—1953, Torts*, 28 WASH. L. REV. 201-4 (1953).

Tort Obligations

In tort cases[152] while there is no presumption to aid the plaintiff, community liability may be found by either of two routes:[153] (1) when the act is one within the managing power of the actor for the community on a basis of respondeat superior, and (2) when the act is done for the benefit of the community. The latter test clearly applies when assets acquired by the tort (*e.g.*, conversion) are community property under the statutory definitions.[154] The former might be called "management" torts, and from recent decisions it is open to argument that, except for the "official capacity" torts, this category will include all tortious conduct, or at least all not within the "benefit" category. A willful, fatal beating gave rise to community liability in *McHenry v. Short*,[155] in which the husband was either ejecting a trespasser from community land or was performing duties as watchman on the land. Community liability was found in *LaFramboise v. Schmidt*[156] when the husband took indecent liberties with the small girl being cared for by him and his wife. Recreational activities,[157] even though somewhat abnormal,[158] have been held to be community activities resulting in community liability. And of course, torts committed in connection with the actor's business affairs either as entrepreneur or employee create community liability.[159] There may yet be, however, an area in which the tortious conduct so clearly has no relationship to community affairs that only separate liability can be imposed. Here would fall the liability in an action against a husband for alienation of the affections of plaintiff's wife, and perhaps the purely personal altercation.[160]

Official Capacity Tort

A peculiar rule exists covering the tort liability of a public official. Despite the fact that the salary earned is community

152. The cases are more extensively analyzed in Pruzan, *Community Property and Tort Liability in Washington*, 23 WASH. L. REV. 259 (1948).

153. Bergman v. State, 187 Wash. 622, 60 P.2d 699, 106 A.L.R. 1007 (1936).

154. McGregor v. Johnson, 58 Wash. 78, 107 Pac. 1049, 27 L.R.A. (N.S.) 1022 (1910).

155. 29 Wash.2d 263, 186 P.2d 900 (1947).

156. 42 Wash.2d 198, 254 P.2d 485 (1953).

157. King v. Williams, 188 Wash. 350, 62 P.2d 710 (1936).

158. Moffitt v. Krueger, 11 Wash.2d 658, 120 P.2d 512 (1941).

159. Local No. 2618 v. Taylor, 197 Wash. 515, 85 P.2d 1116 (1938); Milne v. Kane, 64 Wash. 254, 116 Pac. 659, 36 L.R.A.(N.S.) 88 (1911).

160. Newbury v. Remington, 184 Wash. 665, 52 P.2d 312 (1935). Though perhaps the wife rather than the plaintiff should carry the cost burden of her husband's pugnaciousness.

property and hence it would seem that the spouse's acts as an official are "community" acts, the court has held that only a separate liability arises from torts committed in the officer's official capacity.[161] It was once contended that if the tort of the husband in negligently driving a taxicab in his business caused community liability, the same should be true of the tort of a husband whose whole endeavor was devoted to duties as a public official. The purported explanation by the court was, "The distinction is as clear as any distinction can be. The community drives the automobile; the community does not make the levy. The one is a community tort; the other is an official or separate tort."[162]

Effect of Separate Property Agreement

The effectiveness of a separate property agreement mentioned in Part IV, *supra*, is not limited to the ownership rights of the spouses, but in addition, the court has recognized that property, which would otherwise be community property and available to a creditor, will pursuant to such an agreement be separate property and thus, in the hands of the non-acting spouse, beyond the reach of the creditor.[163] This can be phrased either that the contractual liability is only separate, or that the liability though community and separate does not reach this asset as separate property of the non-acting spouse. Such an agreement is effective against subsequent creditors even though they do not know of the agreement,[164] but not against existing creditors.[165] The existence of the agreement must be satisfactorily proved.[166] The writer has found no cases considering the effect of an existing separate property agreement on the position of the tort judgment creditor.

Out-of-State Creditors

In view of the excellent discussion of the problems elsewhere,[167] mention only need be made of the court's treatment of out-of-state creditors seeking to reach Washington assets. The court has reasoned that a claim arising in non-community property state is necessarily a separate claim, hence enforceable in Washington only against separate property of the actor. The

161. Brotton v. Langert, 1 Wash. 73, 23 Pac. 688 (1890).
162. Day v. Henry, 81 Wash. 61, 64, 142 Pac. 439, 440 (1914).
163. Union Securities Co. v. Smith, 93 Wash. 115, 160 Pac. 304 (1916).
164. Piles v. Bovee, 168 Wash. 538, 12 P.2d 914 (1932).
165. Davison v. Hewitt, 6 Wash.2d 131, 106 P.2d 733 (1940); Marsh v. Fisher, 69 Wash. 570, 125 Pc. 951 (1912).
166. State v. Miller, 32 Wash.2d 149, 201 P.2d 136 (1948).
167. MARSH, MARITAL PROPERTY IN CONFLICT OF LAWS 148-54 (1952).

position has been taken when after incurring the obligation the debtor and spouse moved to Washington,[168] and also when a Washington domiciliary has incurred an obligation outside of the state, either tort[169] or contract.[170] This "bankruptcy" by moving to Washington is unwarranted enough, but this distinctive treatment of the out-of-state creditors of the Washington domiciliary not only is unfair but should boomerang on Washington residents in all dealings with out-of-state businesses.

With the knowledge and consent of the wife (to preclude the argument of unauthorized gift), the separate debt, whether out-of-state or otherwise, presumably could be changed into a community debt if a clear expression of the purpose to do so is shown,[171] but unfortunately such a factual pattern is not common and the presumption usualy controlling is that a debt, just as an asset, retains its character even though it may change its form.[172]

VI. Conclusion

On the whole the community property law is apparently working to the satisfaction of Washington residents. There is no general sentiment expressed in favor of abandoning it even though particular complications are spasmodicaly deplored. Most persons who might be caught on technicalities which make transactions hazardous or cumbersome know (even if they do not understand) the "ground rules" which meet the problems, and immigrants from non-community property states quit "shaking their heads" as the "natives" reveal the ground rules.

Statutory codification of the rules developed by the court plus correction of some of the deficiencies would be desirable, but there is no group with a specialized interest in the problem. Piecemeal changes such as elimination of the "marital bankruptcy" rule have been informally proposed by certain legislators, but until there is established some form of law revision commission[173] it appears probable no comprehensive corrective legislation will be proposed.

168. Meng v. Security State Bank of Woodland, 16 Wash.2d 215, 133 P.2d 293 (1943); LaSelle v. Woolery, 14 Wash. 70, 44 Pac. 115, 53 Am. St. Rep. 855 (1896).

169. Mountain v. Price, 20 Wash.2d 129, 146 P.2d 327 (1944).

170. Achilles v. Hoopes, 40 Wash.2d 664, 245 P.2d 1005 (1952).

171. This was argued in Meng. v. Security State Bank of Woodland, 16 Wash.2d 215, 133 P.2d 293 (1943).

172. Katz v. Judd, 108 Wash 557, 185 Pac. 613 (1919).

173. See Cross, *Law Revision in the State of Washington, The Present Picture and a Proposal*, 27 Wash. L. Rev. 193 (1952).

The Legal Marital Property Regime According to the *Projet* of the French Commission for Revision of the *Code Civil**

*Roger Houin*** and *Marcel Verrier****

Among the problems presented by the proposed revision of the *Code Civil*, one of the most important and pressing, as well as the most delicate, concerned the legal marital property *régime*. The problem is important because the system adopted will apply to all persons married without entering into a marriage contract, that is, to the vast majority of married persons. French law, of course, recognizes the principle of freedom in marriage contracts, and those who wish to modify the legal community property *régime* or submit to a different system (separation of property, dotal *régime*) may execute such contracts before notaries. But as a matter of fact such contracts are rare. The problem is parti-

---

* Translated by Donald J. Tate, Editor-in-Chief, *Louisiana Law Review*.

The purpose of the Commission for Revision of the French *Code Civil*, created by the decree of June 7, 1945, is to prepare a general revision of the *Code Civil*. Placed under the presidency of M. de la Morandière, Dean of the Faculty of Law of Paris, Member of the *Institut*, the commission consists of twelve members, three professors of the Faculty of Law of Paris, three members of the *Conseil d'Etat*, three judges, and three attorneys or ministerial officials. It consists also of a secretariat composed of a Secretary-General, a professor of law, and three secretaries, either judges or attorneys.

The commission has already established a preliminary *projet* of the preliminary book and the first book of the future *Code Civil*. The preliminary book contains particularly the general provisions concerning the application of laws, the status of foreigners, and the international conflict of laws. The first book contains provisions respecting physical persons and the family, and especially the rules concerning the status of persons, marriage and divorce, marital property *régimes*, filiation, and the protection of minors and other persons lacking capacity. The commission is presently studying the provisions of Book II (successions, donations and testaments).

The works of the commission are published by the Librairie du Recueil Sirey, 22 rue Soufflot, Paris (V^e).

** Professor of Law, University of Rennes; Secretary-General of the Commission for Revision of the *Code Civil*.

*** Magistrate in the Ministry of Justice; Secretary of the Commission for Revision of the *Code Civil*.

cularly delicate because the legal system adopted must suit families whose habits, social levels, and ways of life differ profoundly.

As a matter of fact, while recent laws (law of February 18, 1938, and law of September 22, 1942) have given the wife full capacity and have rendered the juridical relations between spouses somewhat more flexible, the legal marital property system is still the one adopted in 1804, the community of movables and acquisitions. Under this system the husband has extensive power over the property of both spouses; and the wife, although she has legal capacity, plays only a minor role. This discord between the principle proclaimed by the legislator and the actual position of the married woman has not escaped attention. During recent years, various proposals to modify the present legal *régime* have been submitted to the parliament.[1] It is therefore not surprising that the Commission for Revision of the *Code Civil* devoted numerous sessions—both of sub-committees and of the plenary commission—to the examination of the problem and the drafting of provisions for the system selected.[2]

I

It was necessary for the commission to resolve at the outset the preliminary question whether it should contemplate a change in the community property system established by the *Code Civil*, a system which, at least in essential principles, has not been modified since 1804. This is, of course, the community of movables and acquisitions. It provides for both common and separate property. Only the immovables belonging to the spouse at the time of the marriage and those acquired by the spouse during the marriage by inheritance or donation remain separate property. On the other hand, the immovables acquired during the marriage under onerous title and *all movables*, regardless of their origin and the date of their acquisition, are common property. As under all community property systems, the husband has far greater powers than the wife. He has the administration of both his separate property and the common property and—at least in principle—can freely dispose of one and the

1. The most recent proposals contemplate the substitution of the *régime* of sharing in acquisitions for the present legal *régime*. See particularly the bills introduced by M. Monneville (1946), M. Caillavet (1950), and by Mme. Poinso-Chapuis (1951).

2. See TRAVAUX DE LA COMMISSION DE RÉFORME DU CODE CIVIL ANNÉE—1948-1949, 333 *et seq.* (1950); TRAVAUX ANNÉE—1949-1950, 123 *et seq.* (1951); TRAVAUX ANNÉE—1950-1951, 351 *et seq.* (1952).

other. Moreover, he has the enjoyment and administration of the wife's separate property, but he cannot dispose of it. Consequently, under this system, the wife has very limited powers. She can dispose of only the naked ownership of her separate property, which is of little practical importance.

This system, established by the Custom (*coûtume*), was retained without difficulty at the time of the redaction of the French Civil Code, since in 1804 it was still suited to the nature of fortunes and the social position of the wife. In that period, immovables formed the essential and stable element of private fortunes and it was considered desirable to keep this element within the family. The system adopted, by excluding the immovables from the community, achieved the desired result. In view of the small value of movables, it was not considered objectionable to include them in the community and divide them between the spouses upon dissolution of the marriage. Moreover, this method had the advantage of avoiding the difficulties of proof often involved in determining the origin and composition of the movables belonging to each spouse. The *régime* adopted, in assigning the wife a limited role in the management of the family property, also reflected the customs of the era. In that period the wife, who lacked juridical capacity, took little part in business and social activities.

It is precisely in regard to these two features that criticism of the community property *régime* is today becoming strong. In the first place, the inclusion of the spouses' movable property in the community does not correspond to the present nature of private fortunes or to the wishes of the interested parties. The considerable development of movable fortunes since 1804 no longer permits viewing movables as negligible; the ancient adage, *res mobilis res vilis*, does not fit our times. Besides movables proper—already more important, generally, than in the past—movables include transferable securities (stocks or debentures of commercial and industrial companies, and government bonds), which are of considerable value today, and commercial enterprises, the importance of which has likewise increased with the development of commerce and industry. Moreover, inclusion of these things in the community and their division upon dissolution of the marriage no longer seems equitable. This inequity is evident when the fortune of one of the spouses consists of immovables and that of the other, equally valuable, consists exclusively of movables. Is it not inequitable that the latter is obliged to divide his fortune with the other without receiving a counterpart?

Furthermore, the system of community of movables and acquisitions, its critics say, no longer conforms to the present position of the wife. In our day, the wife participates in social life. She is advocate, physician, and civil servant. She manages industrial and commercial enterprises. In the field of law, she has won political equality and full civil capacity. Why then, ask these critics, does the woman, who is the man's equal in the social sphere, continue to be regarded in the household as a person lacking capacity, subject like a minor to a sort of tutorship of the husband? Undoubtedly, there is some exaggeration in this last criticism. In harmonious families, the wife is by no means conscious of being under the husband's tutorship. All important decisions are the product of common accord and, generally, the wife knows quite well how to make her point of view prevail.

Moreover, it is important to note that certain Code provisions or ancillary laws assign the wife a more important role than that which the principles of the community *régime* seem to give her. Thus the Code itself requires the concurrence of the wife in a sale of immovables by the husband—the wife must join in the sale in order to renounce her legal mortgage. Since the enactment of a law of September 22, 1942, modifying article 1422 of the *Code Civil*, this concurrence is likewise required for all donations of common property by the husband. The wife also enjoys certain powers, either under certain laws (power to bind the husband for necessities of the household, possibility of having a bank account opened) or by virtue of judicial authorization (possibility of obtaining authorization to represent the husband under article 219 of the *Code Civil*). Finally, it must be noted that, since the enactment of the law of July 13, 1907, the wife who pursues a calling separate from that of her husband may dispose freely of the things she acquires with her earnings (the system of *biens réservés*). However, according to an important body of opinion, the powers thus conferred upon the wife are still greatly inadequate and profound reforms are still needed.

II

Agreement, therefore, was easily reached on the need for revising the legal marital *régime*. But the next difficulty lay in selecting the system to be substituted for the community of movables and acquisitions. To meet the criticisms of the existing *régime*, it was necessary that the new one should, on the one hand, permit each spouse to keep as separate all of his or her property, both movable and immovable, and, on the other, assure the wife more independence from the husband. Among the systems fulfilling these two requirements are notably the *régime* of separation of property and the *régime* of sharing in acquisitions.

The *régime* of separation of property has an immediate appeal in its simplicity. Each spouse remains owner of the property which he owned at the time of the marriage and of that which he acquires thereafter; he has the administration and enjoyment of this property. Consequently, neither a settlement nor a partition takes place upon dissolution of the marriage. This *régime* also has the advantage of assuring the wife complete independence and of making her, in the management of the family interests, the equal of her husband. Moreover, it has been emphasized that the system of separation of property is the legal *régime* in numerous foreign countries.

However, many jurists consider that this *régime* is not fully satisfactory and, indeed, that it has serious disadvantages. In the first place, it is emphasized that its alleged simplicity is more apparent than real. As a matter of fact, upon dissolution of the marriage, the *régime* of separation of property requires a settlement for the same reason as do all other *régimes*. This settlement is generally difficult, owing to the inevitable intermingling of the property of the spouses. It is frequently asserted that, owing to negligence or inexperience, married persons under this system often have but one bank account. How could one in such a situation determine, except arbitrarily, what belongs to each spouse? Furthermore, it is said, if the *régime* of separation of property confers independence upon the wife in principle, it still does not, in fact, assure the protection of her property. As indicated above, the wife often leaves the management of her property to the husband and permits him to make purchases and sales of movable assets without retaining evidence of the transactions. Upon dissolution of the marriage, she is frequently faced with the impossibility of establishing what her property is. Thus, her situation is worse than that of the wife under the community system. Finally, the most serious and most repeated criticism of the *régime* of separation of property is that it fails to provide for the spouses' sharing in the property accumulated during the marriage. The sharing of gains is indeed one of the fundamental elements of the French tradition. A system which does not provide for sharing would not be readily accepted, especially since the rights of the surviving spouse are so restricted in French law (precisely because the community property system exists). Undoubtedly this difficulty could be overcome by joining to the *régime* of separation of property a community of acquisitions. But then the *régime* of separation of property would become a complex system, and experience seems to indicate that it would not function satisfactorily.

The system of sharing in acquisitions seems to be a perfection of the *régime* of separation of property. It is a new system, initially inspired by Swedish legislation. It has been adopted, not only by Sweden, but by various other countries, and, notably by Colombia in South America. This *régime* was also studied in France by a commission formed at the Ministry of Justice in 1925; and a government bill, submitted in 1932 but not passed by the legislature, proposed its adoption.

This system ingeniously combines the *régime* of separation of property with the community property system limited to acquisitions. During the marriage, the spouses live as if they had been married under the *régime* of separation of property pure and simple. Each administers the property he owned when married and the property he acquires thereafter and disposes of one and the other freely. At the dissolution of the marriage, however, a mass is formed consisting of all the property acquired during the marriage by either spouse. This mass of acquisitions is divided equally between them. But the partition, in principle, is not in kind but solely according to value, each spouse having the right to keep his acquisitions on condition that he account to the other for the value of the part to which the latter is entitled. This system offers certain advantages of the two systems whose principles it combines. Like the *régime* of separation of property, it assures the spouses independence during the marriage. Like the community *régime* limited to acquisitions, it provides for sharing by both spouses in the savings made during the marriage.

However, this *régime* has provoked various criticisms. First of all, critics have said that it is a mere product of the mind and has not yet undergone, at least in France, the test of experience. They have also objected that it is a complicated system which will not function satisfactorily unless it is used by experienced spouses; it is especially dangerous for the wife, who, from inexperience, will leave the management of her property to the husband. Finally, they have said that this system is best suited to spouses who pursue independent callings or have separate sources of income—which is not the case most frequently encountered. For example, the wives of working men, small businessmen or farmers usually do not engage in pursuits which provide them separate income. In cases of this type, and they seem the most numerous, the system of sharing in acquisitions seems poorly adapted to the conditions under which the spouses live.

III

Consequently, a majority of the commission favored a third system—the community limited to acquisitions—although some members were firm believers in one or the other of the systems above discussed. The commission was of the opinion that the system of community limited to acquisitions was the one best suited to most spouses at the present time. In those families where the spouses work together (farmers, working men, small businessmen), the *régime* reflects, in simple fashion, the unity of interest existing between them. In families where the husband alone works, it allows the wife to share in the savings which result from good management of the household interests. On the other hand, since the community is limited to acquisitions, each spouse retains as separate all property, movable or immovable, belonging to him prior to the marriage and all property coming to him by succession or donation. Thus, the community system limited to acquisitions escapes, on this score, the criticisms of the existing *régime*. Furthermore, the commission believed that the community system limited to acquisitions would find ready public acceptance, because it is already the system most often adopted by spouses entering into a marriage contract. However, the new legal system differs considerably from the community of acquisitions presently existing as a contractual system under the *Code Civil*. The commission gave consideration to certain criticisms addressed to this latter *régime* by the proponents of the *régime* of separation of property and the system of sharing in acquisitions. Accordingly, while preserving the framework of the traditional system, the commission sought to suppress or attenuate certain provisions now under criticism.

In the first place, in order to give expression to the evolution of the wife's social and juridical position, the commission sought to augment her powers in the management of the family interests. The commission even wished to give the wife the same powers as the husband; but if such a reform seemed practicable in the personal relations of the spouses either between each other (fixing of domicile, pursuit of a calling) or between themselves and their children (paternal authority), it did not seem possible in the management of the family's pecuniary interests, in view of the difficulties which could thereby be created in the relations of the spouses with third parties. However, although the preliminary projet continues to assign the husband the preponderant role, it increases the wife's participation in the management of the common property and the administration of her separate property by requiring her to join in all major juridical acts.

The preliminary projet provides that the husband cannot, without the wife's consent, dispose gratuitously of the common property nor dispose, even by onerous title, of certain important property (immovables, commercial enterprises, movables needed for the family's current living or for the pursuit of the spouses' common calling). The wife's consent is likewise required for certain other major juridical acts (collection of capital, disposition of patent and trademark rights, copyrights, and artistic property rights, leasing of immovables or commercial enterprises).

The commission even considered requiring the wife's consent for the alienation of securities belonging to the community. But by reason of the multiplicity of transactions in which transferable securities may be involved and the rapidity with which these transactions must sometimes be made, it seemed to the commission that the need for securing the wife's consent would result in excessive inconvenience for the spouses which might be detrimental to their interests.

Although the husband remains the administrator of the wife's separate property, she nevertheless enjoys a right of control over the major juridical acts which the husband, as administrator, may be called upon to make. The consent of the wife will be required for the leasing of her most important separate property (immovables and commercial enterprises), for the transfer of interests in patent and trademark rights, copyrights, and artistic properties, and, finally, for the collection of her separate capital. Thus the husband will no longer be able to abuse his power to execute acts prejudicial to the wife, as, for example, in case of separation in fact or on the eve of a divorce. Moreover, the *projet* is not confined to protecting the wife against the husband's abusive exercise of his powers but protects her also against his malicious refusal or inaction. In such cases, the *projet* permits the wife to obtain authority to act from the court, if the contemplated act is justified by the family's interests.

The wife's role in the management of the family property having thus been considerably enlarged, the commission considered it unnecessary to preserve the special *régime* (*biens réservés*) allowing the wife to retain as separate the property acquired by her in pursuit of a professional activity. This system had been instituted solely by reason of the wife's want of control over the ordinary community property. Having given the wife effective powers, the commission believed it inadvisable to preserve this special system, which had created serious problems and which had been little used in practice.

In the second place, the commission also sought to avoid, as well as possible, another disadvantage of the community *régime*, namely, the need for a partition of the common property upon dissolution of the marriage. In most cases this partition is a difficult operation, the results of which are not always satisfactory. If the partition is made in kind, it is not always possible to assign each claimant the property he wishes to retain, and the drawing of lots, required in certain cases by law, usually leaves all interested parties discontented. If the partition cannot be made in kind, resort to public auction becomes necessary and this usually takes the property out of the family. In keeping with the present tendencies of the legislation and the provisions already in force with respect to agricultural enterprises, the commission sought to exempt from the drawing of lots or the public auction certain goods which the claimants, and especially the surviving spouse, may have a great interest in keeping. This purpose was applied particularly to the industrial, commercial or agricultural enterprise which provided the livelihood of the spouses, and the house or apartment in which they lived. The preliminary *projet* provides that the surviving spouse shall have the right under certain conditions to have these things adjudged to her preferentially in the partition. Of course, the value of this property will be fixed as of the day of the partition so that the children or other heirs will suffer no detriment.

The preliminary *projet* introduces into the community of acquisitions numerous other reforms of lesser importance which it is not possible to analyze here. In preparing the *projet*, the commission sought to resolve all difficulties which experience had revealed in both the active and passive components of the community, its administration and its liquidation.

Finally, it should be noted that, according to the preliminary *projet*, the marital system adopted by the spouses at the time of the marriage is no longer an immutable *régime* which governs the marriage until its dissolution. Abandoning the principle of immutability of marriage contracts, the preliminary *projet* allows the spouses to modify, under judicial supervision, the marital *régime* they adopted when the rules of that system prove antagonistic to the family's interests. This important reform seems likely to introduce much more flexibility into the operation of marital property systems by permitting the spouses to submit, during the marriage, to the system which best corresponds to their respective interests.

In selecting the new legal system and specifying its mode of operation, the commission, like the redactors of the *Code Civil* of 1804, was careful not to break with the tradition of French law. It considered the system of community limited to acquisitions the one best fulfilling present needs—at least in most of the cases—and restricted itself to a few amendments designed to "modernize" that *régime* to a reasonable degree. While the reform thus effected may not seem spectacular, it will fulfill the wishes of the public, it seems, and its placement in operation will encounter no serious obstacle. Undoubtedly, certain members of the commission wished to see a more modern system adopted as the legal *régime*, for example, the *régime* of sharing in acquisitions. While their views were not adopted by the majority of the commission, the *régime* of sharing in acquisitions has nevertheless found a place in the new *Code Civil*. The preliminary *projet* preserves that *régime* as a contractual *régime* which spouses who enter into a marriage contract may adopt. Thus the practice will be to put this new *régime* to the test and evaluate its merits. Economic and social evolution will continue and the time will perhaps come when this system will in turn be selected as the legal system. But the transition will be smooth and free of danger.

Index